Open Data Now

Open Data Now

*The Secret to Hot Startups,
Smart Investing,
Savvy Marketing, and
Fast Innovation*

Joel Gurin

New York Chicago San Francisco Athens London Madrid Mexico City
Milan New Delhi Singapore Sydney Toronto

1 2 3 4 5 6 7 8 9 0   DOC/DOC   1 9 8 7 6 5 4 3

ISBN 978-0-07-182977-9
MHID   0-07-182977-6

e-ISBN 978-0-07-182978-6
e-MHID   0-07-182978-4

This publication is designed to provide accurate and authoritative information in regard to the subject matter covered. It is sold with the understanding that neither the author nor the publisher is engaged in rendering legal, accounting, securities trading, or other professional services. If legal advice or other expert assistance is required, the services of a competent professional person should be sought.
—*From a Declaration of Principles Jointly Adopted by a Committee of the American Bar Association and a Committee of Publishers and Associations*

McGraw-Hill Education books are available at special quantity discounts to use as premiums and sales promotions or for use in corporate training programs. To contact a representative, please visit the Contact Us pages at www.mhprofessional.com.

To my parents, Pat and Jerry Gurin, who have inspired me by combining the power of data with deep commitment to social change.

And to my wife, Carol, with much love and appreciation for our life together.

Contents

CONTENTS

PREFACE

My Journey Through
the Datasphere

I'VE BEEN FORTUNATE TO HAVE A VARIED AND SATISFYING CAREER. I began as a science journalist; became a book author and magazine editor; was the editorial director and then executive vice president of *Consumer Reports* for many years; worked in Washington as a bureau chief at a federal agency; and held leadership positions in publishing and nonprofit organizations in between. But nothing has been more fascinating and inspiring than the work I've had a chance to do on Open Data for the past three years.

I've been immersed in the world of Open Data since the fall of 2010. I had joined the federal government almost a year before as chief of the Consumer and Governmental Affairs Bureau at the Federal Communications Commission. I was recruited to join the FCC because I had a strong consumer background and the new chairman, Julius Genachowski, wanted to make consumer issues a priority. As soon as I joined the agency, my bureau and I started to tackle a thorny consumer problem: How could we help people choose from a dizzying array of cell-phone plans to find their best personal choice?

To try to figure that out, I started talking to colleagues who were working on similar consumer problems in financial services, healthcare, and other areas. Eventually I met Danny Goroff, then at the Office of Science and Technology Policy, who suggested that someone should start a White House task force to look at this issue. The result: I became chair of the White House Task Force on Smart Disclosure, cochaired by Sophie Raseman of the Department of the Treasury, which we launched to study how consumers can use government Open Data about products and services to make more informed choices in the marketplace.

Through the task force I met Beth Noveck, who had led the Open Government Initiative for the Obama administration. After working with her on several projects, I joined her team as senior advisor at the Governance Lab at New York University. The GovLab, as we call it, develops new approaches to government through technology, data, and collaboration, and Open Data is a central part of our work.

I've gotten to know dozens of entrepreneurs, business leaders, researchers, academics, journalists, and others who are developing new ways to understand and use Open Data. I've met a new breed of techno-evangelists whose rallying cry is "data liberation!" And I've discovered a growing, vibrant new world of Open Data resources, a kind of datasphere that provides the material for transformational changes in business, government, and society.

I've been lucky in my career to work in the private sector, in consumer advocacy, and in government, and this book reflects all three perspectives. I hope it will be useful to business readers, the primary audience for this book, who want to grow their companies, market more effectively to their customers, find new investment opportunities, and build new businesses. But I also hope it's helpful to the government agencies that work with those businesses, to the advocates who keep both business and government honest, and to consumers who want to use Open Data to improve their own lives.

Acknowledgments

THIS BOOK BRINGS TOGETHER IDEAS AND OBSERVATIONS from many years of my work, and many colleagues have contributed to its development. At *Consumer Reports*, I worked with Rhoda Karpatkin, Jim Guest, and strong management teams using test and research data to improve the lives of American consumers. At State of the USA, Chris Hoenig, Jeri Asher, and our colleagues used public data to develop measures of national progress. And at the FCC, I worked with our chairman, Julius Genachowski; with my deputies in the consumer bureau, Bill Freedman, Yul Kwon, Mark Stone, and Karen Peltz Strauss; and with many others to use technology and data to improve telecommunications for the Internet age.

The White House Task Force on Smart Disclosure that I chaired broke new ground in studying how Open Data can help people make more informed decisions and make markets more efficient. Thanks go to Danny Goroff, Richard Thaler, Myron Gutmann, and Pedro Espina for the initial ideas and groundwork that led to the task force; to Cass Sunstein, Aneesh Chopra, and Todd Park for their ongoing support of our efforts; and to research director Irene Wu and the other members of the task force for their dedication, insights, and hard work. Through the task force I met with dozens of experts in other federal agencies, too numerous to name here, who all contributed greatly to both the task force report and the insights on government Open Data that have informed this book. Special thanks go to Chris Vein, who gave us invaluable guidance as Deputy U.S. Chief Technology Officer, and to Sophie Raseman of the Department of the Treasury, my partner in leading the task force, who has been an extraordinary colleague in the cause of Smart Disclosure.

Thanks also go to Jim Hendler, John Erickson, and my other colleagues on the OrgPedia Project on corporate data—and especially to Beth Noveck for bringing me in first to that project and now to the Governance Lab at NYU. Her commitment to developing Open Government with the use of Open Data is inspiring, and I'm proud to be part of this exciting new work. My colleagues at the Governance Lab—co-founders Aaron Cohen, Shankar Prasad, Manik Suri, and Stefaan Verhulst, project manager Laura Manley, and many others—are a continuing source of ideas, inspiration, and insight.

The many people who agreed to be interviewed for this book contributed immeasurably, and I'm grateful to all of them. In addition to those whom I've quoted in the text, many other people contributed their time, their ideas, and leads, sources, and examples from their own areas of work. Thanks go to Bob Adler, Michael Alford, Jenni Allen, Kay Allen, Jose Alonso, Scott Amey, Victor Asal, Michael Atkin, Mitchell Belgin, Ruth Bell, Yale Braunstein, Mike Byrne, James Cham, Pratap Chatterjee, John Chelen, Michael Chui, David Colgren, John Coyne, Bill Eggers, Greg Elin, Brian Forde, Joe Galarneau, Dan Gaylin, Nancy Gillis, Dan Goleman, Nathan Good, Philip N. Green, Stephanie Grosser, Bob Groves, Peter Groves, David Halpern, Chris Hendel, Maurice Herlihy, Bernadette Hyland, Howell Jackson, Charlotte Kahn,

ACKNOWLEDGMENTS

Tim Kelsey, Gene Kimmelman, Jed Kolko, Jennifer LaFleur, Jesse Levey, Raphael Majma, Phil Mattera, Patrice McDermott, Katherine McFate, Chris Meyer, Michael Nelson, Greg Norris, Sophia Oliver, Norm Ornstein, Stefanie Ostfeld, Hamid Ouyachi, Karl Rothemeyer, Alan Schechter, Dick Sclove, Peter Shane, Rosie Sharpe, Micah Sifry, Alan Simpson, David Smith, John Stadler, Mike Starr, Tom Steinberg, Paul Stieger, Will Tucker, Jemma Venables, Eric Wanner, Steve Young, and Ethan Zuckerman. Sincere apologies to anyone I've inadvertently missed in reviewing my notes.

Because the world of Open Data is changing so quickly, I've launched a website, OpenDataNow.com, that I hope will be used as an ongoing source of current information and insight. Thanks go to Janey Lee and Hanee Designs for their excellent work in developing the site. Thanks also to Jeanne Holm of Data.gov for her work with the Task Force on Smart Disclosure to set up Consumer.data. gov, the government's ongoing hub for consumer-focused data and information.

This book would not exist without the efforts of my agent, Gail Ross, and my editor, Tom Miller. Many thanks to them both for their belief in the importance of this book and to Tom for his clear, insightful editorial guidance, which has made this book much better and more focused. I'm also grateful to the friends and colleagues who reviewed early versions of chapters and key editorial material thoughtfully and expertly, often on very tight deadlines: David Blaszkowsky, Jim Hendler, Bill Hoffman, Hudson Hollister, Alicia Berger Levey, Chuck Lewis, Harvey Lewis, Charlotte Mayerson, Beth Noveck, Howard Parnell, Stefaan Verhulst, and Mark and Julie Wittes Schlack. Their comments and contributions have improved this book greatly, while any remaining errors are, of course, mine.

Finally, I want to thank my family for their love and support and their help on this book. My most important reviewer has been my wife, Carol, who has been the ideal first reader for everything I write. On this book, as in life, she's kept me focused on what really matters.

ACKNOWLEDGMENTS

My parents, who are data experts themselves, have given me great encouragement and valuable advice in this new venture. And I thank my kids, Alison, Joanna, and Ben, for their enthusiasm, interest, and help on this project with everything from next-generation perspective to advice on my website. I hope that Open Data will help bring them a more open, fair, and abundant world in the years ahead.

Open Data Now

INTRODUCTION

The World's Greatest Free Resource

Open Data is "going to help launch more startups. It's going to help launch more businesses. . . . It's going to help more entrepreneurs come up with products and services that we haven't even imagined yet"—President Barack Obama, May 9, 2013.

IMAGINE THAT YOU SUDDENLY HAVE ACCESS TO A MASSIVE NEW business resource. It can be used to build new companies that deliver better healthcare, offer in-depth investment tools, provide energy more efficiently, improve transportation, or offer a wide range of consumer services through mobile apps and the web. It can help established companies learn what their customers really think about them, spot market trends early on, and choose the best business partners while avoiding the riskiest ones. It can speed up scientific research by an order of magnitude. And while it takes money and effort to develop these opportunities, the essential resource itself is free.

1

That resource is Open Data. The concept of Open Data is simple enough: it's public data, from government or other sources, that's available for anyone to access for personal or business use. Anyone who's ever booked a flight online, used a smartphone's GPS, or watched the Weather Channel has used Open Data. This free public data can also be used, with ever-improving methods of data analysis, to launch new business ventures, solve difficult strategic problems, provide new kinds of business intelligence, and more.

Today's Open Data revolution is rapidly leading us into new territory. With more powerful computers, cheaper memory storage, and the exponential growth of digital information, huge databases are now becoming public for the first time. They are taking Open Data to an entirely new level and changing our world in the process.

Open Data is becoming a secret to success for smart business leaders around the world. Investors use it to analyze the risks and rewards of different companies in their search for the best opportunities. Company owners use it to understand subtle clues to their brand's reputation and to develop data-driven marketing strategies. And entrepreneurs are using Open Data on weather, housing, transportation, and more to build businesses that provide new services and benefit the public. These startups are raising tens of millions of dollars and can build value many times greater than that.

In October 2013, McKinsey & Company released a new report on the value of Open Data worldwide. The report calculated that "an estimated $3 trillion in annual economic potential could be unlocked" through Open Data in sectors like education, energy, and health. This is the largest value put on Open Data so far, and may seem too inclusive; for example, it includes the value of using Open Data to increase the population's earning power by improving education. Regardless, this latest McKinsey report demonstrates the growing business interest in Open Data and excitement about its potential.

At the same time, Open Data is having a profound impact outside the private sector in ways that affect the business environment. Government leaders are releasing more Open Data both to enhance trust in government and to foster business innovation. Medical researchers are using it to find treatments and cures for diseases more rapidly. Journalists use Open Data to expose problems ranging from money laundering to Medicare fraud—and increasingly to bring corporate operations to light.

Over the past three years I've met with the leaders of the emerging Open Data movement, first as head of the consumer bureau at the Federal Communications Commission, then as chair of a White House task force, and now as part of a team at New York University. I've met with inspiring entrepreneurs who are using Open Data to build new enterprises and drive progress in areas like healthcare, finance, education, and energy. I've gotten to know high-level U.S. and U.K. government officials, policy makers, academics, and NGOs who are working to release all kinds of new data that businesses and others can use. This book reflects their vision, insights, knowledge, and advice.

The world of Open Data is moving fast, and no book on this topic can be completely current. I've launched a website, OpenDataNow. com, to follow the latest developments, debates, and opportunities. The site hosts a blog, apps, and news links to serve as a hub for the growing Open Data community. I encourage readers to check it out, comment, and contribute. I've posted articles, interview transcripts, and podcasts that focus on several of the experts quoted in this book; a list of these is in Appendix A on pages 251-252.

This book contains several resources to help readers explore the possibilities of Open Data. Most chapters conclude with pragmatic advice on putting Open Data to use. The book also includes an extensive Glossary that should help anyone new to this field. (I could have used it myself when I was doing this research.)

Whether you are an entrepreneur, an executive, an investor, a small business owner, or in the public or nonprofit sector, Open Data will provide new opportunities that could transform the way you work. *Open Data Now* is your guide to understanding this new phenomenon, managing its challenges, and harnessing its power.

PART ONE

The Power of Open Data

CHAPTER ONE

An Opportunity as Big as the Web

I N NOVEMBER 2012 I WAS SITTING IN A PACKED CONFERENCE room at the brand-new Open Data Institute (ODI) in London, a public-private partnership launched with a 10-million-pound grant from the British government. The ODI has all the look and feel of a well-funded tech startup. The Institute is situated in London's equivalent of Silicon Valley, known as Silicon Roundabout for the Old Street roundabout where the nearest tube station is. It's an area much like the tech hives in San Francisco's South of Market neighborhood or Silicon Alley in lower Manhattan—underdeveloped neighborhoods with ample space for new companies to stake out their territory, innovate like mad, and drive up the cost of real estate. While this international gathering happened to be in London, it could have been in either of those technology centers.

I was at the ODI with two dozen colleagues from business, government, and nonprofit organizations who had come together to talk about Open Data—the new movement to make large amounts of data available for public use. On this November Monday, we were in the second of two back-to-back meetings at the ODI, put together with funding from the MacArthur Foundation. We were meeting as representatives of the White House; 10 Downing Street; the U.K. government's Cabinet Office and its Department of Business Development; the World Bank; a major British retailer; two high-tech consulting firms; a leading tech publisher; university departments of law, computer science, artificial intelligence, physics, and cognitive neuroscience; two foundations; and nonprofits working on corporate transparency, civic engagement, and green business practices.

We were greeted by the Institute's CEO, Gavin Starks, an entrepreneur who has done Internet development for two decades in places as diverse as Virgin, Google, the British government, and UNICEF. He was making the provocative case that Open Data would have the same impact as the invention of the World Wide Web.

Open Data today, he said, "is very much like the web was for me in 1994, when I was still trying to convince people that e-mail was a good thing or that they might want to launch a website. Everyone was excited about its potential, but no one knew quite what shape it would take. Over the last 20 years we've seen a lot of innovation, creativity, and disruption. Today, we don't know exactly where Open Data will lead, but we do know that it will be transformative. Some ways of doing business will start, some will evolve, and learning how to navigate that will be a challenge for all of us. But the potential that we saw in the early days of the web is what I see now with Open Data."

This isn't the first time a new tech development has been compared to the dawn of the web. But the leaders of the Open Data movement have the credentials to make that claim. The president and cofounder of the Open Data Institute is Sir Tim Berners-Lee, whose bio says, simply and accurately, that he "invented the World Wide Web" while at CERN, the European Particle Physics Laboratory. The ODI's chairman, Sir Nigel Shadbolt, is a pioneer in web science and artificial intelligence and was instrumental in creating the British government's Open Data policies. They are typical of the visionaries in the United States, the United Kingdom, and other countries who are developing Open Data now.

Open Data can best be described as *accessible public data that people, companies, and organizations can use to launch new ventures, analyze patterns and trends, make data-driven decisions, and solve complex problems.* It's very different from Big Data—more on that in a minute—although the two overlap. Open Data is data with a mission: it's designed to provide free, open, transparent data that can transform the way we do business, run government, and manage all kinds of transactions. Like our gathering at the ODI, the people behind Open Data are a diverse group, including leaders from the corporate world, technology, government, academia, nonprofits, and fields such as health, education, and environmental science.

The Open Data movement began with democratic goals, fueled by the idea that governments should make the data they collect available to the taxpayers who've paid to collect it. But in addition to its social benefits, Open Data has created tremendous new business opportunities, which are the focus of this book. It's worth remembering that the Internet itself began as a government-funded initiative, the ARPANET, created by the Advanced Research Projects Agency that President Eisenhower launched as a response to Sputnik. That government research project became one of the major economic drivers of our time. In a similar way, government's drive to release Open Data is creating a major economic resource and the infrastructure to manage it.

The Open Data policies developed by the U.S. and U.K. governments are driven by a push for economic growth and job creation. President Obama made this clear when he announced his administration's new Open Data Policy in May 2013. This policy, which will make unprecedented amounts of federal data available in highly usable forms, has a business agenda first and foremost. Significantly, the president didn't make his announcement at a Washington press conference or in the Rose Garden but on a visit to a technology center in Austin, Texas. There he promised that government Open Data is going to help launch new businesses of all kinds in ways "that we haven't even imagined yet."

The Open Data Policy includes a detailed description of the criteria for government data to be released as Open Data, drawing on work done by the Open Knowledge Foundation in the United Kingdom, the Washington-based Sunlight Foundation, and others. This book goes further: the Open Data I'm writing about includes data from other sources as well as government.

I use "Open Data" to include data from any source that's made available in an "open" form that anyone can access and that meets a few specific conditions. All Open Data must be licensed in a way that allows for its reuse. It should be in a form that can be easily read by computers, although here there are gradations of "openness." And there's general agreement that Open Data should be free of charge or cost just a minimal amount.

Open Data includes federal, state, and local data; scientific data released by researchers; data that companies release about their own operations; user reviews and tweets written by ordinary people; and any kind of data that can be found through Google or scraped from websites. By using these many kinds of Open Data:

- Entrepreneurs are building new businesses that generate many millions of dollars in revenue. Open Data released by the National Oceanic and Atmospheric Administration beginning in the 1970s and GPS data released more recently spawned new industries that do billions of dollars in business each year. New businesses using open health data may soon match that, and opportunities in energy, finance, education, and other fields are increasing as well.
- Governments are providing new, centralized data resources for business development. Data.gov, a website launched by the Obama administration, now makes hundreds of thousands of government datasets open and available for anyone to use for

free. The United Kingdom has launched its own version, Data. gov.uk, and other countries are using a platform distributed by the United States as "Data.gov in a box" to start their own data hubs.

- Companies are developing new marketing strategies, evaluating competitors and partners more accurately, and building their brands' value. The new technique of *sentiment analysis* gathers information from Twitter, blogs, news feeds, and other public sources, uses text analysis to turn this information into Open Data, and turns the mass of public opinion into quantifiable business insights.

- Investors are finding companies with the greatest promise and avoiding those that pose high levels of risk. Through new data-driven websites, investors can quickly get in-depth information on large and small companies. Open Data is giving investors new insights into companies ranging from innovative startups to globally traded public corporations through websites that provide online tools and data visualizations.

- Companies are becoming more transparent about their operations, to their benefit. Between government-required disclosures and voluntary reporting, companies are making more Open Data available about their environmental, social, and governance practices. By releasing this data, a company can attract new investment, recruit more effectively, and improve its corporate image.

- Scientists and researchers are accelerating the pace of new discoveries. In the physical sciences and biomedicine, researchers are taking the bold step of both sharing their data early and openly so that online networks of both experts and amateurs can work with their data to achieve new breakthroughs. Even the secretive world of drug research is beginning to make more data public.

- Websites are helping consumers make better, more informed choices for all kinds of products and services. New businesses are developing online and mobile "choice engines" that give consumers the data they need to make complex, important decisions. They help consumers access detailed, interactive Open Data to choose the options that are best for them, whether they're choosing healthcare, a mortgage, a credit card, or a college education.

Open Data vs. Big Data: Related but Very Different

Open Data should not be confused with Big Data, one of the most talked-about developments in information science over the last few years. Big Data involves *processing very large datasets to identify patterns and connections in the data*. It's made possible by the incredible amount of data that is generated, accumulated, and analyzed every day with the help of ever-increasing computer power and ever-cheaper data storage. It uses the "data exhaust" that all of us leave behind through our daily lives. Our mobile phones' GPS systems report back on our location as we drive; credit card purchase records show what we buy and where; Google searches are tracked; smart meters in our homes record our energy usage. All are grist for the Big Data mill.

While Big Data and Open Data each have important commercial uses, they are very different in philosophy, goals, and practice. For example, large companies may use Big Data to analyze customer databases and target their marketing to individual customers, while they use Open Data for market intelligence and brand building. National governments may use Big Data to track citizens in the name of security, while they use Open Data to engage with their citizens and foster participatory democracy. It's telling that the recent book *Big Data*, the best general presentation of the field, devotes only two-and-a-half pages to Open Data. The two are not the same.

With Big Data, the data sources are generally *passive*, and the data is often kept *private*. Big Data usually comes from sources that passively generate data without purpose, without direction, or without even realizing that they're creating it. And the companies and organizations that use Big Data usually keep the data private for business or security reasons. This includes the data that large retailers hold on customers' buying habits, that hospitals hold about their patients, that banks hold about their credit card holders, or that government agencies collect about millions of cell-phone calls.

At this writing in the fall of 2013, I've found that every time I mention the word *data* it triggers a discussion about the National Security Agency and its PRISM program. We're still trying to figure out exactly what data the NSA has collected, how much, and why. The NSA revelations have rekindled a national debate about data privacy, which is a good thing (more on that in Chapter 11). PRISM is a prime example of the disturbing side of Big Data: it's a massive collection of data without the participation, or even the awareness, of the people whose data is being collected, and it's been kept hidden from the public until recently. It's also the antithesis of Open Data. In fact, even the idea of Open Data for national security is an oxymoron.

In contrast to most Big Data, Open Data is *public* and *purposeful*. It's data that is consciously released in a way that anyone can access, analyze, and use as he or she sees fit. (I don't count Edward Snowden's revelations as Open Data; to be truly open, data should be released by someone who has the authority to do so, not by someone who has pilfered it.) Open Data is also often released with a specific purpose in mind—whether the goal is to spur research and development, fuel new businesses, improve public health and safety, or achieve any number of other objectives.

Having said all that, Big Data and Open Data do overlap, and when they do, the result can be powerful. Some government agencies have made very large amounts of data open with major economic benefits. National weather data and GPS data are the most often-cited examples. U.S. census data and data collected by the Securities and Exchange Commission are others. And nongovernmental research has produced large amounts of data, particularly in biomedicine, that is now being shared openly to accelerate the pace of scientific discovery.

While Open Data is related to Big Data on one hand, it's also related to the Open Government movement on the other. Open Government includes collaborative strategies to engage citizens in governing as well as the government releasing Open Data to the public. This book's Appendix B, "Defining Data Categories," gives a more detailed analysis of how Big Data, Open Government, and Open Data are related, complete with a Venn diagram.

The Open Business Opportunities

Although there's widespread agreement that both Big Data and Open Data will be important business resources, no one is sure exactly what they'll be worth. Determining the overall value of Open Data is far from easy. Many companies that use it are so new that it's too early to measure their success. On the other hand, many established companies use open government data as just one resource for their work, making it hard to figure out how much it contributes to their business.

The Open Data 500 study, which I'm now directing at the GovLab at New York University, will give economists and other researchers a new information base to help assess Open Data's value. This study, which is funded by the Knight Foundation, is the first real-world, comprehensive study of American companies that use government Open Data in health, finance, education, energy, and other sectors. We're identifying 500 of these companies and surveying them to see how they use government Open Data and how they think government agencies can make their data more useful. We plan to make our findings available on a website by early 2014 where researchers can download our data, new companies can complete our survey, and members of the Open Data community can suggest future research.

To identify different kinds of Open Data companies, my colleagues and I began by looking at other research that had already been done.

Since 2012, the Open Data Institute in London has been working with the consulting firm Deloitte to study Open Data's potential. In a series of studies led by Harvey Lewis, a research director in Deloitte's Insight Team, the firm has identified five Open Data business "archetypes":

- *Suppliers* publish their data as Open Data that can be easily used. While they don't charge for the data—if they did, it wouldn't be Open Data—they increase customer loyalty and enhance their reputations by releasing it.
- *Aggregators* collect Open Data, analyze it, and charge for their insights or make money from the data in other ways.
- *Developers* "design, build, and sell web-based, tablet, or smartphone applications" using Open Data as a free resource.
- *Enrichers* are "typically large, established businesses" that use Open Data to "enhance their existing products and services," for example by using demographic data to understand their customers better.
- *Enablers* charge companies to make it easier for them to use Open Data.

I've found these categories useful and have also come up with two simple categories of my own.

The first I'd call Better Business Through Open Data. Open Data can improve healthcare, energy, education, finance, transportation, and many other aspects of consumer society. (In an interesting insight, the Deloitte team has noted that many sectors "will benefit most from open government data that has direct relevance to consumers, and stimulating interest from consumer-driven businesses may yield the greatest economic impact.") In many of these areas, Open Data may become such a seamless part of daily life that most people won't notice it's there. Patients will still go to doctors, but now they'll get better, more informed care. Households will still use electricity, but now they'll use Open Data to help manage their energy use. Consumers will use data-powered websites to choose credit cards and financial services as easily as they now use the web to book a flight. All kinds of daily activities will seem largely the same, but better, as consumer-focused companies improve their services by using Open Data behind the scenes.

In contrast, there are other opportunities that I'd call Open Data Pure Plays—companies, even whole industries, that simply would not exist without Open Data. They include startups that are revolution-izing agriculture by analyzing weather data; companies using Open Data to predict trends in healthcare, financial markets, or other fields; companies that manage and market government data; and companies developing market insights with data from the vast universe of social media.

Like the web itself, Open Data will be a major driver for new businesses and economic growth in the United States, the United Kingdom, and other countries. It will create new jobs, fuel new start-ups, and launch new industries with revenue in the billions. This book covers the full range of Open Data opportunities and the factors that will shape how Open Data is used in the years ahead.

About This Book: Four Open Data Promises

This book describes the business applications of Open Data with examples from dozens of companies, many of which I've interviewed myself. Part 1, which begins with this chapter, describes the four big Open Data promises for businesses and their clients: the potential for *hot new startups*, tools and services for *smart investing*, strategies for *savvy marketing*, and new forms of *fast innovation*.

Chapters 2 through 4 describe the *startups* that are rapidly devel-oping by using Open Data.

Chapter 2 describes companies that are turning government data into dollars using the huge data resources that the U.S. government and others now make available for free. This chapter profiles a variety of companies using GPS data in new ways; the boom in the use of government health data; the startup "incubator" at London's Open Data Institute; and The Climate Corporation, recently bought for about $1 billion, which is working to revolutionize agriculture and increase farmers' profits worldwide.

Chapter 3 covers choice engines for smart disclosure, a category of new companies that help consumers make informed choices in complex areas like healthcare, financial services, and transportation. Several well-known companies, from Kayak to Zillow, are already providing Smart Disclosure, but there's room for growth here, particularly in the United States. In the United Kingdom, where several large companies provide Smart Disclosure on energy providers, credit cards, and insurance, an estimated 24 million people use these price-comparison websites every month. Based on population, that's the proportional equivalent of 100 million monthly customers in the United States, a huge potential market.

Chapter 4 describes new companies whose goal is to "manage the data deluge" and profiles several new and old companies that help others work with government Open Data. While several large companies have provided government data services for years, the release of more Open Data is creating new opportunities and new startups. One of them, Enigma.io, recently won the prize as the hottest new startup at TechCrunch Disrupt NY, beating out about 30 other contestants. That's the tech world's equivalent of winning *American Idol* and is a sign of the potential of Open Data.

Chapters 5 and 6 describe how Open Data is creating new companies and tools for *smart investing*, providing business opportunities for both the entrepreneurs who create these services and the investors who use them.

Chapter 5, on data-driven investing, shows how Open Data and new analytic techniques are giving investors valuable tools and insights. A company called Capital Cube has developed software to analyze more than 40,000 globally traded public companies, update its data on them every day, turn the data automatically into narrative descriptions of current trading, and provide tools for comparing prospective risk and return of different companies in different sectors. In the United Kingdom, Duedil (for "due diligence") provides data on small- to medium-sized companies in the hope of encouraging hundreds of billions of dollars in new investment. With the Securities and Exchange Commission now adopting XBRL, a computer language that can encode large amounts of information, investors will soon have even more Open Data on public companies in a highly usable form.

Chapter 6 covers green investing, driven by Open Data, which has rapidly gone from being an idealistic goal to a mainstream investment strategy. Investors are increasingly looking for companies that operate sustainably and have the data to prove that they do. Sustainable companies aren't just good for society and the environment—they tend to be models of good corporate governance and low operational risk. A large majority of S&P 500 companies now use sustainability measures from the Global Reporting Initiative to report on their practices. Bloomberg has begun offering sustainability data to its subscribers, and the number who use it is growing by almost 50 percent a year.

Chapters 7 and 8 describe how Open Data provides new opportunities for *savvy marketing*.

Chapter 7, on how reputational data defines your brand, covers a powerful form of Open Data that's created by ordinary people. The complaints, experiences, and opinions that people post online add up to a body of reputational data that's open for the world to see. Smart companies are now learning how to mine this data, understand it, respond to it, and use it to build their brands through sophisticated online marketing. The founders of PublikDemand, a new company that channels consumer complaints, describe how companies can turn complaints to their advantage: they're championing a new approach called "social customer service" that companies can use to improve their reputations by responding openly to public complaints.

Chapter 8 covers the marketing science of sentiment analysis, a cutting-edge technology for turning thousands of consumer opinions into quantitative business intelligence. Countless websites now invite consumers to write reviews of hotels, restaurants, or just about any other kind of product or service, and untold numbers of consumers tweet or blog about these products or services on their own. It can all be synthesized and analyzed as Open Data, creating datasets out of the collective consciousness of everyone who uses the web. Sentiment analysis extracts data from social media with particular attention to words that have a positive or negative "sentiment" attached to them. In this chapter, Seth Grimes, a guru of sentiment analysis, describes how companies can use this technology for new kinds of business and market intelligence.

Chapters 9 and 10 explore the fourth promise of Open Data—the way it can be used for *fast innovation*.

Chapter 9 shows how new forms of crowdsourcing can help research-focused companies find solutions using Open Data. It describes academically based "citizen science" projects that have recruited close to a million volunteers to analyze and refine different kinds of scientific data, providing a possible model for the private sector. And it examines companies such as TopCoder, Kaggle, and InnoCentive that use prizes and competition to recruit expert help for tough data problems.

Finally, Chapter 10 explores how Open Data is fueling open innovation—a dramatically new scientific approach that shares data early and openly to foster collaboration across many research labs. By sharing data that would normally be kept secret, open innovation runs counter to the prevailing cultures of scientific research and drug development. But it's so effective that it may justify a new business model. Companies ranging from biomedical startups to the pharma giant GlaxoSmithKline are now using open innovation productively.

Looking Ahead: The Changing Business Environment

The 10 chapters in Part 1 show that Open Data's potential is immediate and real and include pragmatic advice for any company that wants to apply it. But companies based on Open Data also have to watch the social, legal, and political factors that will shape how we use data in the years ahead. Part 2, "The Business Environment: New Trends in Open Data," includes three chapters and a conclusion that describe the most important trends to watch.

Chapter 11 explains how privacy concerns, heightened by National Security Agency revelations, may change the rules around personal data of all kinds. Personal data can become Open Data in a special sense: with new technology, individuals can choose to make their personal data "open" for certain purposes, securely and selectively. Companies such as Personal.com and Reputation.com are betting that a new market in personal data, controlled by individuals, will open up new business opportunities while protecting personal privacy.

Chapter 12 shows how financial regulators, advocacy groups, journalists, and others are using Open Data to make business and government operations more transparent. It describes the new rules that successful businesses will have to follow to do well in this new "see-through" society. And it shows how some data-driven organizations are making transparency their business.

Chapter 13 describes the growing push for Open Data by national governments in the United States, the United Kingdom, and Europe, by state and local governments, and in other parts of the world. The United States has instituted an Open Data Policy that may have a historic impact, and the U.K. government, the European Union, and the G8 have made similar commitments to Open Data. These changes all promise that government Open Data will be a growing resource that businesses around the world can use for innovation and growth.

Finally, Chapter 14 summarizes the most important lessons of this book and gives a preview of the years ahead.

While Open Data has many sources and many uses, the Open Data movement began with a push to make government data more accessible, meaningful, and usable. Today, federal data is a huge, free resource that's just beginning to be tapped. The next chapter explores the potential of government Open Data and the companies that are starting to put it to use.

CHAPTER TWO

Hot Startups: Turning Government Data into Dollars

GOVERNMENT OPEN DATA HAS THE POTENTIAL TO INCREASE public knowledge, empower citizens, and build American businesses. In recent years, business innovation has been a major driver for the federal government's Open Data initiatives. The U.S. government may turn out to be the largest single source of free Open Data in the world. Its business potential is just starting to be realized, and it's fueling a wave of startups that's beginning to build.

The Obama administration has developed its Open Data Policy as part of a larger commitment to Open Government, described in Chapter 13. Under this policy, announced in May 2013, more government data will be made available to the public in more ways than ever before. The policy builds on decisions made long ago, under different administrations, when the U.S. government released weather data as Open Data in the 1970s and decided to release GPS data about a decade later. Today, government weather data is worth more than $30 billion annually—the value of accurate weather predictions plus applications such as weather insurance. The value of GPS data has been estimated at $90 billion by an industry study; it may be less, but it's likely to be in the tens of billions of dollars.

Vivek Kundra, who served as the first U.S. Chief Information Officer under President Obama, has summed up the value of government geographic data, weather data, and GPS data, respectively, with these numbers: "Zillow is valued at over $1 billion, the Weather Channel was sold for approximately $3.5 billion in 2008, and Garmin has a market cap of $7.24 billion. These are all companies that were built using raw government data."

Some companies have used government data to create entirely new kinds of services. For example, Panjiva, started in 2006, uses government data "as a platform for international trade." By using government Open Data on shipping and financial and reputational evaluations of buyers and sellers, Panjiva is helping to build a stronger, more transparent, and more efficient international trade network.

State and local Open Data also provide opportunities for entrepreneurs. Several cities, for example, have released Open Data on transportation that developers use to build apps for commuters. The popular NextBus app, available in Boston, Los Angeles, San Francisco, Toronto, and Washington, DC, tells commuters when they can expect their bus to appear, letting them know whether they have to wait at the stop or have time for a cup of coffee.

There seems to be a paradox here: If Open Data is free, how can anyone build a business on it? The answer is that Open Data is the starting point, not the end point, in deriving value from information. In general, governments have focused more on making the data itself available than on developing public-facing applications. The private sector can then add value by taking Open Data and building something great with it.

You can see the innovative power of government Open Data in a stream of startups and new business applications that grows year by year. Remarkably, even the weather and GPS datasets that have been available for decades continue to spark new ideas and new companies.

Google, one of the world's best-known data-driven companies, has used GPS and other government Open Data in a growing number of applications. Google Maps and Google Earth are produced by combining Google's own data with government data, and have become sources of Open Data themselves: the company counts more than a million websites and apps that use data from Google Maps.

Google's ultimate application of GPS and other mapping data may be its self-driving cars, which could be available by the end of the decade. In addition to making money for Google, the technology used in these vehicles could provide significant public benefit. One analyst believes this technology will reduce the number of auto accidents and save drivers huge amounts of time and fuel lost to traffic jams, for a total economic value of $200 billion a year or more in the United States. The navigation system for Google's autonomous cars uses data that the cars themselves collect through sensors and cameras, together with Google's own map data, which ultimately draws on GPS.

GPS and location data now help power some of the most popular and creative smartphone apps. Consider these:

- Foursquare, which began as a follow-your-friends app that let you see where people were "checking in," has developed new features to let you recall your experiences over time or get recommendations for restaurants where your friends have been.
- Uber is reinventing taxi service by letting you know which cars for hire are close to your location—making it possible, as the company's cofounder has said, to "push a button and get a ride."
- Waze provides real-time navigation, with information constantly improved by data from your fellow drivers, while Inrix offers improved navigation for both smartphones and enterprise

clients like auto manufacturers. (Inrix counts among its partners the I-95 Corridor Coalition. As a New Yorker who's been stuck on I-95 far too many times, I'm glad to see such an organization exists.)

- RedLaser lets you scan the barcode on a product you're considering buying and instantly find out what it's selling for in other stores nearby. According to its website, this app has been downloaded 27 million times.

- Instagram and Flickr let you add mapping data to the photos you post; Vine does the same for short videos; and Evernote lets you track where you were when you wrote those notes to yourself.

No one could have envisioned these developments in 1983 when President Reagan announced that the GPS system then in development would be made available for civilian as well as military use. (That promise was later fulfilled under President Clinton.) At the time of Reagan's announcement, the first truly mobile phone had just become available—it was about the size of a large flashlight—and phones with screens (but no computing capability) were still a decade away. But that's exactly the point. The value of government Open Data is that it's a long-term, permanent public resource that innovators can use for decades, developing new ideas and new companies as technology makes them possible.

Weather data, which has been available longer than GPS data, also continues to offer surprising benefits. Weather Underground, which was the original online weather service, continues to add new data as it makes use of new tablet platforms. The latest iteration lets you switch on and off maps showing weather alerts, fires, and radar and webcam images. A new company, Stormpulse, offers a business-to-business service for sophisticated weather prediction; the company website says it "reduces weather risk for a broad range of industries including energy, transportation, defense, healthcare, and retail." But the most striking new applications come from applying sophisticated new data analytics, out of reach even a decade ago, that can analyze weather patterns in a way that could revolutionize agriculture.

In researching this book, I've had a chance to interview many companies and organizations that are pioneering new uses of government Open Data. To explore the scope of innovation, I visited a company that's using weather data in a powerful new way; a major gathering for innovators in health Open Data; and a government-sponsored "incubator" launching new Open Data companies in the United Kingdom.

The Climate Corporation: From Insurance to a New Green Revolution

In the spring of 2013 I met with David Friedberg, the cofounder and CEO of The Climate Corporation in San Francisco. Founded in 2006, the company has grown to more than 150 employees, including 30 based around the country and 25 in a new Seattle office. When I met with Friedberg, the Climate Corporation had recently received a $50 million investment of venture capital. Six months later, in October 2013, the company was sold to Monsanto for almost $1 billion, described as "one of the largest buys of a new-era data analytics company."

Originally called WeatherBill, The Climate Corporation was started to sell a better kind of weather insurance, but it's grown into a company that could help farmers around the world adapt to climate change, increase their crop yields, and become part of a new green revolution. It's a perfect example of Open Data entrepreneurship that shows what can happen when brilliant, creative people start looking deeper and deeper into what government data can tell them.

Walking into The Climate Corporation's headquarters, which occupies a high floor in a building behind San Francisco's Museum of Modern Art, feels a bit like walking into a hip, high-tech science museum. Each conference room is named after a famous scientist or inventor—Nikola Tesla, Aristotle, the Wright brothers. And each is decorated with relevant designs, such as the radar map on the wall of the Christian Doppler room.

But the centerpiece of the headquarters is in the lobby: a six-foot-diameter globe that beautifully displays the world's weather in real time. Using a system of projectors controlled through an iPad, the globe can display hundreds of different data-driven views of the planet, showing changing wind patterns, temperature, ocean currents, or whatever you'd like to look at. It can also reproduce the surface of the Moon or Mars—or, if you need to set a certain tone for a staff meeting, a replica of the Death Star. These globes, developed by the National Oceanic and Atmospheric Administration, are usually found in science museums. The Climate Corporation, which may be the only private company to own one, often hosts local school groups, who are awed by it. (If you feel that you absolutely have to have one of these, and you have a really big living room, you can search online for "Science on a Sphere.")

David Friedberg has genuine geek cred: he was an astrophysics major and then worked at Google before founding The Climate Corporation. He and his colleagues realized that they could build a successful data-driven business, surprisingly enough, without having exclusive rights to any of the data it is based on. With a few exceptions, the terabytes of data that fuel the company are freely available to anyone. But the analytic expertise The Climate Corporation has brought to bear has created unique value.

As Friedberg tells it, the company began with the simple insight that the weather affects the profits of a large number of businesses every year. "Ski resorts shut down when there's not enough snow, golf courses don't open when there is rain, city governments have to plow the city streets when there's too much snow, even the lemonade stand on the corner is closed down if it's drizzling," he told me. "The concept was that, if we could simulate the weather, we could allow businesses to create a customizable insurance policy that would pay them automatically for the specific weather events that would cause them financial loss."

The company started by working with data from 200 weather stations across the country. As a prospective policyholder, a business would go to the company's website, pick a nearby weather station, and buy insurance against bad weather that the station would measure. The company would analyze historical weather data for that station, predict the likely weather mathematically, and write an appropriate policy.

"Over time," Friedberg told me, "we found that the best market for this model was in agriculture. Farmers in the United States generate about $500 billion a year in revenue, and they make about $100 billion a year in operating profits. So farming's about a 20-percent-margin business on average. The one source of variability for revenue nowadays is the weather, because all the other risks of farming have largely been eliminated through herbicide, fungicide, and insecticide technologies. Weather can be a very big driver for outcomes: farmers can end up losing everything. Slight variations in weather can cause significant losses in profit. And farmers were significantly underinsured under the federal crop program."

As The Climate Corporation began to turn its attention to farmers, the company found that data from 200 weather stations across the United States simply wasn't precise enough to model the weather at local farms. They expanded to get data from 2,000 stations, but that was still not enough. "If you're a farmer and the nearest weather station is still 30 miles away over a hill," said Friedberg, "how often am I going to match your exact experience—your exact rainfall or temperature on a daily basis?" So they used what is called Common Land Unit data that shows the location, shape, and size of all the farmed fields in the country. Even though this is free, public data, it took many Freedom of Information Act requests and a collaboration with Stanford University and other research institutions to get the

U.S. Department of Agriculture to release it. (The company is still trying to get updates on a regular basis.)

Next, The Climate Corporation used government data to assess the weather at all those fields more precisely. Using Doppler radar, said Friedberg, it's now possible to measure how much rain falls on a given farmer's field in a day, to an accuracy of almost 1/100th of an inch. The company also got maps of terrain and soil type from the U.S. Geological Survey, built from on-the-ground soil surveys and satellite imaging, that give accurate pictures of squares of land 10 meters on a side (roughly the size of a suburban backyard). "Farmers don't necessarily care about how much rain fell," said Friedberg. "What they really need to care about is how much water is in their ground," which is determined by both rainfall and the soil.

"Ten years ago," Friedberg told me, what they do "would have been nearly impossible." Putting the data together, he said, "now we've actually got a better estimate of what's going on at your field than you do. We're seeing a huge improvement in satellite imagery. The cost is zero: you can get the images and process them for free. I can now use the infrared imagery of farmers' fields and estimate exactly what date they planted their crop and what the growth stage is."

At some point, Friedberg and his partners realized that they weren't just in the business of selling insurance: they were getting into the business of improving agriculture on a global scale. They've continued to improve their models, adding data on crop yields and tying weather conditions more accurately to agricultural output. The company has developed a service, Climate.com, that is free to policyholders and available to others for a fee. "On a daily basis, we'll tell you what fields you can go to work on, what field should have spraying and planting done today, what field is at a growth stage where you should fertilize it, where you should wait five days to plant." Their goal is to be able to increase a farmer's profitability by 20 or 30 percent—a huge increase in this vulnerable industry.

What's next may be the Green Revolution 2.0. The U.S. government's satellite data doesn't stop at the border: it covers the entire planet. The Climate Corporation is now looking for ways to apply its work internationally, probably starting with Australia, which has relevant data of its own. Ultimately, Friedberg said, "Corn farmers in central Africa could start to get a Climate.com service delivered through an iPhone or a text-messaging service that will tell them on a daily basis what's the optimal thing to do."

In the end, it can seem like a conundrum: the U.S. government has invested huge amounts to generate data, but it's taken a private company to put the data to use. In fact, though, this is exactly how many advocates for Open Data think it should be. "I believe strongly that you need to have a capitalist incentive to make these things work," said Friedberg. "In the government, your goal is not to fail, so your goal is not to take risks." You have to go outside government to use "the capitalist economic model that says, 'Take risk and make more return.'" But without government support, none of that innovation could happen. "I'm a huge believer," Friedberg concluded, "in the government providing infrastructure services."

That final point is a critical one. Through an Open Data infrastructure, government can spur innovation by providing the foundation for data-driven businesses. It's been true for GPS and weather data, and it's starting to be true for health data as well.

"An All-Out Crazy Party" of Health Data

The next boom in using government Open Data is likely to come in health and healthcare. A McKinsey study valued Big Data on health in the United States at $300 to $450 billion. While some of that is private data, such as hospital and patient records, much is Open Data on Medicare fees, drug effectiveness and side effects, and other aspects of healthcare and public health.

In June 2013, I was live-blogging from a packed hall at the Omni Shoreham Hotel in Washington, DC, at a meeting devoted to "unleashing the power of open health data." This convention-style hotel had been taken over by the fourth annual Health Datapalooza, one of the largest Open Data events in the world. I had gone to the Health Datapalooza two years before, in 2011, when it was held in an auditorium at the National Institutes of Health. Now I was in a huge ballroom with about 2,000 other people, a hundred or so of them standing in the back because all the seats were taken.

The very first Health Datapalooza, held in 2010, was a meeting of about 45 people at the Department of Health and Human Services (HHS) brought together by the hope that government health data could be put to greater use. By 2013, at a meeting about 40 or 50 times larger, the serious players were in evidence. "The industry is here. The VCs are here," noted one reporter who's covered these events from the start. Health data is indisputably big business, and the federal government is trying to help realize its business potential.

The Health Datapaloozas were launched by Todd Park, now U.S. Chief Technology Officer, in his earlier position as CTO of the Department of HSS. Park had been impressed by the way government weather data had built an entire industry. He saw the same potential in health, particularly given that about 80 percent of adult Internet users were getting health information online.

Park has become the Obama administration's most visible and enthusiastic spokesperson for Open Data. He's given the Open Data movement its rallying cry: he popularized the term *data liberation*, or, as he likes to pronounce it in his speeches, "*data liberación*." In addition to the Health Datapaloozas, Park has now put on Datapaloozas in energy, education, and other areas, all to encourage the private sector to do "awesome" things with government data at no taxpayer cost.

As one observer noted, a Datapalooza could be defined literally as "an all-out crazy party of data," and that's a pretty good description for these events. At the 2013 Health Datapalooza, Park praised the way that government experts were now working to make more data available at a rapid rate. "We will make the rising tide of government data available and easier to use by the public, including talented innovators and entrepreneurs like all of you, while rigorously protecting privacy," Park told the crowd. "This isn't our data, it's your data—you paid for it as taxpayers—and our feeling is that we should give it back to you in easily usable, machine-readable form, for you to use to create new applications, services, breakthroughs, businesses, jobs, and general awesomeness on a massive, massive scale." (Machine readability, a core concept of Open Data, means that the data is in a form a computer can process.) Park continued: "You will irrevocably change healthcare in America for the better. You will literally save lives and improve lives beyond measure. . . . I can't think of more important work for American innovators to be doing."

Health data is vast and diverse, and the 2013 Datapalooza showcased work being done both with Open Data from the government and with confidential, very un-open data from hospital, clinic, and patient records. But I found several companies using truly Open Data to gain new insights and build their businesses.

Some are veterans in the field who are now using data in new ways. On the exhibit floor I talked to representatives of Archimedes, which began as part of Kaiser Permanente in 1993 and split off as a separate company in 2006. Archimedes has spent two decades developing algorithms and predictive models for healthcare. Using data from sources including the Centers for Medicare & Medicaid Services (CMS), databases of clinical trials, and the National Health and Nutrition Examination Survey, Archimedes develops models of health status and the effect of medical interventions in different populations and provides tools to help match patients to treatments at the point of care. In a somewhat similar way, Impaq International (for-profit) and the National Opinion Research Center (nonprofit) are research organizations that use government Open Data to analyze the potential impact of healthcare policies and programs.

I also talked to people from iTriage, a five-year-old health data company that's been a favorite example of the Obama administration. Started by an ER doctor, iTriage lets you use a website or your smartphone to log your symptoms, get quick advice on the kind of care you need, and get a list of nearby facilities that can help. The iTriage booth at Datapalooza showed a video testimonial from a man who had woken up in a hotel room in a strange city in the middle of the night with crushing chest pain. The iTriage app on his smartphone directed him to the nearest ER, where doctors treated his heart attack and saved his life. This company relies on Open Data from the National Provider Identifier Registry, developed by CMS, to identify physicians, hospitals, and other healthcare providers who can give their users immediate care. It has now been bought by Aetna, where it is part of the company's new CarePass program for personalized medicine.

Also at Datapalooza was a new company called MedWatcher that could have an important impact on both personal and public health. MedWatcher is a contractor to the Food and Drug Administration and works to make FDA data more valuable. The FDA has long maintained a database of "adverse events"—reports of side effects from different drugs—but too few people have contributed to the database or seen the alerts it generates. MedWatcher makes the database accessible by cell phone, so patients can get alerts on the drugs they're taking and also report any problems directly to the FDA. Over time, the company could significantly increase our knowledge about drug safety and how to improve it.

While companies like iTriage and MedWatcher help patients take charge of their own healthcare, another new company, Aidin, is building quality controls into the healthcare system itself. Aidin was started by a young data analyst whose grandmother had a bad experience at a rehabilitation facility. "She was hallucinating for a week," he told National Public Radio. "She was overmedicated, and it was a really traumatic experience for my grandfather and my family." The company takes government Open Data on the quality of healthcare facilities, including data from patient reviews, and integrates it into hospitals' systems so they can use it for discharge planning and avoid such bad results.

A Government-Funded Incubator for Open Data Startups

First with weather and GPS data and now with health data, the U.S. government has defined its responsibility as collecting, gathering, and presenting data on important subjects in easily usable forms. In the United Kingdom, the government has gone further: the British government, under the Prime Minister's direction, has provided funding to foster and "incubate" new Open Data companies. The model is being tested at London's Open Data Institute, and it's off to a good start.

Five months after the November 2012 meeting that I described in Chapter 1—which, incidentally, inspired me to write this book—I went back to the Open Data Institute to see how it was accomplishing its goals. I knew the ODI had an ambitious agenda. Sir Nigel Shadbolt, the ODI's chair, put it this way: "The ODI is trying to increase the quality of data supply, stimulate the demand, build the ecosystem, enable capability, and communicate the stories of success," he told me.

The Institute's work had begun with a project to establish the right mindset. "What we're trying to do here," CEO Gavin Starks told me, "is really about catalyzing Open Data culture." When the ODI launched, the Institute immediately sent out a call for artwork that would express the theme of "Data as Culture." They got close to 100 responses from more than 20 countries and commissioned 9 of them. On my April 2013 visit, the artwork was proudly on display, giving the ODI an atmosphere of geek chic. One eye-catching piece was a life-size, translucent, rectilinear humanoid with lights and wires placed on different levels of its see-through body. I was told that this entity is connected with a facility in South London about 10 miles away and that the flashing lights reflect activity at that other spot, though exactly what activity wasn't quite clear.

My own favorite piece was a somewhat subversive example of conceptual art—a vending machine full of potato chips (excuse me, "crisps" here) located in the ODI's kitchen area. It looks unremarkable until you notice that several bags of crisps have fallen to the dispensing drawer at the bottom of the machine of their own accord. A closer look shows that the machine is connected to a flat-screen TV that shows *BBC News* nonstop. An explanation posted on the wall says that this artwork, unsurprisingly titled *Vending Machine*, is rigged up to a text analyzer that releases a bag of crisps any time the BBC reports something bad about the economy. Why so many bags at the bottom? "There's been a lot of news about the budget the past few days," one staffer told me.

The artwork is fun, but it makes a serious point: Open Data has the potential to connect to all different kinds of human activities and all aspects of our world and our lives. Again, Gavin Starks sees a parallel to the Internet here. "One perspective is that the creation of the Internet, e-mail, and the web itself were social responses to global changes, such as the increased fragmentation of communities," he said. "I have a similar perspective on Open Data: it is a social response to local, national, and global systems issues. If we are entering an era of data-driven decision making to tackle social equity, environmental sustainability, and economic growth, we will need Open Data to help inform those decisions."

The Institute provides space, technical assistance, and a collegial environment to help startups that are creating business value while doing some social good. When I visited the ODI in April 2013, four of the five young companies in its "incubator" were on the premises. My conversations with their founders reflected the variety of new Open Data applications. (When I caught up later with Starks in the fall of

2013, he told me that the number of companies ODI was incubating had doubled.)

Mastodon C: Open Data Meets Big Data. I started by talking with Fran Bennett, CEO of Mastodon C, a Big Data analytics company that was the first to join the ODI incubator. Mastodon C had specialized in using cloud computing to analyze Big Data more efficiently and with a lower carbon footprint than its competitors. The company is now focusing on big sets of Open Data from the U.K.'s National Health Service (NHS). Mastodon C has just done a government-funded analysis of variations in prescribing patterns across the United Kingdom, finding areas where expensive drugs are being prescribed for no apparent reason when generics would work as well. If this analysis helps the NHS change how some doctors prescribe medication, the NHS could save more than one billion British pounds per year.

Locatable: Data on Where to Live. After meeting with Fran Bennett I talked to Vasanth Subramanian and David Prime, two of the three cofounders of Locatable. Each is a former physics student four or five years out of college, and together they decided to apply their scientific training to a basic human question: Where should I live? They built a website showing commuting times from different locations into London and then added data on demographics, rental prices, crime rates, schools, and other statistics available as government Open Data. As I was finishing this book, I learned that Locatable's initial business model had not panned out. But following the classic startup strategy of pivot and reboot, the company is now developing a new approach in the real estate space.

Open Corporates: Tracking Tens of Millions of Companies. I then caught up with Chris Taggart, the head of Open Corporates, whose work on corporate transparency is related to my own work at the GovLab. Taggart came to Open Data from a successful career as a magazine publisher and is a bit older than his young compatriots at the ODI incubator. He described Open Corporates as "the largest open database of companies in the world. In the two years we've been going, we've gone from 3 million companies and 3 territories to over 52 million companies now in about 72 jurisdictions." The database is growing rapidly; by the time you read this, those numbers will be higher. Taggart estimated that there are about 250 to 500 million companies out there to be brought into the database, although no one can know the exact number. Open Corporates has now developed a powerful way to visualize complex corporate structures; more on that in Chapter 12.

Honest Buildings: A LinkedIn for Commercial Real Estate. Finally, I talked with Nick Katz, the Associate Director for Europe of Honest Buildings, the only U.S.-based company in the ODI incubator. Quoting a write-up in *Forbes*, Katz described his company as "like LinkedIn for builders." Picture a LinkedIn profile, he said, and then "picture one for a building. Architects and construction companies can connect to them and show off the work they did. They can have lots of data that underlies pictures and descriptions as well, and they can all be hypertagged, sort of like Twitter is now. We're building this whole search functionality that has never been done before." With Honest Buildings, a builder can search to find the best possible firms for a project, read about their past work, and assess their reputations.

These startups, and others around the world, are showing the great diversity of what can be done when Open Data is applied creatively. Large companies are also seeing the potential of Open Data. Virgin Media has teamed up with the ODI to use the company's data for innovation, and dozens of other companies have joined ODI's corporate membership program to put their data to use.

Realizing the Business Potential

A number of government Open Data initiatives—including contests, "hackathons" for programmers, and publicity events—have focused on using government data for web or smartphone applications. While that's valuable, the "app economy" may not be the most robust source of revenue for new businesses. In July 2013, one study found that 90 percent of all apps were free and ad-supported: the average price of an app was 19 cents for the iPhone, more for the iPad, and less for Android.

Anyone who wants to use federal data for business development in a serious way should begin by learning what's there. The United States' centralized data hub, Data.gov, has not been easy to use; it's included too many datasets without enough filtering and organization. At this writing, however, Data.gov is being redesigned in ways that should make it a more valuable resource. (In the United Kingdom, Data.gov.uk plays an equivalent role.) The website also has a number of communities that bring together datasets in different areas of interest, including business, energy, health, law, and manufacturing. Federal agencies are also developing application programming interfaces (APIs) to make their data easier to access and use.

The government now sponsors a number of conferences, events, and challenges to encourage the use of federal data. Among the best information sources are:

- The White House blog, at www.whitehouse.gov/blog
- The blog of the Office of Science and Technology Policy, at www.whitehouse.gov/administration/eop/ostp/blog
- The blog of the Open Government Initiative, at www.whitehouse.gov/open/blog
- The online publication FedScoop, which covers federal technology issues, at fedscoop.com

- Information Week, which covers similar ground, at www.informationweek.com/government
- The various federal data challenges posted at Challenge.gov

For healthcare, a number of resources from the Department of Health and Human Services (HHS) can provide access to data and insight about how to use it.

- HealthData.gov, produced under the Health Data Initiative—a partnership between HHS and the Institute of Medicine—makes a number of datasets available for entrepreneurs, researchers, and policy makers to use.
- CMS.gov, the website for the Centers for Medicare & Medicaid Services, now publishes a wide range of data on the U.S. healthcare system in machine-readable form.
- Medicare.gov includes comparative quality information on physicians and other healthcare providers, hospitals, nursing homes, home-health agencies, and dialysis facilities, all of which can be helpful to consumers and fuel information-based business applications.
- The Health Data Consortium, which now runs the annual Health Datapaloozas together with HHS, is "a collaboration among government, nonprofit, and private sector organizations working to foster the availability and innovative use of data to improve health and healthcare." You can learn about their work at www.healthdataconsortium.org.

Two other general resources can help people looking to develop new applications and companies from government Open Data. Project Open Data, available on the software development site GitHub at project-open-data.github.io is a government project to help developers understand and make use of federal Open Data resources. And the Application Developers Alliance, at appdevelopersalliance.org, supports the work of app developers and advocates on their behalf.

Finally, a few general strategies can be helpful to anyone hoping to find business value in government data:

Track Information from Agencies of Interest. The new Open Data Policy, described in Chapter 13, directs federal agencies not only to make their data open and useful, but also to publish lists showing what datasets they maintain. That will make it possible to study those inventories as they're released, find creative opportunities, and ask the agencies involved to make data publicly available.

Push Agencies for the Data You Need. An instructive anecdote: one of the first startups to use government data directly was Brightscope, which provides ratings of 401(k) plans for employers, pension fund managers, and individual investors. Brightscope's cofounders, brothers Mike and Ryan Alfred, realized that they could develop this service with data the Department of Labor collects on Form 5500, which pension plans use to report their financial condition, investments, and operations. After the brothers submitted more than 50 Freedom of Information Act requests, the Department of Labor finally began giving them the data they wanted—in boxes and boxes of paper forms. The Alfred brothers ultimately helped persuade the Department of Labor to begin collecting and publishing the Form 5500 data online, making it much more accessible to Brightscope and anyone else who wants to use it.

The lesson is clear: if you figure out a use for a government agency's data, push until you get it. With the new Open Data Policy, it should be much easier than it was for the Alfred brothers to get valuable government data in usable forms, unless there are significant issues of privacy or confidentiality. The Open Data Policy specifically instructs agencies to get input from data users on the kinds of data they need and the formats they need it in. Entrepreneurs should not hesitate to approach federal agencies and ask for the data they want.

Use Government Data for Business Intelligence. As massive amounts of government Open Data become available, companies will be able to use the data to help analyze their own business and their competitors'. Data on demographics, healthcare costs, wage and labor issues, and other factors will be available in ways that can be mashed up with a company's own data to provide new insights. Knowing how to use this resource will give any company an edge in business strategy and planning.

CHAPTER THREE

Consumer Websites: Choice Engines for Smart Disclosure

FOR CONSUMERS WHO WANT TO BE CAREFUL SHOPPERS, TODAY'S products and services pose some mind-numbing challenges. In the past, being an informed consumer meant knowing how to shop for a car, resist outrageous sales pitches, and avoid unsafe products. Today, consumers have to sort through a complex array of options and conditions to shop intelligently. A single cell-phone company, for example, may have more than a thousand different options for its customers, when you take all the combinations of handsets, services, limits, and fees into account. Choosing a mortgage, credit card, college, energy plan, or health insurance provider can be equally baffling.

In the past, many companies have profited from consumer confusion, encouraging people to buy expensive services and making it almost impossible for consumers to find the best choice for their individual needs. Now a new type of Open Data, called Smart Disclosure, is helping consumers navigate these confusing markets. And it's providing new business opportunities for startups as well.

Smart Disclosure combines government data, company information about products and services, and data about an individual's own needs to help consumers make personalized decisions. Since few people are database experts, most will use this Open Data through an intermediary—a "choice engine" that integrates the data and helps people filter it by what's important to them, much the way travel sites do for airline and hotel booking. These choice engines can tailor the options to fit an individual's circumstances, budget, and priorities. A growing number of companies are building choice engines into successful businesses. They range from travel and financial sites in the United States to large-scale "price comparison" websites in the United Kingdom.

To understand the consumer need here—and the business opportunity in meeting that need—imagine for a minute that you're traveling from Minneapolis to Memphis and that there are no websites to help you choose your flight (no Kayak, no Orbitz, no Expedia). Your first impulse may be to call a travel agent, but for this exercise, imagine that the travel agents have all gone on strike. If you have an assistant who usually handles this for you, imagine that he or she is out with the flu.

How would you book your flight? You would have to call airline after airline, write down the times and prices of different options, figure out which airlines that fly out of Minneapolis connect with the ones that go to Memphis, try to get an itinerary without a three-hour layover, ask what aircraft they're using because you hate those commuter jets, and finally call to book the flight you want—only to find the price has gone up 50 percent in the time it took you to figure this all out. You could spend half a day making a decision that would have taken 15 minutes with the right website and end up with no confidence that you'd even found the best option.

If any of us had to plan our travel this way, we'd consider it an archaic, anticonsumer, and fairly infuriating ordeal. But this is the kind of decision process that people go through every day to make even more important decisions. Many high-stakes consumer choices involve complex calculations that people now have to do on their own. Financial services, cell-phone plans, higher education options, health insurance, and many other services present an intimidating array of options. There's no simple way to rate them *Consumer Reports* style, because the best choice for each person depends on that individual's circumstances, budget, and priorities.

Smart Disclosure is designed to help solve this problem with Open Data from government and other sources and choice engines to make the data usable. Smart Disclosure has obvious benefits for consumers and also presents opportunities for business. The ultimate opportunity is to provide choice engines for every important, complex consumer decision—in other words, a Kayak for everything. The market for choice engines is open for entrepreneurs who can find new ways to deliver valuable, individualized data to the public.

On another level, every consumer-focused company has an opportunity to give its customers more data about the options they provide. Companies that embrace this trend and provide useful Open Data about their products and services can reach new customers and increase customer loyalty.

A Mandate from the White House

As chief of the Consumer and Governmental Affairs Bureau of the Federal Communications Commission, I had the opportunity to chair the White House Task Force on Smart Disclosure working with cochair Sophie Raseman of the Department of the Treasury. To study how government agencies can help promote this kind of consumer empowerment, the task force met for more than a year and talked with experts in more than 25 government agencies and more than 40 businesses.

Our group came up with the term *Smart Disclosure* and helped craft its official definition: *the timely release of complex information and data in standardized, machine-readable formats in ways that enable consumers to make informed decisions.* From mid-2011 to late 2012, the task force helped plan the first Summit on Smart Disclosure, hosted by the White House and the National Archives, which drew more than 300 people; launched a government website on Smart Disclosure called Consumer.data.gov; and helped shape a memo from the Obama administration urging government agencies to promote Smart Disclosure in their work. Our report was released in May 2013 and is available through the White House website.

Our work on Smart Disclosure was largely inspired by a concept called RECAP—Record, Evaluate, and Compare Alternative Prices—from the book *Nudge*, which influenced both behavioral economists and regulators in the Obama administration. *Nudge* was written by University of Chicago economist Richard Thaler and Harvard Law School professor Cass Sunstein, who was head of the Office of Information and Regulatory Affairs during President Obama's first term.

The idea of RECAP is for companies to give customers feedback on the fees they have paid for different services—for example, wireless voice, text, and data—in a simple annual summary that consumers could use to evaluate their service plans. Thaler and Sunstein used cell-phone plans as an example, with good reason. A study by NYU Law School professor Oren Bar-Gill has found that two-thirds of American consumers have the wrong cell-phone plan for their needs and that consumers pay a total of $13 billion a year more than they need to as a result.

The coauthors of *Nudge* were supportive of our task force and of Smart Disclosure in general: Sunstein wrote the administration memo urging federal agencies to use Smart Disclosure, and Thaler wrote the first thorough article about Smart Disclosure in a piece for *Harvard*

Business Review coauthored with Will Tucker. In that article, Thaler and Tucker described the impact of Smart Disclosure as a concept and the choice engines that it will make possible.

"For businesses, [Smart Disclosure and choice engines] can be both a threat and a huge opportunity," they wrote. "Firms that gain market share through deception and obfuscation—or just by taking advantage of consumer laziness—may lose out as better disclosure makes markets more efficient. Firms that are providing high-value products at reasonable prices should thrive." Their conclusion: "The rise of choice engines will do more than create super shoppers. It will make markets more efficient, create new businesses, and improve the way governments serve their citizens. Big stuff."

In his recent book, *Simpler*, on new approaches to government regulation, Sunstein was equally positive. "The idea of Smart Disclosure is sparking enthusiasm not only in the United States but all over the world. . . . With Smart Disclosure, it should eventually be easy for consumers to get secure access to their own healthcare, energy, finance, and education data. Smart Disclosure also promises to provide new opportunities for the many entrepreneurs and startups now creating new apps and services. What has been complex and hard to find can be made simple and accessible in an instant."

Personal Data for Personalized Decisions

As the RECAP model implies, Smart Disclosure works best when it brings together data about the services a company offers with data about the individual consumer. Smart Disclosure includes giving consumers data about themselves—such as their medical records, cellphone charges, or patterns of energy use—so they can choose the products and services uniquely suited to their needs. This is Open Data in a special sense: it's "open" only to the individual whom the data is about and has to be released to each person under secure conditions by the company or government agency that holds the data. It's essential that these organizations take special care to be sure the data is not seen by anyone else.

Many people may balk at the idea of having their personal data released in a digital form. But if the data is kept private and secure, giving personal data back to individuals is one of the most powerful aspects of Smart Disclosure.

In the federal government, managing personal data has become a matter of pushing the right "buttons." The trend began when the Veterans Administration launched Blue Button, a web application that lets veterans download their medical histories by clicking a virtual button on a computer screen. The VA thought these clickable records would help veterans take better charge of their healthcare by tracking their vital signs, test results, family history, and other data that's helpful to them and their doctors. The VA launched Blue Button nationally in October 2010, hoped that at least a few thousand vets would find it useful, and waited to see what would happen. By fall 2012, a million veterans had used Blue Button.

This same application has now been adopted in the private sector, where it has proved popular with patients. As of this writing in 2013, companies including UnitedHealth Group, Aetna, and Kaiser Permanente are providing it for their members. More than 80 million Americans now have access to their health records via Blue Button.

U.S. Chief Technology Officer Todd Park has promoted more projects modeled on Blue Button in what he's calling a "MyData" initiative. It's apparently limited only by the number of button colors he can persuade government agencies to use. The Department of Energy and the Environmental Protection Agency together launched Green Button, a set of standards developed with industry to give consumers timely data about their energy usage. With this information, consumers can use new websites and apps to make cost-saving, environmentally friendly energy choices. Beginning in the Western states, Green Button is already used in more than 16 million homes with tens of millions more to be covered by the program soon. A similar program is now being developed for educational data to give students and parents easy access to school records and learning resources.

In the United Kingdom, the government's Smart Disclosure agenda has begun with personal data. With leadership from the government's "midata" team, a half dozen energy companies agreed to give their customers both electronic access to their individual records and better information about the fees they were being charged. More recently, the giant supermarket chain Tesco has begun to give British consumers help based on their shopping records. Shoppers who sign up for Tesco's loyalty program can have their receipts scanned, learn instantly whether they could have gotten lower prices at a local competitor, and get cash back if that's the case.

Some of the most successful commercial choice engines combine personal data with other information to help consumers find the right options for them. Credit Karma, a California-based company, will tell you your credit score and will then present you with personalized credit card offers based on your credit profile. Personal data thus becomes a tool for the consumer as well as a marketing tool for vendors. As the company describes itself, "Unlike the traditional credit marketing world where businesses buy and sell your personal information without your knowledge and then chase you with offers, Credit Karma tries to give the power and the choice back to you." The startup is doing well; at this writing, it had just received a new round of $30 million in venture funding. A similar young company, Credit Sesame, is using government demographic data to help its users assess their creditworthiness.

The Business of Choice Engines

With all the decisions consumers have to make and all the Open Data that now exists, entrepreneurs have plenty of opportunities to build choice engines that can be both useful and profitable. The Task

Force on Smart Disclosure identified four major business models for choice engines:

- Paid subscription: Choice engines provide a service to consumers, business users, or other individual customers who pay them for it.
- Payment from institutional clients: Choice engines work for large institutions, such as utilities, companies managing employee benefits, or others that pay them a fee.
- Payment for lead generation: Choice engines recommend vendors (airlines, hotels, credit card companies, or others) who pay a commission for each new customer.
- Nonprofit: Foundations support a choice engine to do work for the public good in areas such as education or health.

When the White House and National Archives held their Smart Disclosure summit in March 2012, with input from the Task Force on Smart Disclosure, we invited a number of choice-engine companies to attend and present over lunch. They included companies helping consumers make choices in health, finance, energy, education, telecom, and car buying. As the concept of Smart Disclosure takes hold, all kinds of creative businesses, websites, and apps are being launched. Here's a brief overview of several of the most active areas.

Healthcare. Thanks largely to Todd Park's leadership at the Department of Health and Human Services, consumers now have access to Open Data about healthcare and health insurance as I described in Chapter 2. Several related government websites make this information directly available to the public. At the same time, new companies are using federal, state, and other data to help consumers make healthcare choices.

The website FAIRHealth has been a model for using Smart Disclosure to help control healthcare costs. This nonprofit was founded in 2009 with funding from the New York State Attorney General's

Office after a settlement with the insurance industry over the way companies set their reimbursement policies. FAIRHealth collects data from hundreds of private payers and others involved in handling health claims, with all identifiable patient information removed. In return for contributing data, payers get discounts on license fees—an innovative incentive for taking private data into the public realm. As of 2012, FAIRHealth had data on 13 billion different cases from across the United States, all coded by zip code. The result is a website that gives consumers unique tools to predict their out-of-pocket costs, choose among health plans, negotiate with providers, and decide whether or not to go out of network. At the same time, the database has been a valuable resource for researchers and industry analysts trying to reduce our national healthcare expenditure.

Now other, commercial websites are also providing Smart Disclosure to help people find quality healthcare and control their costs. CakeHealth promises to organize all your medical billing online so you can "know what you're paying for and find a plan that's optimized specifically for your needs." HealthGrades and ZocDoc help you find and book a doctor quickly, choosing by specialty, location, the insurance he or she takes, and patient reviews.

Perhaps most significantly, major insurance companies are now providing similar services. UnitedHealth Group, for example, offers the myHealthcare Cost Estimator to its more than 20 million policyholders. The online tool combines quality estimates with data on the actual fees charged by each provider or healthcare facility. It's a win-win for both patients and the company that insures them.

While much of the focus has been on federal health data, state data is becoming increasingly available as well. Colorado, for example, made its All Payer Claims Database available in the fall of 2012 to help consumers and help keep costs down. Phil Kalin, the head of the project, told National Public Radio that "patients will be able to go online and see how much something is actually going to cost them and compare prices across hospitals and doctors. . . . We've looked at initial kinds of data that show, for example, an MRI can cost as little as $450 to as much as $3,500 [according to Colorado Public News], with no obvious distinction in terms of quality. Other states with databases like these"—NPR counted more than a dozen at the time—"see prices vary as much as double from the lowest price to the highest, with no evidence of difference in outcomes."

Personal Finance. The Department of the Treasury has set up an online hub for federal data about finance, and the Department's blog has highlighted some of the applications being built with this data. They go well beyond typical financial websites, such as Mint.com, that focus on personal financial management and basic general advice. For example, GetRaised uses Bureau of Labor Statistics data to help people determine whether they're underpaid and calculate how much of a raise to ask for. GetRaised reports that about two-thirds of women who have used the site to ask for raises have gotten them, for an average of $6,700. HelloWallet uses other Department of Labor and Federal Reserve statistics to motivate consumers to save by comparing their financial situation with their peers'. And BillGuard helps consumers find and correct fraudulent charges on their credit and debit cards, using the new credit card complaint database maintained by the Consumer Financial Protection Bureau (CFPB).

More financial tools may be forthcoming if and when consumers get access to more of their personal data. Consumers would benefit not only from access to government-held financial records, like the tax forms the IRS holds, but from better access to data held by their financial institutions. As part of the financial reforms of 2010, Congress gave consumers the right to request access to their own personal financial information, with a few exceptions. The law specifies that financial institutions have to provide this information "in an electronic form usable by consumers" and gives the Consumer Financial Protection Bureau the authority to set standards for this information. Making this data available would help consumers and make it possible to develop new consumer services.

Real Estate. These familiar websites include Open Data and tools to help consumers find housing and evaluate neighborhoods for factors such as walkability, education, and crime. Their information comes from federal data, state and local data (such as records of deeds), and other sources.

In August 2013, President Obama held a live national conversation hosted by the real estate site Zillow, both to emphasize his administration's commitment to affordable home ownership and to stress the importance of his Open Data agenda. A post on the White House blog noted that "Zillow is powered, in part, by open government data—including freely available data from the Bureau of Labor Statistics, the Federal Housing Finance Agency, and the Census Bureau. Zillow uses these datasets to do things like help home buyers in a given region understand the point in years at which buying a home is more financially advantageous than renting the same home." The post also gave a nod to real estate sites Realtor.com, Estately, Trulia, and Redfin.

Zillow, which is essentially a choice engine for home buyers, is an Open Data success story. After the government's Open Data Policy was announced in May 2013, the Zillow blog stressed the importance of making data publicly available. "At Zillow, we built our business taking public real estate information that was previously only accessible by spending hours in dusty registry of deeds offices or courthouses poring over paper documents and making it easily accessible to consumers, for free," the post read. "And since our start in 2006, we've been heartened to see just how much the national conversation about real estate has changed since we helped free this data from the shadows. We think people are making smarter decisions based on this abundance of information." It's been a good strategy for Zillow: the company was founded in 2005, had over $66 million in revenue when they launched an IPO in 2011, and had a valuation of $2.3 billion in 2013.

Education. For the Obama administration, a public commitment to affordable education has been on a par with supporting homeownership. In his January 2013 State of the Union Address, President Obama announced a new Smart Disclosure website to help tuition-phobic parents throughout the country. He promised that "tomorrow, my administration will release a new 'College Scorecard' that parents and students can use to compare schools based on a simple criterion: where you can get the most bang for your educational buck."

The College Scorecard goes beyond the kind of information that college-bound students and their parents have gotten in the past. The new federal website zeroes in on true costs, which can differ from a school's advertised tuition as much as the price you pay for a new car can differ from what's on the sticker. Calculators on the site let prospective students enter information about themselves and find out how much students like them paid to attend each college the year before, after taking grants and scholarships into account.

The Scorecard builds on a Congressional requirement, implemented in 2011, that almost all colleges must provide a "net price calculator" to help students figure out what they will really pay. The College Board, Princeton Review, and *U.S. News* college websites all now include information on how to calculate net price. With the cost of college continuing to rise and a continued push for greater cost transparency, websites like these can provide more useful Smart Disclosure to students and parents. (In August 2013, the president announced a plan to push even harder on college costs. He proposed rating schools on the basis of factors including tuition, graduation rate, student debt and post-college earnings; making those ratings available to prospective students; and basing federal financial aid partly on each school's rating. But the plan would need Congressional approval and has not yet moved forward.)

The success of another education website called GreatSchools.org shows the high level of consumer interest in choice engines for education. GreatSchools, a nonprofit, was started a decade and a half ago by an affable, dedicated teacher named Bill Jackson. Educated in mechanical engineering at Yale, Jackson taught in the United States and China through the 1980s until the lure of the web brought him to Silicon Valley in the 1990s. He soon realized that he could marry his passion for education with his technical knowledge to create a website that would help parents choose between different educational options.

GreatSchools.org, remarkably, is now used by more than 40 percent of households with K-12 students. The website presents data both from official measures and from public opinion. It shows a "GreatSchools score" on a scale of 1 to 10 that's based on state data and a "community rating" of 1 to 5 stars based on reviews from parents, students, and school staff. The organization works closely with the U.S. Department of Education, where Jim Shelton, who directs innovation for the Department, has said that GreatSchools is "the only organization of its kind." While the website is mostly funded by foundations and contributions, about 30 percent of its roughly $10 million budget comes from advertising, licensing, and other revenue.

Energy. The Green Button experiment, described previously, is proving to be a success. With federal leadership and industry participation, Green Button has developed standards that utilities can use to make their customers' data available to them. Standardization fosters innovation, and startups with names like WattzOn, PlotWatt, and FirstFuel are using Green Button data to give both consumers and businesses individualized tools to help them save energy.

While Green Button gives you your own energy data in a form that can be easily analyzed, a company called Opower goes one step further: it compares your energy data to your neighbors' data as well. This creative approach to Smart Disclosure has been successful. Launched under a different name in 2007, Opower has grown to more than 400 employees, with headquarters in Arlington, Virginia, and offices in San Francisco, London, and Singapore.

In March 2013 I met with Ogi Kavazovic, VP of Strategy & Marketing for the company. "The problem we set out to solve," said Kavazovic, "is that energy efficiency hasn't really taken hold in the mainstream. If you look at energy efficiency programs that exist out there, customer participation at any given year is about 1 percent." Opower found a strategy in behavioral research: "With respect to energy, it's much more motivating to tell people what their peers are doing, versus telling them what their personal financial gain would be."

Homeowners have experienced the power of social norms in another context, said Kavazovic: those ubiquitous blue recycling bins. They encourage recycling because everyone can see whether or not their neighbors are using them, and no one wants to seem environmentally negligent. Opower makes your neighbors' energy consumption as visible as their recycling habits and motivates you to be energy conscious as well. Opower then provides tools to help you analyze your personal energy usage and reduce it.

Opower contracts with utility companies, which pay the company an annual licensing fee. Many operate in states where the utilities are virtual monopolies and regulatory commissions require them to run energy efficiency programs so they don't take advantage of their customers. But Opower also works with utilities in states that don't have this requirement: they see Opower as part of their commitment to customer service.

As of October 2013, Opower had saved more than 3 billion kilowatt hours in energy. A 2011 study by the Environmental Defense Fund showed homes with Opower reduced energy use by 1.8 percent on average, significantly better than other programs, and that consumers would save $3 billion a year if Opower was in every home in the country.

Broadband Service. The National Broadband Map, developed by the Federal Communications Commission and the National

Telecommunications and Information Administration, shows the speed and availability of different broadband options in almost every neighborhood in the United States. It was developed when I was at the FCC as a form of Smart Disclosure to help consumers choose the best available broadband service. As useful as the map has been, it depends on data provided by Internet service providers themselves. The FCC and others have developed ways to test broadband speed and performance independently as a check on the providers' claims.

When I was chief of the consumer bureau at the FCC, my bureau and the agency's Office of Engineering and Technology ran a national test of broadband speed, working with a consortium of industry representatives and an outside technical consultant. We published our findings in 2011 in the report, "Measuring Broadband America," and as Open Data that we made available online. The Internet service providers accepted our data as legitimate since they had helped design the tests, and most were fairly pleased with the results. But one company, Cablevision, showed up in the tests as having poorer than advertised performance at peak hours.

What happened next was a classic demonstration of how Smart Disclosure can shape a market. Another service provider began trumpeting that its service was better than Cablevision's. Cablevision got to work improving its service nationwide. We retested, saw that Cablevision's service had indeed improved, and made the results public. Cablevision then put out its own commercials promoting its performance. And, in the process, millions of Cablevision customers got better broadband service. "Measuring Broadband America" has now become an annual project for the FCC.

Another ongoing project invites consumers to run a simple test to see how their Internet service is working—and help monitor the functioning of the global Internet at the same time. These tests, which have been done more than 200 million times since 2009, are run by Measurement Lab, or M-Lab, a self-described "consortium of research, industry, and public interest partners dedicated to providing an ecosystem for the open, verifiable measurement of global network performance." M-Lab provides a network of servers around the world that run tests designed by academic researchers. When Internet users run these tests on their laptops or smartphones, M-Lab collects the data. The resulting Open Data is available for anyone to review and use, as is M-Lab's methodology.

M-Lab was launched in 2009 when Vint Cerf, an Internet pioneer and Chief Internet Evangelist at Google, convened an expert group to discuss how to gather scientific data on network performance. After a couple of days of debate, the group of researchers and policymakers decided to form M-Lab through a partnership including PlanetLab at Princeton, The New America Foundation, and several academic and research institutions as well as Google.

In the fall of 2013, I asked Cerf how M-Lab's work had progressed. "It's been very satisfying," he told me. "Eight hundred terabytes of data has been accumulated and it's publicly available for analysis by anybody who wants to participate in the program. We have tools that are geographically sensitive and can say something about the performance patterns in various parts of the world, in some cases down to the city. Our purpose here is to create an environment where measurements can be openly accessed and evaluate and analyzed." M-Lab data, Cerf told me, can "help people understand how the network works so that the technical community can infer what steps could be taken to make the network perform better." The project is aligned with Google's mission "to organize the world's information and make it universally accessible and useful" through an open, high-functioning Internet.

M-Lab data is now an important check on how both businesses and governments affect Internet performance. The data can show differences between Internet service providers that could ultimately help consumers decide which provider will best meet their needs. On the political front, one study using M-Lab data found the Iranian government slowed down the network to make the Internet almost unusable during politically sensitive times. A French research team is using M-Lab data to create a global map of network neutrality, showing those countries where the Internet serves all kinds of traffic equally and those that may give special preference to some content providers. In sum, M-Lab has become a key resource for keeping our most important means of global communication operating effectively and impartially.

One-Stop Shopping and Meerkat Marketing

While Smart Disclosure has been the basis for many successful consumer-information businesses, it has not yet reached its commercial potential. When people are shopping for credit cards, cell-phone plans, or various kinds of insurance, they don't automatically go to choice engines for help, at least in the United States. One likely reason: people just don't think very much or very often about changing these services, even though they might save a lot of money by doing so. Other kinds of Smart Disclosure are an easier sell. For example, frequent travelers may book airline flights and hotels once a month or more; people look for a new medical specialist when something new goes wrong; and anyone shopping for a house or planning for college will go online again and again to look for information before making a decision.

One strategy would be to attract consumers by creating a single website for several kinds of choices. BillShrink tried this: the company began by offering a choice engine for cell-phone plans and grew to include tools for choosing credit cards, TV service, savings plans, and cheap gas stations. BillShrink invested heavily in creating data for its choice engines, scraping wireless companies' websites for data and analyzing bills that consumers sent in. But according to Schwark Satyavolu, its founder and CEO, BillShrink was not able to survive as an independent company, despite good publicity and consumer appeal. BillShrink's parent company, now called TruAxis, was sold in 2012 to

MasterCard, which uses its data as a basis for offering personalized rewards to customers.

BillShrink, Satyavolu told me, had two problems. First, it was too expensive for the company to reach consumers when they were at the point of making a buying decision. And second, only 10 percent of the people who used BillShrink actually went ahead and made a purchase while they were on the site, which was the way that the company earned revenue.

In the United Kingdom, however, several all-purpose choice engine sites have had mass-market success. All of them cover a similar range of services: insurance, gas and electric plans, mobile phones, broadband, credit cards, and mortgages. In 2010, *The Guardian* reported that an estimated 24 million Britons used a "price-comparison" site every month, out of a population of 62 million. (Price comparison is not the only element of Smart Disclosure, but it's a core factor.) That's the proportional equivalent of more than 100 million Americans a month using online choice engines. It's hard to know why British sites like MoneySupermarket.com, Confused.com, and GoCompare.com have been so successful. But one of the newer British sites, Compare TheMarket.com, seems to be succeeding through brilliant marketing.

CompareTheMarket's spokescreature is a meerkat (as in, CompareTheMeerkat—get it?) named Aleksandr Orlov. This meerkat's success would make America's GEICO gecko, well, green with envy. Shortly after his introduction in TV ads in 2009, the Russian-accented meerkat was a massive hit, spawning a line of stuffed toys, children's books with adult appeal, and a half dozen other meerkat characters. As *The Guardian* reported just after Christmas 2009, the Orlov toy "was due to go on sale in Harrods for £19.95 until excessive demand prompted Mohamed Al Fayed," then the owner of Harrods, "to give the entire stock to children's charities." Aleksandr Orlov, whose catchphrase is "Simples!," may demonstrate a simple truth of consumer behavior: most people don't think of credit card or insurance shopping as fun, and anyone who can make it seem entertaining will have a competitive edge.

It turns out, though, that the story of these British choice engines is not so simple after all. *Which?* magazine, the British equivalent of *Consumer Reports*, published an analysis of 10 price-comparison websites and found that consumers were not thrilled with them. The best of the sites achieved less than 50 percent customer satisfaction. Equally disturbing, the sites' recommendations varied greatly when the same consumer went to several of them with the same search criteria for car insurance, which the magazine used as a test. Two of the sites offered quotes from only about 10 percent of car insurance companies.

These findings raise a troubling question: Are choice engines, both in the United States and the United Kingdom, gaming the system? It wouldn't be surprising. While choice engines follow several different business models, the most common is lead generation—they're paid when a consumer signs up for a service the website has recommended. It's tempting to structure choice engines to promote companies that pay more for leads or provide more revenue through advertising. Choice engines could become victims of their own success: the more widely they're used, the more consumers may start to suspect their motives.

Realizing the Business Potential

Smart Disclosure has significant business potential, both as a basis for commercial choice engines and as a tool that service providers themselves can offer. Anyone interested in exploring it can begin with the report of the Task Force on Smart Disclosure, available on the White House website. The federal site Data.gov also has a community on Smart Disclosure at Consumer.data.gov, with relevant datasets, apps, and resources.

An unusual firm, New York–based ideas42, is dedicated to "using behavioral economics to do good" and does various projects on consumer decision making. The company, described as a "behavioral design and consulting firm," worked on the March 2012 Summit on Smart Disclosure and does some other work in that field. They're at www.ideas42.org.

The principles of Smart Disclosure lead to a number of insights and opportunities that different kinds of businesses can use.

Give Customers Their Own Data to Build Customer Loyalty. There's growing evidence that giving people access to their own data—health records, energy usage, or shopping history, for example—will meet a consumer need and increase customer loyalty. Some 20 to 30 percent of the utilities that work with Opower, which gives consumers their own energy data, are in states like Texas that have competitive energy markets, where utilities are not required to offer energy-saving plans. These utilities choose to work with Opower because they've decided it's good for their business.

"They've done the math on this phenomenon and found that an energy-efficient customer is a happy customer," Opower's Ogi Kavazovic told me. "The value of them retaining the customer over-shadows the 30, 40, 50, or even 100 dollars they may lose in revenue in energy savings. So they both win. The customers get a utility that's proactively trying to help them reduce energy waste and their bill. In return, the customers pay the utility back in loyalty."

Sir Nigel Shadbolt, chairman of the United Kingdom's Open Data Institute, has seen similar examples in his country. As an example, he described the telecommunications market, "which is quite competitive in the United Kingdom. We have six major providers, and they compete fairly aggressively." For a long time, said Shadbolt, these companies were concerned that giving personal data back to their customers would make it easier for customers to switch to another company in search of a better deal.

"But what they've noticed," he told me, "is that the telecoms are a channel now—the device formerly known as the telephone is the channel through which so much is happening, from advertising to payment. They see this huge wave of the customer's activity going through that channel, and they've realized that they've got an amazingly complete view of the customer. They have the ability to give information back and have a conversation with the consumer about the information that is incredibly rich." To start with, they have a clear opportunity to cross-sell products that their data predicts a customer might be interested in.

In an Open Data world, every consumer-service company should ideally give its customers access to data about their own transaction history, such as cell-phone records or energy use. There's no clear business benefit to hanging on to customer data: a company can share data with its customers and still analyze the data itself for marketing insights. By giving consumers access to their own data, companies can build a connection that increases customer loyalty. And there's a growing sense in government and among consumers that people have a right to their own data in the first place.

Build a Successful Choice Engine. Several companies are trying to figure out how to make consumer choice engines affordable to build, compelling to use, and profitable to run. As more and more people come to expect Smart Disclosure, the market for choice engines will grow. By using smart applications of Open Data, enticing website design, and clever marketing, consumer choice engines can have a chance of success.

Commercial choice engines would be wise to make their business models transparent. As more choice engines are built, consumers will wonder whether they have hidden agendas. People may notice when websites that profit from lead generation leave out well-known companies that don't agree to their terms. By telling consumers clearly how they operate, choice engines can build the trust they will ultimately depend on.

Even in competitive areas like travel advice, new choice engines can succeed by providing a better, more compelling user experience.

When Kayak launched in 2005, it took on Expedia, Orbitz, Travelocity, and Priceline. To make matters worse, Google and Microsoft started providing travel information soon after. Kayak has no unique data to offer: it aggregates data from other travel sites (and unlike those sites, it earns money from advertising rather than lead generation). But Kayak developed a website with a simple, appealing style, highly personalized filters, and clear data presentation that helped it develop a loyal customer base. In an interview with *Fortune* after Kayak's July 2012 IPO—a few months before it was bought by Priceline for $1.8 billion—Kayak cofounder Paul English described the company's strategy:

> *What we do at Kayak is very simple. We help people find flights and hotels and cars. By focusing on that, we've been able to create a product that consumers have really loved. . . . We really invest in product design and development because at the end of the day, that's the asset we have. . . . If you were to compare Kayak to other companies . . . you would notice first that we have monitors all over the walls that show live data about what's happening with our customers—the latest feedback coming in, feeds from Twitter, how many searches a day we're getting in each country. Everything we do is very focused on what's happening today with the customer.*

Profit from Consumer Connection, Not Consumer Confusion. Though no one likes to admit it, many consumer-focused industries rely on confused customers to choose more expensive options than they need or to pay fees they aren't aware of. In an Open Data world, this kind of profit by obfuscation is no longer a durable business model. Web-savvy consumers have become used to sophisticated websites that help them sort through their options for everything from an airline flight to a pair of jeans. Before long, any company that requires its customers to read through long terms of service or static, confusing web pages will look like it's either antiquated or hiding something.

Consumer-focused businesses that want to lead in an Open Data world will need to be clear about the products and services they offer and make it easy for consumers to find their best options. Forward-thinking businesses have historically succeeded by providing consumer-friendly information. In 1970, for example, Giant Food hired consumer advocate Esther Peterson to help develop unit pricing and nutrition information for its customers. The company's credo, "You have a right to be informed," became part of its unique selling proposition and growth strategy. Today, faced with complex products and services, consumers have even more reason to reward companies that give them useful information as part of good customer service.

Use Choice Engines to Make Your Own Business Decisions. Businesses aren't just providers of services, they're also consumers of them. Some Smart Disclosure choice engines are now helping companies make choices that will meet their needs at the best possible price. Two leaders in Smart Disclosure for businesses—one focused on healthcare, one on telecom—show why companies that use these kinds of tools will come out ahead.

Castlight Health, which was cofounded by Todd Park before he joined the government, has helped businesses reduce their overall healthcare costs by about 10 percent. I visited the company's offices in mid-2012 and contacted Peter Isaacson, the company's chief marketing officer, for an update in August 2013. "Castlight has been growing very quickly," Isaacson told me, "moving from about 200,000 covered lives in January 2012 to over three million covered lives today."

Isaacson summed up Castlight's business rationale: "As healthcare costs continue to soar, more companies are shifting the increased cost burden to their employees. However, medical services have huge price variation, and almost no correlation exists between cost and quality, making it difficult for employees to make informed healthcare decisions. Castlight Health provides cost and quality transparency that helps companies lower healthcare spending while improving the

65

quality of care." The company does this by providing Smart Disclosure tools to their clients' employees. Castlight, which now has more than 20 Fortune 500 clients, uses healthcare quality and other data from the Centers for Medicare & Medicaid Services in HHS.

In the same way that Castlight helps reduce companies' healthcare costs, Validas can help them save money on phone bills. I first met Validas's principals when I was at the FCC and they were focused almost entirely on business-to-business telecom solutions. In January 2013, they launched a free consumer service, SaveLoveGive.com, that provides important information for consumers and can also meet the needs of small businesses. Through SaveLoveGive.com, consumers give Validas permission to access data from their phone bills, and Validas gives consumers guidance on how to save money—which the website encourages users to donate to charity. Half a year after launch, the service had signed up more than 100,000 people, saved them more than $5 million, and raised more than $110,000 in charitable donations.

"This is the crux of both our B2B and B2C operations: helping the decision-making process of mobile plan configuration by better understanding near real-time usage demands, whether a family with 5 lines, a business with 25, or a corporation with 50,000," said Dylan Breslin-Barnhart, director of SaveLoveGive.com, in an e-mail to me. "Our business clients save an average of $20 per line per month— meaning the average 25-line business saves around $6,000 per year through us. Scaled up, a 1,000-line, moderate-size company would likely see savings of nearly a quarter of a million dollars per year." At the time of this writing, the company was planning to make a solution for businesses with 10 to 100 lines available through SaveLoveGive. com; larger businesses can contract their services through the Validas. com website.

CHAPTER FOUR

New Companies to Manage the Data Deluge

F OR THE LAST FEW YEARS, THERE'S BEEN A GROWING MOVEMENT in Washington to make federal spending more transparent to the public. The focal point of the movement is the DATA Act, a not-quite-perfect acronym that stands for the Data Accessibility and Transparency Act . . . Act. It's a key Open Data initiative that would improve government accountability and change how we track the country's finances. It's had strong bipartisan sponsorship in the House and Senate and has attracted support from both consumer advocate Ralph Nader and antitax zealot Grover Norquist. Equally noteworthy, it's attracted strong support from a coalition of technology companies that was formed to push for its passage.

At this writing the Data Transparency Coalition, started by former Congressional staffer Hudson Hollister, includes 15 tech companies that support the DATA Act and Open Data legislation more generally.

There are plenty of policy reasons for citizens to support the DATA Act (more on those in Chapter 13), but why does the tech industry care? It's enlightened self-interest. The boom in government Open Data—spending data, health data, and more—will create a need for companies to help manage it. As Hollister told me:

> *Some companies want to build the next TurboTax for regulatory compliance, platforms that allow grantees, contractors, agencies, or state governments to do all their reporting related to federal spending automatically. As agencies start collecting information from regulated companies with Open Data in mind, they will generally replace paper and plain-text documents with searchable electronic data. In many cases, this means the companies could use software to submit information that they now report manually, and a new Open Data software industry will develop to help them do that.*
>
> *Other companies want to build platforms to republish the data and add value—Google is probably the prime example—and make money off advertising or subscriptions. And still other companies offer analytics. They recognize that published, standardized spending data is more grist for their mill. Finally, there are companies that offer different kinds of infrastructure—companies that design databases or cloud hosting systems that can help run these systems more cheaply.*

In May 2013, Hollister and his coalition put on a Data Demo Day in Washington to showcase two dozen companies that are part of the Open Data ecosystem. It included companies in all the categories Hollister described: those focused on regulatory compliance (such as WebFilings and RR Donnelley), companies that republish data (Govini and Spikes Cavell), those that do analytics (Informatica, Esri, EMC, IBM, Oracle), and those that provide infrastructure (such as Socrata). With more Open Data, they said in their presentations, they could help the government detect fraud, oversee contracts and grants, map the impact of federal spending, analyze government Big Data, and even prevent future Solyndra-like collapses.

When you read the list from the Data Demo Day, a few things are obvious. Managing government data is a big business, and Open Data will make it much bigger. The government's data management needs are many and varied, and the companies that can meet those needs range from well-established giants that everyone's heard of to startups known only to the tech elite. What's exciting is that the opportunities are growing rapidly for new companies—like the enterprising New York startup Enigma.io, which I'll profile later in this chapter.

Why Open Data Will Help Launch Data Startups

There's no shortage of big companies tackling big government data problems. If you're not especially tech oriented, you may think of them—as I did until recently—as those companies that buy large, luminous billboards in major airports, offering enterprise solutions to problems many of us can't quite conceptualize. They include SAP, "the market and technology leader in business management software, solutions, services"; SAS, "business analytics and business intelligence software"; Esri, a long-time leader in sophisticated mapping software; IBM; and several others. These companies work both with large businesses and with large government entities and have for years.

Some significant players are fairly new on the scene. Take Palantir Technologies, "founded in 2004 by a handful of PayPal alumni and Stanford computer scientists." (Not exactly a startup but not a long-standing tech giant either.) Since its founding, Palantir has developed an eclectic and high-impact portfolio. The company began with funding from In-Q-Tel, the venture capital arm of the CIA, and works on counterterrorism projects for the U.S. intelligence community and Department of Defense—quite the opposite of Open Data. At the same time, it's developed software to analyze Open Data on government spending and detect potential fraud. Its website also features the company's campaign to fight human trafficking through data analysis, with funding from Google's philanthropic arm.

With several companies already providing expert data analytics, why will the Open Data world need scrappy new startups? The basic reason is that the volume and variety of data, the data management challenges, and the wide range in the scale of datasets will open up room for innovators. The case was made in a recent blog post by David Eaves, Canadian blogger and self-described "public policy entrepreneur, open government activist, and negotiation expert." As he wrote:

> I do hope there will be big wins—but what I really think Open Data is going to do is lower the costs of creating lots of small wins—crazy numbers of tiny efficiencies. If SAP and SAS were about solving the five problems that could create tens of millions in operational savings for governments and companies, then Socrata, CKAN [more on them below], and the Open Data movement is about finding the 1,000 problems for which you can save between $20,000 and $1M. . . . Cumulatively over time, these savings are going to add up to a lot. But there probably isn't going to be a big bang. Rather, we are getting into the long tail of savings. Lots and lots of small stuff . . . that is going to add up to a very big number, while no one is looking.

As Open Data provides new opportunities, the federal government is starting to open up its contracting process to make it easier for lean, innovative tech companies to compete. This long-overdue change has been championed by Clay Johnson, a technologist with an impressive track record on the Howard Dean and Barack Obama presidential campaigns. Johnson started an organization with the tongue-in-cheek name The Department of Better Technology to simplify government procurement. His open-source software package, Screendoor, can be used by cities, states, or the federal government.

Johnson began with a concern about the cost of federal contracts and a desire to make the contracting process more democratic. As he has pointed out, the hard-to-navigate system of government contracting favors established, expensive vendors who know the system.

His iconic example was a federal website that cost $181 million to build—$81 million more than the new initiative to map the human brain—and that was built, ironically enough, to catalog databases on government contracts.

In October 2013, we all saw an even stronger argument for reforming government tech contracting: the epic failure of Healthcare.gov, the website that was supposed to make it easy to buy insurance under the Affordable Care Act. This site, which cost roughly half a billion dollars to build, proved unable to serve the hundreds of thousands of people who tried to use it to sign up for insurance. Although the front end of the website—the part that users interact with—was designed by a team at the Department of Health and Human Services, the technical architecture of the site, which was supposed to actually make it work, was built by long-time government contractors who apparently botched the job. Johnson and others wrote persuasively that this failure exemplified the need to reform how the federal government manages contracts for IT services.

While we're a long way from transforming how the government issues contracts, some first steps have shown that federal technology leaders understand the problem. The White House brought Johnson in for a year as a Presidential Innovation Fellow, one of an elite group working on new technology for Open Government. Screendoor (originally called Procure.io) came out of the work of that team, which developed a system called RFP-EZ that makes it easy for small companies to bid on modest government IT contracts. RFP-EZ has brought in bids about 30 percent lower than those that came in through the standard contract process. The program is now being developed further by the White House and the Small Business Administration and will help open the way for tech startups to compete for the government's business.

New data technologies used by government will create opportunities for new companies as well. The SEC now requires financial data to be filed using the computer language XBRL, described in more detail in the next chapter. The move has caused some controversy and posed some challenges for companies that report to the SEC. But it's also given birth to a company, WebFilings, that's now helping businesses use XBRL and comply with SEC regulations.

Some government agencies are helping promote advanced technologies that are particularly adept at handling complex, diverse datasets. The EPA, the Department of Health and Human Services, and the Government Printing Office have started to use a new data-management technology called Linked Data, also called Web 3.0, Semantic Web, or the Web of Data. Linked Data manages data relationships through the web itself by giving each piece of data its own web address. Unlike conventional databases, which are limited by their defined rows and columns, a Linked Data structure forms a network of connections that can be expanded in any way that's needed.

Linked Data is especially useful for analyzing data that comes from diverse sources and contains different kinds of information—the challenge posed by government data from different agencies. The hub for the British government's Open Data, Data.gov.uk, is being built in a Linked Data structure, and so is DBpedia, a spinoff of Wikipedia that manages massive amounts of data in the same way that Wikipedia organizes information and text.

The World Beyond Washington

Data management companies have opportunities to work with local governments as well as with the feds. Open Data can help democratize city government: through the global participatory budgeting movement, municipal governments around the world have given residents financial data and let them decide how to spend part of the city budget. But many cities have failed to make their data usable. "They're using old software systems and their data is not stored in a uniform or accessible way," said Nate Levine, cofounder of a software company called OpenGov, when I visited their Mountain View, California, office. "You can look at five different cities, and there is a wide variation in the data and the mechanisms used to access, analyze, and share the data."

OpenGov, originally called Delphi Solutions, was launched to fix these problems. (Joe Lonsdale, the company's chair, was a cofounder of Palantir.) The company has developed an appealing, intuitive web application that turns endless budget spreadsheets into accessible charts and graphs. "It's the kind of thing you can actually put on a big screen at the city council meeting," said Zac Bookman, cofounder and CEO of OpenGov. For example, city managers could show multiyear trends in spending on emergency services or police overtime. The company launched in Palo Alto and is now working with about 20 cities, including Springfield, Illinois; New Haven, Connecticut; and many in California.

Because every city handles its accounts differently, OpenGov still does some data formatting manually, but the company is working to automate the technology for large-scale application. The result, said Bookman, "could be dramatic. You'll have financial data in the hands of citizens, engaging citizens in actually knowing what their government is doing and how government works. You'll be increasing efficiency for government officials when they can actually see and use their data. You'll be able to get analysis with the system, compare spending between cities, and establish best practices for how governments spend their money."

Levine described his vision more colorfully: "I don't know if you've ever played Sim City," he said, "but analogously I hope we end up enabling city administrators and finance officers to run important functions right from their computers. They'd have all their key financial data accessible to them all the time."

Other companies are working on state and local data as well. CKAN, "the world's leading open-source data portal platform," provides free software to governments large and small as well as to companies and nonprofit organizations. And Socrata, based in Seattle, has become a leading vendor for governments of all sizes.

"Socrata is the first and only software company in history to focus exclusively on enabling governments to open and 'consumerize' their vast reserves of untapped data," the company's president and CEO, Kevin Merritt, wrote me by e-mail. The company's goals are to help city, county, state, and national governments improve transparency, measure performance, use data for decision-making, and make their Open Data available and usable.

"Socrata has been entirely focused on helping governments open their data," Merritt wrote. "More than 80 governments now rely on Socrata Open Data and performance management solutions. . . . As they have made more Open Government datasets available, they've attracted more interested citizens, developers, and entrepreneurs to their data. . . . These customers are pioneers in the Open Data movement. . . . Some of the biggest consumers of Open Government data are internal stakeholders. Socrata's customers have discovered that the Socrata Open Data Portal—which makes it easy for external stakeholders to find and use data—makes sharing of data between departments easier and even allows for internal, private data sharing, too." It's been a successful strategy: as of August 2013, Merritt told me, Socrata had more than tripled in size over 24 months.

Demystifying the Enigma of Open Data

Some of the most ambitious ventures are a handful of new companies trying to become large-scale brokers for government Open Data. Companies like DataMarket and Import.io have been developing this approach for a while. But probably the hottest startup in this area is a new company called Enigma.io, which may become one of the most interesting Open Data businesses.

Enigma.io was launched because two friends working with very different kinds of data realized they faced some common problems. Hicham Oudghiri was a currency trader working in New York; Marc DaCosta was an academic working on climate issues in Amsterdam.

Both were working with public data that should have been easy to access and use. And both were having a hard time of it.

They quit their jobs, started working together to solve their common data problems, and soon brought in a third colleague, Jeremy Bronfman, who had worked in the capital markets and founded an energy exploration company. Bronfman, who became the startup's CEO, was brought on, as he told me, "to turn it into a business." The founders decided to call the company Enigma.io—both in honor of the code-breaking machine developed by computer pioneer Alan Turing during World War II and because they were finding that too much public data was more enigmatic than it should be. Enigma.io would demystify it. "The idea," said Bronfman, "was to create something like the Internet for public data that really made it easily accessible and digestible."

On May 1, 2013, Enigma.io was selected out of 30 contestants as the top new company at the annual TechCrunch Disrupt NY. In addition to a $50,000 check, the company received invaluable recognition. When I met with Bronfman in Manhattan three weeks after this victory, he had been fielding calls from a number of companies that wanted to work with Enigma.io, as well as several government agencies that thought the startup could help them get their data into shape.

The company's strategy, Bronfman explained to me, was to take valuable public data, beginning with data that was "relevant to corporations or economic activity," and make it much more usable. Two challenges here. The first was to help their clients with data accessibility—the problem you have when you know what you're looking for but you can't get to it in a usable form. The second was what's being called data discovery—the ability to search about a topic you're interested in and discover data that you didn't know you needed.

"Let's say you're an analyst who's following McDonald's," Bronfman said. "Every time a new McDonald's opens, it has to file for an FCC license to operate the intercom at the drive-through window. That means you can track new franchises by looking at FCC license data. However, you might very well not know that."

"We've all been trained by Google," said Bronfman. "So the approach you take is, 'I want to learn everything about McDonald's,' not, 'I want to look for FCC licenses.'" It's Enigma.io's job to connect you to the data you need and help you discover that the FCC has data that's relevant to the fast-food business. "We want people to be able to interact with data just by searching based on the topic they're interested in rather than having to figure out where that information lives," said Bronfman.

To build Enigma.io, the team—now a little over a dozen people, all based in New York—has had to figure out how to take data in all kinds of formats, from data mailed to them on CDs to data scraped from company websites, and put it into an easily usable form. And they've had to make it possible to search through the entire dataset—not just the metadata used to describe it—at a rapid rate. Maintaining the speed of search gets harder as Enigma.io adds more data; by mid-2013, the company had 100,000 datasets (essentially, 100,000 large data tables) and more than 20 billion individual data points. On the other hand, figuring out how to incorporate new datasets gets easier over time, because there are only so many different kinds of data problems to solve.

Today, Enigma.io charges for access to its data on a sliding scale—more for hedge funds, less for academics, nonprofits, or government agencies. Eventually, the company wants to make more of its data and search capability available for free. (If they were to do it today, the traffic would crash their system.) In this model, Enigma.io's revenue would come less from access to data and more from analytic or other premium services.

You could define their mission as turning public data, or "public sector information" as the Europeans call it, into Open Data. Public data is data that's theoretically available to anyone who wants it but that may be difficult or expensive to find and use. It includes both government datasets and some data from companies, such as Nike's public list of its suppliers. For it to become Open Data, it has to be put into an accessible, searchable system, which is what Enigma.io does, and has to be made available for either a low cost or for free, which is what Enigma.io hopes eventually to do.

While the value of many Enigma.io datasets is apparent, some have a more mysterious meaning. I was curious about why the company makes aircraft registry data available. "It was part of the inspiration for Hicham and Marc," said Bronfman. "They read an article by someone who figured out that Sarah Palin was going to be the 2008 vice presidential nominee a few days before it was announced by using this dataset. He took a list of aircraft and went to each of the web portals of all the top Republican donors, then figured out which companies they were involved with, looked at the planes that they owned, and saw that all these planes that never flew above Chicago suddenly were flying to Wasilla."

"Another database that is getting an enormous amount of use, though we only have it for a few states now, is sales tax receipt data," said Bronfman. "Every time a retailer makes a transaction in a state that has sales taxes, there is a filing associated with that. Each state has a different level of granularity with which they report it and a different update schedule. But, for example, we can tell you what every restaurant or hotel in the state of Texas's revenues were for the month of March, location by location. That's an enormously powerful indicator both macroeconomically as well as microeconomically."

Even at this relatively early stage, Enigma.io has developed a robust data resource and an impressive set of tools. Bronfman described a few things you'll be able to do with Enigma.io:

- Mash up your own proprietary data (for example, a customer list) with Enigma.io's public data behind a secure firewall
- Create alerts for events of interest that are reflected in new data
- Do geographically based searches using data that Enigma.io will geocode
- Take a company—say, Boeing—and see what government agencies it contracts with to see how it may be affected by cuts in government spending

- Link news articles to Enigma.io data—enabling you to click on a company mentioned within an article in the *Wall Street Journal* and read Enigma.io data about its lobbying, campaign contributions, or other activities

Ultimately, said Bronfman, just as there is one Internet, "we think there is going to be sort of one central ecosystem around which all this stuff happens. We want that to be us. There are a lot of incredible businesses that can be built on top of this data in powerful ways. There's amazing innovation that can be built when you provide the right ecosystem and tools."

Realizing the Business Potential

The need for government data management is creating new opportunities for individuals, for entrepreneurs, and for existing businesses. Several young companies are challenging the giants that have dominated data management and are providing essential services more cost-effectively. With more than 100 federal agencies, the potential is great. And the needs of state and local governments make the potential greater still.

Across the board, the federal Open Data Policy will establish both a government mandate for agencies to release their data and a new market for data management companies and developers that can work with Open Data. For contractors offering IT and data management services, the new federal procurement system, RFP-EZ, opens a new way to connect with agencies that could use these services. While RFP-EZ only covers contracts up to $150,000, it should begin to make it easier than it's been in the past to bid on a job and have a good chance of success.

On the government side, state and local governments can learn from a number of effective Open Data programs. CKAN, "the world's leading open-source data portal platform," provides information about itself at ckan.org. Socrata, whose website gives information about the company at www.socrata.com, profiles its customers at www.socrata .com/customer-spotlight. Cities can also get help from Code for America, founded by Jennifer Pahlka in 2009 and often referred to as a "Peace Corps of Geeks." Code for America recruits talented young coders to work for a year helping city governments across the United States solve their problems through technology. More information is at www.codeforamerica.org.

For government agencies and others considering Linked Data solutions, 3 Round Stones in the Washington area has developed a Linked Data software platform and is a leader in using Linked Data with both government and commercial clients. (Full disclosure: 3 Round Stones has done some work for my team at the GovLab on a current development project.) The company's website, www.3roundstones. com, has links to various resources, including books on Linked Data written by David Wood, who serves as the company's chief technology officer. The World Wide Web Consortium, or W3C, at www. w3.org, sets best practices and standards for the web with a focus on Linked Data. And a web research group called the Tetherless World Constellation at Rensselaer Polytechnic Institute has put almost 2,000 government datasets into a Linked Data format; you can find them at logd.tw.rpi.edu.

Finally, on the broadest level, government Open Data is part of a nationwide data boom that is creating a demand for new experts. A McKinsey & Company report estimates that the United States needs about 150,000 or more data scientists beyond the number we have today. We will also need web developers, computer graphics geniuses, and others with the knowledge and skills to help process, visualize, and use Open Data. Anyone involved in training and developing this growing part of the workforce can expect busy and productive years ahead.

CHAPTER FIVE

Data-Driven Investing: New Tools for Business Analysis

THE SECURITIES AND EXCHANGE COMMISSION COLLECTS data on about 10,000 public companies and thousands of regulated entities. It's information that's critical to investors, businesses, and financial professionals. And over the last two decades, it's gone from hard-to-get expert data to one of the most important kinds of government Open Data we have.

The saga of SEC data is one of the iconic stories of the Open Data movement. It began when Carl Malamud, one of the earliest and most effective advocates for Open Data in government, essentially shamed the SEC into releasing what has now become core public financial information. In 1993, the SEC was maintaining the Electronic Data Gathering, Analysis, and Retrieval System, universally known as EDGAR, with data from the documents that corporations submit to the SEC. This valuable data was available to anyone, at a price—$15 per document, $39 per hour to connect to the database, and about $1 per page to print. Malamud, as well as some members of Congress, thought this was wrong, and he set out to do something about it.

With funding from the National Science Foundation, New York University, some other donors, and some of his own money, Malamud bought access to more than three million documents and made them available online over two years. Then, having established the value of this public data, he asked the SEC itself to make EDGAR available and began to shut his own service down. After a short attempt at resistance, the SEC agreed and adapted Malamud's database as its own public service.

Today, the SEC has made a significant shift: rather than protecting its data, the Commission is working to provide more and more Open Data about American business. Since mid-2012, more than 8,000 companies that are traded on U.S. exchanges and meet certain accounting criteria have been required to provide parts of their annual and quarterly reports—the 10Ks and 10Qs—using eXtensible Business Reporting Language, or XBRL. This computer language uses a tagging process to associate large amounts of standardized, comparable information about a company's performance with the numbers and text of the report. Every company works with a library of 11,000 different tags to describe its business information and can add even more tags if needed. All of this data in XBRL is Open Data for the public to use.

The move to XBRL was a major transition that involved technical, policy, and other difficulties. But David Blaszkowsky, the SEC official who was responsible for the office that developed and runs the program, points to its benefits. As he described it to me, "All users of this critical public financial information, down to the smallest public watchdog group or retail investor, have equal access to it—instantly, in its full detailed glory, and for free. And it's in a format that's ready to use in the spreadsheet or analytical tool of their choice."

While XBRL is a great example of Open Data in principle, the SEC's rollout has not been unchallenged. Company accountants have complained that the system is overcomplicated, overdetailed, and difficult to use, while its defenders think that companies will get used to it in time. In December 2012, a report from the Columbia Business School found fault both with the system and with its critics. While expressing "numerous reservations about whether XBRL will succeed" as the SEC intended it to, the authors also recommended that "filers should spend the effort they are investing in attempting to destroy the SEC's XBRL regulation on improving the quality of their own data, as well as on making their own data more useful and accessible to users."

There are good reasons to hope that XBRL will make the SEC's data faster and easier to access and analyze. About 20 other countries, including Australia, China, France, Germany, India, Japan, the Netherlands, and the United Kingdom, are now using XBRL in financial reporting. In the United States, the Federal Deposit Insurance Corporation uses XBRL for the Call Reports that include the financial and performance data that banks submit to the FDIC every quarter. Since the FDIC standardized this reporting with XBRL in 2005, Call Reports have become significantly more timely, more accurate, and easier to produce. Recently the SEC has used XBRL data in new, real-time fraud detection programs (dubbed "Robocop" by some reports). Investment analysts and commercial data and analytics firms are increasingly using the XBRL data as well.

An advisory committee to the SEC has now endorsed the use of XBRL and asked for even more data, more quickly, in a more usable form. The Dodd-Frank Act set up this 21-member Investor Advisory Committee to give the SEC input from the investment community. The membership, announced in mid-2012, includes top executives from several investment firms, the executive director of the Council of Institutional Investors, and representatives of pension plans for the AFL-CIO, the California Teachers' State Retirement System, and the California Public Employees' Retirement System.

In July 2013, the Committee issued a report asking for more machine-readable, usable data from the SEC. It began by noting that "massive amounts of data are regularly submitted to the SEC. Since the vast majority of this information is not currently machine readable, it is difficult to retrieve, analyze, and compare. . . . Modern technology provides the opportunity to unlock far greater value from the information that it collects and stores." The report went on to endorse the use of XBRL and similar systems, saying that they will make it easier for investors and regulators to retrieve information, monitor securities markets, and "facilitate investor participation in the governance process."

Algorithms for Investment Advice

The SEC's data in all its forms—including data on mutual funds as well as individual companies—has made possible a new breed of digital investment advisors. These websites use Open Data and apply new computational power to provide sophisticated investor tools for a wide range of clients, from ordinary investors to financial mavens.

On one end of the spectrum is SigFig, a web service that helps individual investors track their portfolios and gives them advice on reducing fees and maximizing returns. The company, which recently raised $15 million in new funding, is actually registered as an investment advisor, but its advice comes from algorithms that crunch data to deliver "unbiased, scientific portfolio recommendations." SigFig tells you when its analysis suggests you might do better with different investment funds and lets you compare your portfolio allocations to those of other people at your stage of life. The company doesn't charge a management fee. Instead, it earns its revenue through publishing arrangements with several websites and referral fees when users go to a new broker.

SigFig's users now have more than $50 billion in their collective portfolios, according to the company, and represent a younger demographic—mid-30s to mid-50s—than traditional investment advisors usually attract. Other new companies, such as Personal Capital and

Motif, are also making investor advice user friendly in the hope of reaching a similar group.

Next on the spectrum is Capital Cube, which is targeted at more serious investors while remaining remarkably user friendly. This subscription-based website uses SEC and other data to provide information on more than 40,000 globally traded public companies—"essentially every company traded," according to John Ballow, Capital Cube's founder. Unlike conventional investor tools, Capital Cube updates its data on all these companies every day, automatically creates narratives from the numbers, and provides analytic tools and data visualizations to help users assess risk and potential reward. The company was recently bought by Analytix Insight, Inc., and Ballow, who is now a managing partner at Marshall Place Associates, no longer has an operating role.

I had been in touch with Ballow for about a year and followed the company's development. When I contacted him by e-mail around the time of the acquisition, Ballow was confident that Capital Cube provided unique value. "No one has anywhere near the coverage or timeliness," he wrote. "Our dividend analysis and earnings quality analysis is essentially without competitors."

Capital Cube has not built its business on cutting-edge analysis of XBRL but has used established third-party data providers like FactSet, Thomson Reuters, and Capital IQ for its data feeds. "When we last looked at XBRL," Ballow told me, "the database had too many holes (i.e., missing lines), inconsistent definitions (i.e., extensions), and very limited coverage. If the objective of XBRL was to make finance data 'user-friendly' to the average investor, then I think it has a way to go." For example, he points out, there is no consistent definition of "revenue" in the XBRL system—a complaint I've heard from others as well. "Rather than thousands of lines of accounts," Ballow said, getting "standardized, quality assured, consistent" data at a high level "would be of greater use."

At the expert end of the spectrum, the first popular investment site to make use of XBRL has been Calcbench. Calcbench serves professionals in corporate finance, auditing, investment research, and academia with in-depth, highly detailed data on about 9,000 public companies. As its website says, "Calcbench is one of the first companies to fully harness the power of the new, government-mandated data standard called XBRL. This gives us an unprecedented direct line into the SEC's corporate financial data repository. Result: we are able to provide data with a whole new level of detail, faster, and at a much better value." Calcbench's founders acknowledge that XBRL is hard to use—"Priceless data being created, BUT *extremely complicated* to decipher," their website says—and their business opportunity has been making this rich data usable for the financial community. Calcbench also helps improve SEC data quality by using "advanced computing techniques to identify and correct errors (close to half a million corrections made so far), and increase comparability between companies."

All of these websites use hard data—even if it's flawed data—about the companies they analyze. But another, very different technology is also being used to help investors gauge the market. This approach relies on the emerging science of sentiment analysis, described in detail in Chapter 8. Using sophisticated text analytics, sentiment analysis extracts meaning from huge numbers of online reviews, tweets, and blog posts to detect positive, negative, or more nuanced "sentiments" about people, products, and companies. Inevitably, some analysts are now applying the technology to try to predict shifts in the financial markets.

I heard about some of their work at a New York conference on sentiment analysis in May 2013. One presenter was a cofounder of KredStreet (since renamed PsychSignal), which analyzes market analysts' predictions to develop synthesized assessments of the market and individual stocks. Another speaker, from Bloomberg LP, described his team's efforts to develop a system that can respond to news about companies almost instantly during the trading day. Because news can affect trading within a few seconds, their analysis has to be advanced, automated, and fast.

No one is yet sure how well sentiment analysis can spot trends in stock prices, either for individual equities or for the market as a whole. It's only one approach, and used alone it could lead to a lot of bad investment decisions. But it makes sense to look at public sentiment as one indicator of business issues and trends. That's true whether you're investing in equities or considering a more extensive investment or partnership with a publicly visible company.

Who Are You Investing In?

As investors look for deeper information on the companies they're interested in, they're likely to ask some basic questions: How is the company identified, who owns it, and who does it own? These questions are simple to ask but hard to answer. The problem of unique identifiers—consistent ways to identify a company or other legal entity—seems technical and obscure to people who don't work with financial or corporate data, but it's critically important to those who do. It's a problem that bedevils anyone looking for in-depth company information and a problem that many organizations are now trying to solve.

Identifying companies now is as difficult as it would be to identify individuals without Social Security numbers. For example, I appear on different documents as Joel Lawrence Gurin, Joel L. Gurin, Joel Gurin, and J. Gurin; receive mail addressed to Joel C. Gurin, some odd androgynous amalgam of my wife's and my first names that appears to be on a zillion mailing lists; and also get letters for Joel Gurion, Guerin, Gruin, and on ad infinitum. It doesn't matter, because I can use my Social Security number and a credit card number to identify myself clearly whenever necessary.

Companies don't have such a simple option. Like people, they're known by many different names. The difficulty is compounded by human error and by the confusing ownership structures that exist in the corporate world. There are some standard corporate identification systems, notably the DUNS numbers used by Dun & Bradstreet, but that is an expensive, proprietary system that's not available for wide public use. The DUNS numbers are essentially a code that only people who pay for access to the codebook can figure out.

Open Corporates, one of the startups being incubated at London's Open Data Institute, is putting together a resource to catalog as many as possible of the world's corporations and uses a unique identifier for each one. "This is one of the core datasets of our world," said Open Corporates CEO Chris Taggart. In contrast to the DUNS numbering system created by Dun & Bradstreet, Open Corporates' data is Open Data.

Several other organizations are also trying to create a new, open identifier system, most notably the Financial Stability Board, which has worked with the G20 to help implement a Legal Entity Identifier (LEI) system focused initially on financial companies. At this point, there's a fair amount of skepticism about how successful the LEI effort will be. But one way or another, we're likely to move to a system of unique corporate identifiers over the next several years. And that system, whatever it is, will give investors organized, useful, and reliable business data.

Open Data to Spur Investment

Small businesses face a challenge in raising capital: because they're small, investors don't want to put in the effort to assess their business potential. As a result, investors are missing some good opportunities and promising businesses can't get the capital they need. Now a few new companies are using Open Data to fill that information gap and help small business owners.

The New York startup On Deck Capital has delivered some $600 million in loans to small businesses since 2007. As its website explains, traditional banks can't afford to spend the time required to evaluate applicants for relatively small loans. To help small businesses, On Deck Capital automates the application process. The company uses software to analyze a company's performance data, such as cash flow, together with Open Data from many sources, including the company's legal records, its Yelp reviews, and public data on the company's industry and region. Using this system, On Deck Capital can approve business loans up to $250,000 in as little as one day.

In the United Kingdom, a startup called Duedil—derived from "due diligence" but pronounced "doodle"—is building an ambitious database and website to help businesses on the other side of the Atlantic. By providing in-depth analysis of British and Irish corporations, Duedil hopes to spur investment. The company's goal is to give lenders the information they need to invest in small and medium-size companies with confidence.

I caught up with Duedil's top executives in their London office, where their growing pains were apparent. Rows of busy programmers took up most of the available conference space; we had to go to a nearby Pret a Manger sandwich shop to talk. At the time, in April 2013, Duedil had just received a new round of funding and was planning to move to larger digs.

Damian Kimmelman, the company's CEO, explained what had driven him to launch Duedil in 2011. "Our goal has always been to grow transparency for private businesses because they make up such an overwhelming part of the economy," he said. "The data is siloed: it's siloed in businesses, it's siloed in providers, it's siloed in government agencies, it's siloed on the web. We think by bringing these silos together and linking them, we can create a huge amount of value for the small to medium-size enterprises [SMEs]." The business case is simple and compelling: data will give potential partners and investors enough confidence in these SMEs to work with them and help them grow. "Transparency leads to trust, and business is built on trust," said Kimmelman.

Duedil has calculated the potential financial benefit of transparency, and it's high. "A number of very strong, healthy businesses don't receive funding because they don't have relationships with financial institutions, or because they don't have the level of transparency that those financial institutions require in order to make that lending decision," said Justin Fitzpatrick, Duedil's chief operating officer. "What you end up with is a shortfall of somewhere in the neighborhood of $250 billion across Europe." That estimate doesn't even take into account the cost in lost opportunity and productivity when businesses don't have the information to work together effectively. "This data has the potential to become a force multiplier for these businesses," said Fitzpatrick.

Much of Duedil is built on Open Data, like data from Companies House, the United Kingdom's central corporate registry, although the company also uses some proprietary data sources. "We love all types of data," said Kimmelman. Like other Open Data–driven companies, Duedil adds value through its analysis and functionality rather than by having exclusive rights to any dataset. In addition to analyzing data, Duedil serves as a platform where SMEs can provide information about themselves, look for potential business partners, and develop the groundwork for productive deals. For this business community, data is the gateway to collaboration.

You might wonder why Kimmelman and Fitzpatrick, who come from New York and Boston respectively, decided to start their company in London. In fact, Kimmelman told me, they based Duedil only on British and Irish corporations because the data they would need on American corporations simply isn't available. Surprisingly, the United States has less public data on corporate ownership than many other developed countries. The state of Delaware, in particular, limits access and charges high fees for much of the data it collects on corporations that register there. It's a gap in Open Data that has made life easier for money-laundering operations and more difficult for business analysts and law enforcement. With growing international attention to this problem, there's hope that it will be addressed.

Nonprofits Are Corporations, Too

While most advocates for better investment data have focused on large multinational companies, there's been increasing pressure for Open

Data on nonprofit corporations as well. Governments and companies don't invest in these organizations the way they invest in for-profit entities, but anyone who contributes to a nonprofit expects a return on investment through the work the organization does. Nonprofits are obligated to show that the funds they collect are well spent, that their organizations are well managed, and that they don't engage in fraud.

These organizations report to the Internal Revenue Service using different versions of Form 990, which the IRS keeps on file and releases on request. But the IRS has released those forms as scanned print files, stored on DVDs that it then charges the public for. Not exactly a model of effective transparency.

In January 2013, the Aspen Institute issued a report and recommendations on nonprofit transparency written by Beth Noveck of New York University and Daniel Goroff of the Sloan Foundation. The report recommended that the IRS encourage electronic filing and that data from the Forms 990 be easily available online. Months later, the Obama administration showed that it had been listening. The president's 2014 budget included a proposal to have the IRS do what the Aspen Institute had recommended. "The administration proposes to phase in a requirement that all tax-exempt organizations file their tax returns electronically and requires the IRS to release those data in a machine-readable format in a timely manner," it read. At this writing, it's not clear whether that proposal will be implemented, but the push for greater nonprofit transparency seems certain to continue.

Realizing the Business Potential

The websites mentioned in this chapter—SigFig, Capital Cube, Calcbench, and others—all provide investment tools and, in some cases, advice for investors with different levels of expertise. It's now possible to get more complete data on publicly traded companies, in more usable forms, more rapidly than ever before. Any investor will benefit from checking these sources out.

Some investment information sources, like Marketwatch.com, now track the "sentiments" of analysts as one indicator of the markets' direction. If this approach interests you, take a look at PsychSignal. It's still in a private beta version at this writing, but you can see a video about the company and track its progress. PsychSignal has been launched by a startup called SmogFarm, which analyzes large open datasets—also a company to watch.

We're just beginning to see the benefits of Open Data in XBRL, and it's worth understanding this system now. Complicated though it may be, XBRL seems to be here to stay as a reporting requirement for public companies and a potential tool for investors. There are a number of resources available for understanding XBRL. The SEC maintains an information portal at xbrl.sec.gov. An organization called XBRL US (at xbrl.us) works on business reporting standards. The company WebFilings, at www.webfilings.com, provides software solutions to help companies report to the SEC, including meeting their XBRL requirements; the company's website claims that more than 60 percent of Fortune 500 companies are clients. The Data Transparency Coalition also reports regularly on the use of XBRL and developments in government Open Data more generally; you can follow their work at datacoalition.org.

Private companies don't have the same reporting requirements as public ones, of course, but they're still subject to scrutiny. The principals of Duedil argue that insufficient data has made it hard for investors to trust these companies and has kept away hundreds of billions of dollars in potential investment. If you're running a British or Irish company, check to see how your Duedil profile comes across: it's the persona you're showing to an increasing number of potential investors. And if you're with an American company, check out Duedil and consider whether your company should provide the same kind of data.

CHAPTER SIX

Green Investing: Betting on Sustainability Data

EIGHTY-SEVEN TRILLION DOLLARS, BY ANYONE'S STANDARDS, is a lot of money. It's slightly more than the GDP of all the world's countries combined. It's just over five times the size of the U.S. national debt. It's the amount of money you would spend in a year if you spent $2.76 million per second. And it's the numerical expression of the investment community's commitment to reducing carbon emissions worldwide.

For the last several years, the Carbon Disclosure Project, based in London and New York, has collected data about different companies' carbon emissions and has provided that data to institutional investors who now represent $87 trillion in assets. The participating companies, which include most of the Fortune 500, submit their data voluntarily through a questionnaire. Recently, the Project has also taken on the global water supply as a major issue.

This kind of environmentally aware, voluntary business reporting is a new, more compelling version of what had been termed "corporate social responsibility," a concept that goes back to the 1950s. Corporate social responsibility, or CSR, has covered environmental, labor, charitable, and community-focused practices, among others. The last decade or so has seen renewed interest in CSR, followed by cynicism, and then followed by a new, more meaningful approach.

Today's version of CSR—often called environmental, social, governance (ESG) reporting or corporate sustainability reporting—is more focused and more data-driven than it's been in the past. It uses new reporting systems to put comparable Open Data in usable forms. And it recognizes that any credible commitment to sustainability has to be backed up by data, not just by lofty statements from the CEO.

While the push to disclose this kind of data began with better-business advocates, it's now being driven by enlightened self-interest. Many investors are demanding ESG data because they see sustainable practices as a sign of good corporate governance and a predictor of long-term profitability. And, in fact, there's evidence that companies that release ESG data are more profitable than those that don't.

Investors also look for good ESG ratings to reduce their investment risk. Open Data on a company's structure and finances will help any investor calculate potential risk and return. But what about the risk that a clothing company will be involved in the next factory collapse in Bangladesh? Or the risk that a soda company operating in India will find itself in a battle over water rights? Or that an oil company will be responsible for the next major oil spill?

There's also the risk that new government regulations will require increased disclosure and bring questionable corporate practices to light. The Dodd-Frank Act, for example, includes some notable transparency requirements under its "miscellaneous provisions." That act mandates the SEC to require companies to report on their use of conflict minerals: "blood diamonds" and certain components of electronic products that are mined under inhumane conditions in the Democratic Republic of the Congo. (The SEC implemented this requirement in 2012.) Dodd-Frank requires the SEC to report on mine safety from a number of perspectives. And it requires online disclosure, through the SEC, of payments that companies make for licenses to extract oil, gas, and minerals from countries where they operate. This last provision echoes the work of the Extractive Industries Transparency Initiative, an international effort launched in 2002 to ensure that developing countries' resources are not exploited unfairly.

More and more companies are deciding that their best strategy is to operate sustainably and release Open Data that shows it. They don't want to wait for a government regulation that could make them release embarrassing data or retool their operations to avoid public criticism. They're also finding that a solid ESG strategy is good for branding and recruiting, helps attract investment, and can improve their operations.

A Short History of Sustainability

Corporate social responsibility came into vogue with the turn of the 21st century, and a number of companies had launched CSR programs by about 2005—but to no one's real satisfaction. Some on the business side warned that focusing on "good" corporate behavior could be a distraction from focusing on business performance, while CSR advocates considered the growing number of CSR programs to be largely superficial. Giving money to charity is laudable, but it doesn't mean as much if a company exploits its own workers. (CSR is still a strong concept in the United Kingdom, where the government adviser for corporate responsibility, Philip N. Green, oversees Trading for Good, a national CSR initiative aimed at local businesses.)

The new trend toward sustainability reporting—and its emphasis on ESG factors—is similar to the concept of corporate social responsibility, and the terms are still often used interchangeably. But the movement to ESG reporting has clearer benefits for the companies that embrace it. Just when CSR was starting to be questioned, some popular books began making the case that attention to environmental, social, and governance factors is simply good business.

In 2006, *Green to Gold,* by Daniel Esty of Yale's Center for Business and the Environment and speaker and consultant Andrew Winston, laid out in detail "how smart companies use environmental strategy to innovate, create value, and build competitive advantage." Much of their argument described the ways in which green practices make business sense—for example, by improving relations with the local community or lowering energy costs. But they also stressed how a genuine, public environmental commitment can build a company's brand, writing that "companies face a growing spectrum of stakeholders who are concerned about the environment." Their conclusion: "In the very near future, no company will be positioned for industry leadership and sustained profitability without factoring environmental issues into its strategy."

Esty and Winston focused on five categories of stakeholders: Rule Makers and Watchdogs; Idea Generators and Opinion Leaders; Business Partners and Competitors; Consumers and Community; and Investors and Risk Assessors, such as stock market analysts and bankers. In 2006, many of these stakeholders might have been satisfied by a company's assurances in its annual report, its CEO's speeches, or a good marketing campaign. But today, stakeholders want reliable Open Data, like the data that the government collects and releases or data that companies submit to independent groups like the Carbon Disclosure Project. They've seen too many branding campaigns turn out to be "greenwashing," calculated attempts to put a green veneer on business-as-usual practices. In one memorable example, BP's green "Beyond Petroleum" campaign attracted skepticism even when it was launched in the year 2000 and seemed downright surreal in hindsight after the Gulf of Mexico oil disaster of 2010.

The same year that *Green to Gold* came out, Andrew Savitz and Karl Weber published *The Triple Bottom Line.* They argued that companies should consider economic, environmental, and social measures together as metrics for success. They considered all these factors to be part of a company's *sustainability*, under the definition that "a sustainable corporation is one that creates profit for its shareholders while protecting the environment and improving the lives of those with whom it interacts." More important, the authors suggested using the term *sustainability* rather than *corporate responsibility*, "because responsibility emphasizes the benefits to social groups *outside* the business, whereas sustainability gives equal importance to the benefits enjoyed by the corporation itself."

Both books argued that enlightened corporations would do well by doing good. *Green to Gold* showed that companies the authors identified as environmental leaders—their group of 50 "Wave Riders"—significantly outperformed the S&P 500 and the FTSE 100 in their stock valuations. Savitz and Weber noted that companies in the Dow Jones Sustainability Index and the similar FTSE4Good Indexes have outperformed the market at large. In addition, they wrote, "Companies that belong to the World Business Council for Sustainable Development outperformed their respective national stock exchanges by 15 to 25 percent over the last three years [before 2006]." The authors quoted John Prestbo, president of Dow Jones Indexes, as saying that "sustainability becomes a proxy for enlightened and disciplined management—which just happens to be the most important factor that investors do and should consider in deciding whether to buy a stock."

Unilever, under CEO Paul Polman, may exemplify the business case for sustainability more than any other large global enterprise. Polman, who calls himself a "hard-core capitalist," has made sustainability the core of an increasingly successful company. A year after Polman's arrival in 2009, Unilever adopted a Sustainable Living Plan to simultaneously double its sales and cut its environmental footprint in half by 2020. "The essence of the plan," Polman told *Fortune*, "is to put society and the challenges facing society smack in the middle of the business." Sustainability, he told the magazine, "drives costs out, it motivates our employees, it links us with retailers." And, whatever the cause and effect, the company's drive to sustainability has coincided with increased company value. Unilever's stock increased by about 75 percent from 2009 to 2013, more than twice the stock increase of the company's closest rival, Procter & Gamble.

The Evidence for ESG

Some recent analyses have supported the idea that sustainability is good for a company's value. One showed that resource-efficient companies—a core definition of sustainability—had almost twice the investment returns of a general grouping of companies, the MSCI World Index, and were more innovative as well. Another analysis showed that the top 100 sustainable companies, based on a list of 11 factors, outperformed the MSCI by more than one-third over a seven-year period.

An extensive study by Deutsche Bank in 2012 found that 89 percent of companies that did well on ESG factors outperformed the market. An even more comprehensive analysis done in 2009 pulled together data from 251 studies over 35 years. It concluded circumspectly that "the preponderance of evidence indicates a mildly positive relationship" between measures of corporate social responsibility, as those studies had called it, and financial performance. But this analysis did support the idea that Open Data about ESG factors should be an important part of any investor's risk calculation. As the authors noted, "Doing bad, if discovered, has a more pronounced effect on financial performance than doing good."

As important as they are, stock price and financial performance are not even the full picture. Robert Kaplan, who developed the "balanced scorecard" that many companies use as a strategic tool, now considers ESG goals a key part of corporate strategy. "Good ESG performance directly contributes to a company's financial performance," he's written. "A good ESG reputation helps to attract and retain high-quality employees, thereby making human resource processes more efficient and effective. Reducing environmental incidents and improving employee safety and health improves productivity and lowers operating costs. Finally, companies with outstanding ESG reputations generally enjoy an enhanced image with customers and socially conscious investors."

In his 2012 book, *Creating a Sustainable Corporation*, sustainability and environmental management consultant Peter Soyka reviewed studies done over two decades. His review found that:

- "Well-chosen pollution prevention, eco-efficiency, and similar initiatives more than pay for themselves. . . .
- There is a strong positive correlation between improved, beyond-compliance, proactive environmental and ES&G management practices and the firm's value. . . .
- The evidence suggests that the cost of equity capital is lower for firms with . . . superior sustainability performance. . . .
- Several studies have shown that a tailored and sophisticated approach to ES&G portfolio construction can enable an investor to outperform the relevant benchmarks . . . .
- Robust evidence has been published showing that higher GHG [greenhouse gas] emissions are viewed as a negative valuation factor, particularly in emission-intensive industries. . . .
- Recent surveys . . . indicate that the greater the depth of a business leader's knowledge of and experience with sustainability, the more likely it is that he or she will understand and value its perceived benefits. . . ."

What Are the Best Measures?

While the general case for sustainable business is clear, there's also agreement that Open Data is essential to show how well companies are following sustainable practices. It's "crucial," says Peter Soyka, for companies to release specific ESG data in addition to making policy statements and showcasing their companies' sustainability initiatives.

"There is no substitute for hard data for all kinds of reasons," he told me, "starting with the need to overcome skepticism of intentions and follow-through, demonstrate effectiveness of policies and programs, and provide the means to determine whether performance is improving or otherwise."

Curtis Ravenel, Bloomberg's Head of Global Sustainability Initiatives, puts it in similar terms. "Data is critically important for the investment community," he told me. "They speak in numbers. But data alone is not very helpful; you have to contextualize it. So we really need data, policies, and some insight from management."

Ravenel came to Bloomberg over a decade ago. He told me that in 2006 "I felt that Bloomberg had an opportunity to demonstrate that sustainability could make good sense from both a business and environmental perspective, so I wrote a business plan for it. A year later the chairman called me up and asked me to come run it." The decision to publish more ESG measures grew out of this program to make Bloomberg itself a more sustainable company. Publishing ESG metrics has been a successful strategy. "We see 50 percent user increases year over year" in the use of sustainability data, Ravenel said.

Bloomberg's program is based on the belief that ESG data is becoming fundamental data for investors and should be integrated into traditional investment analysis. Bloomberg now reports on publicly available measures like greenhouse gas emissions and waste production. When a company has not released this data, Bloomberg will contact them to push for disclosure.

Others in the field give credit to Bloomberg, along with the Carbon Disclosure Project and others, for the rapid growth in the demand for Open Data on sustainable operations. "I've never witnessed so much actual data, or interest in such data, as I have over the last few years," said Mike Wallace, U.S. director of the Global Reporting Initiative (GRI), which has a presence in about 80 countries. Recently, he told me, the number of companies reporting on sustainability has skyrocketed. Sustainability reporting is now common not only for public companies, but also for companies funded by private equity firms like Kohlberg Kravis Roberts and The Carlyle Group. As Wallace points out, they want to be ready when those companies go public.

The cofounder and former CEO of the GRI, Allen White, recently wrote that "the remarkable advancement of sustainability reporting in little more than a decade from an extraordinary, to an exceptional, and then to an expected business practice stands as one of the most notable business innovations in recent years." And the change is accelerating.

The Governance & Accountability Institute, which is the Data Partner for the GRI in the United States, studied the number of Fortune 500 companies and S&P 500 companies reporting on sustainability in 2010 and again in 2011. In one year, the proportion of Fortune 500 companies reporting went from 20 percent to 57 percent; for the S&P 500, it went from 19 percent to 53 percent. Most of these companies use measures derived from the framework created by the GRI, which is now the de facto standard for sustainability reporting around the world. A study by KPMG in 2011 found that 95 percent of the world's 250 largest companies report on their corporate responsibility activities, and 80 percent of the 250 use GRI standards to do so.

As these measures show, U.S. companies still lag behind the rest of the world in sustainability reporting, although they're closing the gap. In addition to reporting more frequently, European companies are more likely to seek some sort of third-party verification, an assurance that they're reporting accurate data. Wallace points out that half of European companies now take this additional step. American companies may become more rigorous, however, if the SEC incorporates more sustainability measures into its reporting requirements. The SEC is now reviewing which measures should be considered essential, or "material," factors in a company's performance and may require more of these to be reported using XBRL. Some companies are already beginning to increase their reporting in anticipation of this change.

The GRI's reporting system is continually being improved as it is used by thousands of stakeholders from business, nonprofits, governments, accounting firms, and others. But the GRI uses a large number of specific metrics, and other groups are using still other measures. Sustainability experts are concerned that a flood of sustainability indicators could make the field too complex and confusing for analysts to compare companies easily. Three different groups—the Global Initiative for Sustainability Ratings (GISR), the Sustainability Accounting Standards Board (SASB), and the International Integrated Reporting Council (IIRC)—are working to develop higher-level systems for sustainability reporting.

Given the close connection between sustainability and performance, some analysts have argued that companies should have only one bottom line that incorporates both. The authors of the book *One Report*, Robert Eccles of Harvard Business School and Michael Krzus of Grant Thornton LLP, describe an approach that was developed at a meeting of investors, companies, standards organizations, and others in London in 2009. In their definition, "One Report means producing a single report that combines the financial and narrative information found in a company's annual report with the nonfinancial (such as environmental, social, and governance issues) and narrative information found in a company's 'Corporate Social Responsibility' or 'Corporate Sustainability' report."

This is much more than an editorial change: it's a way of integrating information that makes it more useful as Open Data. As the authors describe it, One Report "involves using the Internet to provide integrated reporting in ways that cannot be done on paper, such as through analytical tools that enable the user to do his or her own analysis of financial and nonfinancial information." Krzus told me that several companies now use One Report to integrate ESG measures in their reporting: American Electric Power, Novo Nordisk, UTC, Pepsico, and Pfizer are leaders. The IIRC, based in London, is now working to refine and promote this approach.

Supply-Side Sustainability

A company's ESG record isn't just based on how its own factories or facilities operate: it also reflects the entire supply chain—from raw materials through finished products—that it uses to run its business. Peter Soyka notes that attention to ESG factors is growing rapidly, especially "in consumer-facing businesses and their supply chains. Supply chain expectations are driving more focus on ESG data collection and reporting every year." Several major retailers are now pushing their suppliers to follow more sustainable practices and publish the data to prove it, even giving their suppliers software tools they can use to gather and report data easily. While Walmart has been the most visible leader, Mike Wallace notes that Ford, McDonald's, Intel, Microsoft, and others are also asking their suppliers for this kind of data.

Supply-chain data is attracting the attention of another critical group: the consumers who ultimately buy these companies' products. Discussions of corporate social responsibility, ESG measures, and sustainability have taken place among corporate leaders, investors, and shareholders for years. Now consumers are increasingly part of the conversation.

Daniel Goleman, author of the paradigm-shifting book *Emotional Intelligence*, made that argument in *Ecological Intelligence*, published in 2009. Goleman wrote about the market-changing potential of giving consumers fully transparent data about the products they buy. In his words, "as we [consumers] are able to make choices based on full information, power transfers from those who sell to those who buy. . . . Just by going to the store . . . we will create an entirely new competitive advantage for companies that offer the kinds of products our collective future needs. . . . As control of data shifts from sellers to buyers, companies would do well to prepare ahead for this informational sea change."

In *Ecological Intelligence*, Goleman described in detail an innovative new company, GoodGuide, that had recently been launched to provide data on the sustainability of consumer products and the companies that make them. After several years, GoodGuide remains the standard-setter for conscious consumerism. It's not yet clear how much the GoodGuide website and app will actually change the public's shopping habits. But by making sustainability data available in a form that consumers can use, GoodGuide has raised the bar on corporate transparency in a way that's begun to influence several industries. Increasingly, GoodGuide is finding that the manufacturers and companies it rates are asking for advice about how to improve their ESG profiles.

Dara O'Rourke founded GoodGuide in 2008 to help consumers choose products that are good for the environment, for workers, and for their own health. He had the background to know just how difficult this would be and the expertise to make it possible. An associate professor at the University of California, Berkeley, he teaches courses on globalization, environmental justice, and sweatshop labor and has written articles for publications ranging from *The Journal of Industrial Ecology* to *The Policy Studies Journal*.

The GoodGuide website and mobile app now draw on more than 1,500 data sources, run them through GoodGuide's algorithms, and score consumer products on that basis. An evaluation of a baby shampoo, for example, might incorporate data on the manufacturing facility, EPA data on toxic substances, the company's CEO compensation, Morgan Stanley data on the company's social responsibility record, a search of the product recall database, and much more. In a conversation in his San Francisco office, O'Rourke told me how his own work inspired him to launch GoodGuide:

> *GoodGuide came together out of a couple of different threads in my own life. My research is on global supply chains that produce the things we consume here in the United States. For the last 20 years, I've looked at Nike factories in Vietnam, toy and electronics factories in China, and clothing factories in El Salvador. Then one day I had a personal epiphany with my first daughter: I was putting sunscreen on her face and I just*

wondered, What's in this chemical formula that I'm smearing all over her face every morning? She's 10 now and she was four at that time.

I went back to campus, where I have a team of post-docs and grad students who work with me, and we found that the number-one selling kids' sunscreen in the United States has problematic chemicals that have been phased out in Europe, Canada, Japan, and Australia but remain here because of loopholes in the U.S. regulations. I went from my daughter's sunscreen to her baby shampoo and found it had a suspected human carcinogen. Her favorite toy had lead. Her mattress was covered in brominated flame retardants. And on and on, throughout my own home. I realized that despite the fact that I study these things, I have PhDs working for me, and we have all the information we do, I really knew almost nothing about the products I was bringing into my own house.

That motivated me to move the research off campus, away from academic debates to a public tool that average citizens could use. I want people to make decisions that match their own values, their own ethics, their own concerns, their own health issues. If you're concerned about climate, and I'm concerned about labor rights, with GoodGuide we can each find the product or brand that matches our values.

GoodGuide, which was bought by Underwriters Laboratories in 2012, has recruited science advisors and staffers with expertise in environmental science, chemistry, data analysis, and government regulation, among other fields. As they draw on a wide variety of Open Data sources to build consumer information, they're learning things that are important to companies as well. "Industry is going to be under pressure to disclose the material facts about their products and their supply chains, because more and more consumers, more and more NGOs, more and more labor groups are going to demand that," said O'Rourke.

Several years into the consumer-information business, O'Rourke has found that some of the biggest customers for his data are turning out to be businesses themselves. "The first round of phone calls we got after launching was from irate brands who didn't like how we rated them. We turned most of those into positive conversations. But then we got phone calls from retailers and from institutional purchasers in some cities, some states, some hospitals, and some universities that wanted our help. 'We pledged to buy green,' they said, 'and we have no idea how to do it. We need a tool to screen products and vendors for key issues.' That has grown from a handful of small companies to now most major retailers."

Many American companies are worried about new regulations that could affect their products—not from an ineffective and antiregulatory Congress but from states and even cities on the one hand and foreign countries on the other. Global retailers face new regulations against toxic chemicals in, for example, Europe, Canada, and parts of Asia. Even those that market only in the United States face increased regulations, such as a new Children's Safe Products Act in Washington state that covers 66 chemicals. Manufacturers have to either remove those chemicals from their products or publicly disclose that their products contain them.

Maine, California, and even the city of San Francisco have also passed laws that require manufacturers to disclose their use of chemical toxins. These transparency laws give companies an incentive to make sure they know what's in their products and to consider reformulating them: once a toxic ingredient is disclosed in California, for example, it takes only one blog post to make it public all over the world. It's increasingly in manufacturers' best interests to know what's in their products before they're forced to find out.

"In most of the projects we've done with brands and retailers," said O'Rourke, "there's a lot they do know. But there are also many things they don't know about their own supply chains, their own vendors, the raw materials, or whatever. And that's true of some of the biggest brands in the world." Clothing companies may not want to know much about where their products are manufactured, for example, so that they don't have to acknowledge responsibility when a factory in

Bangladesh collapses. "But increasingly they are forced to know," said O'Rourke, "by these kinds of scandals and exposés."

Realizing the Business Potential

The status of sustainability reporting is both exciting and somewhat frustrating. There are many different measures—perhaps too many. With no clear, widely accepted definition of what sustainability is, it's difficult for companies to know exactly what to report as Open Data and how, and it's difficult for potential investors, market analysts, and others to compare companies on this dimension.

At this point, the measures developed by the Global Reporting Initiative are the closest thing to a broadly accepted standard. The GRI's website, www.globalreporting.org, has full information on measures, resources, reports, conferences, and other material for anyone interested in using the GRI's framework.

If you're seriously interested in how sustainability reporting is becoming standardized, and even want to have input into the process, check out the work of the several organizations that are now tackling this problem. You can learn about the GISR at ratesustainability.org; about the IIRC at www.theiirc.org; and about the SASB at www.sasb.org.

Beyond the mechanics of corporate reporting, some best practices for companies are becoming clear:

Run Your Business Sustainably. Easy to say, harder to do. But there's growing evidence that sustainable companies have lower operational risk and stand to become more profitable. They also have a demonstrated edge in recruiting new talent. Trends in investors' requirements, consumer demand, and general best practices suggest that sustainability will become more of a corporate priority in the years ahead. Both nonprofit watchdogs and investigative journalists are becoming better at identifying companies that don't have good environmental, social, or governance practices as well.

Release Open Data on ESG Measures. Companies of all kinds would do well to release Open Data that shows they follow good corporate practices, including good ESG practices. Investors are demanding it: they see sustainability as a sign of good corporate governance and a predictor of long-term profitability. And with the success of organizations like the Carbon Disclosure Project, we are at a tipping point where so many companies are voluntarily releasing ESG data that it may soon seem suspicious not to. Consider using the One Report format to integrate financial and ESG data into a single corporate statement.

Learn What Your Critics Will Find Out. Organizations like Good-Guide are making a science out of discovering chemicals in products that could hurt consumers, and manufacturing processes that could hurt workers. The 2013 fire in a Bangladesh factory suddenly put American and European clothing manufacturers under a harsh spotlight—resulting, among other things, in an online petition signed by 900,000 people asking H&M and Gap to change their manufacturing policies. In the past, companies have often followed a strategy of plausible deniability, deliberately avoiding knowing too much about their supply chains so that they could claim ignorance if the worst happened. With more Open Data about supply chains and ESG issues, that strategy may no longer work. Companies need to know what their critics will inevitably learn and figure out how to improve their operations where necessary.

Anticipate Regulatory Mandates. Before Dodd-Frank, it might have seemed unlikely that the SEC would require companies to report on their conflict minerals policy, mine safety, or payments made to foreign countries. But all of these were hot public-interest issues that ultimately led to government disclosure requirements. Today's topics of concern—worker safety in developing countries, carbon emissions, water usage—could come under more official scrutiny in the future.

Even in a generally antiregulatory environment, federal regulations and legislation could require increased transparency on such high-profile issues. And if the feds don't act, other countries, states, and even cities may pass disclosure requirements that force greater transparency on ESG practices. Companies that manage these issues now will be well prepared for new regulatory requirements, wherever they come from.

CHAPTER SEVEN

Savvy Marketing: How Reputational Data Defines Your Brand

I'M WRITING THIS CHAPTER ON AN ULTRABOOK LAPTOP THAT I acquired by gambling. I didn't win it in a poker game, a raffle, or a bet. I bought it used on eBay.

Gambling? Think about it: I authorized a chunk of money to go to someone I'd never met, for a preowned machine that I'd never seen, described in a way that I couldn't verify. I knew that eBay's Buyer Protection Policy offered me some backup if things went wrong. But that policy involves going through a resolution process with no guarantee of the outcome—not the same as simply being able to return a laptop to the store where you bought it.

Fortunately, my gamble worked out fine, as I expected it would. The deciding factor for me was that the seller had a 99 percent positive rating on eBay, which I figured gave me good odds. By those standards, it didn't seem like much of a gamble at all.

eBay is a classic example of why reputation ratings matter on the web. A controlled study of eBay about a decade ago, which found that people paid more for vintage postcards when the dealer had a good track record, concluded that eBay customer feedback "illustrates Yhprum's Law. (Yhprum is Murphy spelled backward.) Systems that shouldn't work sometimes do, or at least work fairly well." What's true for an individual postcard seller has become true for local restaurants, major hotel chains, and a lot of businesses in between. Customer reviews, ratings, and complaints have been shaping online commerce for years.

But as review sites have become more powerful, their accuracy has come into question. No one knows how many businesses try to game the system. It's not even clear how meaningful that 99 percent rating I relied on was. One recent study found that four-fifths of eBay sellers receive a 99 percent positive rating or higher. The reason may be that the people rating them—who may use eBay to sell as well as to buy—don't want to get a bad rating themselves in retaliation.

Successful businesses need to understand how online reputation systems work, and how, despite their flaws, they're shaping consumer markets. Reviews on a wide range of sites, plus the increasing torrent of comments on blogs and Twitter, can now be analyzed quantitatively as a new form of Open Data. Understand it, and it can help you build your business; ignore it at your own risk.

Today, success comes from knowing how to build a good relationship with your customers online—including even the customers who contact you to complain. In *Can't Buy Me Like*, Bob Garfield and Doug Levy argue that "if you are still selling goods and services by blanketing the world with advertising, trying to persuade or entertain or flatter consumers into submission, you are doing things all wrong." A more authentic kind of customer connection, built by listening to customers as well as speaking to them, will be both more effective and less expensive than a traditional advertising strategy. And to do that kind of "social listening" in volume requires data analysis through methods this chapter will describe.

In the new reputation economy, companies that know how to manage their online presence will have a significant edge. The old adage that there's no such thing as bad publicity isn't exactly true online. But savvy companies can turn negative reviews, or even outright complaints, to their advantage.

How Government Agencies Became Complaint Centers

As the former head of the FCC's consumer bureau, which includes the FCC's consumer complaint center, I've heard from a lot of unhappy wireless customers. Our bureau saw cases of people who had received cell-phone bills in the thousands or tens of thousands of dollars. We dubbed the problem "bill shock"—a term that, for some odd reason, the industry didn't especially like—and we made some of our biggest cases public to show why bill shock had to be fixed.

One memorable case involved Kerfye Pierre, a young woman who had gone to visit her sister in Haiti, gotten caught in the 2010 earthquake, and stayed to help with the relief effort. She used her phone to stay in touch with friends and family in the United States. When she returned home, she found a $34,872.82 bill from T-Mobile. She had checked with T-Mobile after the earthquake hit, and the company had assured her that any calls she made during the emergency would be free. But when they said, "free," they meant only that voice calls were free, though Pierre said they didn't tell her so. T-Mobile charged her for text and data at their usual sky-high international rates.

After mediation by the FCC, T-Mobile agreed to write off all but $5,000 of the charges. At this point the FCC invited Pierre to an October 2010 press conference about bill shock and our proposed rules to prevent it. CNN built a story on bill shock around her case. Surprisingly, T-Mobile still held on to its $5,000 claim for some time before agreeing to write it off. This was arguably not the best decision that a multibillion-dollar company could make in this situation.

Eventually, not only T-Mobile but the entire wireless industry saw the light and decided to do something about bill shock. The FCC negotiated an agreement, bolstered by our complaint records, in which the wireless carriers agreed to send out warnings to their customers before they racked up any extra charges for voice, text, or data. The agreement was announced in a joint press event with the chairman of the FCC, the head of CTIA-The Wireless Association, and a representative of Consumers Union, which endorsed the plan. The agreement made national news, including the front page of the *New York Times*, and gave the wireless industry a chance to repair its reputation.

The moral? Consumer complaints matter. Stonewalling a public complaint (and T-Mobile is hardly the only company that's done this) is ultimately futile. Cognitive psychologists have various explanations for why people and companies persist in such stubborn behavior, but here, let's just say that it's a bad idea. And it's an especially bad idea at a time when there are more and more ways for consumers to take their complaints public and for those public complaints to go viral.

Several government agencies, including the FCC, have for decades tracked complaints about the companies they regulate. Others have just started recently. And many are now taking a more active approach by releasing their complaint records to the public. They hope that turning these complaints into Open Data will embarrass companies into becoming more consumer-friendly without regulators forcing them to. For example:

- For several years, the Department of Transportation has released public rankings of airline carriers based on the number of complaints it receives about each.
- The National Highway Traffic and Safety Administration has run a Safety Complaints Search Engine that allows searches by make, model, and year.

- In 2011, the Consumer Product Safety Commission launched www.saferproducts.gov, which lets consumers submit product-safety complaints and review the complaints that others have made. Previously, individual complaints to the CPSC were not made public.

In 2012, the Consumer Financial Protection Bureau (CFPB) launched a public database of credit card complaints that anyone can download, analyze, and use. The following March, the Bureau announced that it was expanding that database and adding data about complaints regarding mortgages, bank accounts, private student loans, and other consumer loans. The complaint data collected by the CFPB is especially significant, both because it's so directly relevant to major consumer concerns, and because so many people want to complain about the financial services the CFPB regulates. By July 2013, the CFPB had received 177,000 consumer complaints and sent more than 80 percent to companies for them to review and respond.

The CFPB doesn't evaluate financial service providers based on its complaint statistics, but because the bureau makes its complaint data available as Open Data, others can do that analysis. A 2013 paper by Ian Ayres and his colleagues at Yale University, provocatively titled "Skeletons in the Database," found that "(i) Bank of America, Citibank, and PNC Bank were significantly less timely in responding to consumer complaints than the average financial institution; (ii) consumers of some of the largest financial services providers, including Wells Fargo, Amex, and Bank of America, were significantly more likely than average to dispute the company's response to their initial complaints; and (iii) among companies that provide mortgages, OneWest Bank, HSBC, Nationstar Mortgage, and Bank of America all received more mortgage complaints relative to mortgages sold than other banks."

Thanks to the CFPB, financial institutions now have more exposure than ever when it comes to customer satisfaction. A recent article in *American Banker* quoted several bank executives who said they're taking customers' complaints more seriously so they won't have to go to the CFPB. By addressing customer issues effectively, they can both avoid negative publicity and generate positive word of mouth about their brands. As the head of service strategy at TD Bank put it, "I firmly believe if you learn the rules of the game, you can play to win."

One management consulting company, Beyond the Arc, is now working with financial institutions to help them manage consumer complaints in a positive way. They've identified companies that respond to complaints more slowly than others and presented this as an opportunity to improve customer service. And in some cases—for example, billing issues with Discover and concerns about Citibank's APR—they found a spike in negative comments on social media about a month before complaints to the CFPB increased. This shows that analyzing social media quantitatively is an increasingly important strategy that could help stave off official public complaints.

Turning Complaints into Social Customer Service

While Beyond the Arc has made a business out of anticipating consumer complaints and handling them, a new company, PublikDemand, is helping consumers complain more loudly. While PublikDemand focuses on consumers, the company also has advice for consumer-facing businesses. Its founders are urging companies to turn complaints into opportunities by practicing what they call "social customer service," using social media to help their customers and build their reputations in the process.

Courtney Powell, cofounder and CEO of PublikDemand, is improbably young to be an entrepreneur on her third startup. She was a 20-year-old student at the University of Texas in Austin when she joined a startup called Boundless Network that was applying technology to the promotional products industry. She was their first employee; five years later, they had 300. She left to start her own venture, a company called LeedSeed that automated marketing systems for Fortune

500 companies. After three years, she sold part of that company to her partner and was contemplating what to do next. Then fate intervened. In short succession, two major companies did what no company should do to Courtney Powell: they really ticked her off. As she told me in an interview:

> *I was moving offices and I tried to get my cable set up with Time War-* *ner Cable. They informed me that I had a cable modem that was past* *due. I didn't have it; I had never had it. They told me that they were* *going to charge me $900, which they auto-debited from my account.* *It took me about three months to get the money back. It was a terribly* *frustrating experience. That was my "Aha!" moment.*
>
> *Then, I jumped on a flight to go visit a friend in Chicago; it was a* *United flight. The customer service was just outrageous. It was terrible,* *and they were rude. On that flight I began sketching out the idea for* *PublikDemand.*

Powell teamed up with A. T. Fouty, a friend in the startup world who became the tech lead for the new company, and they got to work. Shortly after they launched at the beginning of 2012, said Powell, "we had a guy who used the site for his complaint against AT&T. His complaint was about unlimited data throttling"—a practice AT&T was using to slow down data transmission for some high-volume customers who had unlimited data plans. "He had taken AT&T to court and won, and then AT&T refused to pay. It was at that point that he used the site to get attention, and it got massive attention. We had several thousand supporters on the site, and we were covered by every major newspaper, blog, you name it." AT&T settled within hours.

The founders of PublikDemand say that they're not out to get these companies: on the contrary, they want to help them do better. They believe that companies can turn complaints into a positive for themselves by committing to social customer service. Powell sees more and more companies developing teams that handle complaints coming in from Facebook, Twitter, and other social media sources.

They do this, said Powell, because "the negative impact of these complaints that escalate through social media is huge. We've looked at how we can engage these teams and work with them to answer these complaints as quickly as possible."

"In many of my initial conversations with these companies," she said, "they immediately asked what they could do to stay off the site. They would be more than willing to pay. We are very clear up front that that's not what we are. Everybody has the same chance to resolve problems, and if you do, you'll look good." This policy isn't just good business ethics, it may be essential to PublikDemand's credibility. Another complaint site, Ripoff Report, has been sued (unsuccessfully) for practicing extortion by publishing complaints about companies and then offering a paid "Corporate Advocacy Program" to help restore their reputations. While PublikDemand may offer some paid services to companies in the future, it's offering them free advice at this time.

Some industries, and some companies, do better than others. Eighty percent of complaints to PublikDemand involve telecom companies: the majority of those are complaints about wireless service (no surprise there), while the rest are about cable and Internet. Next comes the banking industry, followed by airlines. Among telecom companies, Verizon Wireless has gotten unusually good at social customer service, said Powell; "that's a huge win for them" and saves them money, since helping customers through social media is cheaper than going through a call center. American Express and JetBlue are also quick to respond. In contrast, said Powell, "we struggle massively with AT&T Wireless," which gets more complaints on PublikDemand than any other company. And Apple "notoriously doesn't respond at all."

"A lot of companies," Fouty added, "see customer service as a cost center and try to minimize the amount of money they're spending there." But, he said, "companies have an opportunity to keep the social media part of the operation in house and really merge it with customer service. You're going to see some real differentiation between companies that get it and companies that don't."

User Reviews: Who Are These People?

Consumer complaints—especially when they go viral and attract media attention—are a worst-case scenario for any company. Less stark, but just as powerful, is the Open Data contained in the consumer reviews that now crowd the web—on Yelp, Zagat, TripAdvisor, Hotels.com, Amazon, Best Buy, and who knows how many other sites.

Studies have now demonstrated, if proof were needed, that these sites influence where people eat and sleep and what they buy. Harvard Business School professor Michael Luca and his colleagues have studied a number of rating systems, including book reviews and the *U.S. News* college rankings, and have quantified Yelp's impact. According to their research, an additional star on Yelp brings with it a revenue increase of 5 to 9 percent. Another study, this one at UC Berkeley, found that even an extra half-star increases the chance that a restaurant will sell out at peak times, boosting its profit margins.

Now consider the potential impact of Glassdoor, where anyone can rate his or her employer anonymously. Glassdoor was founded in 2007 when one of the cofounders asked another, "What would happen if someone left the unedited employee survey for the whole company on the printer and it got posted to the web?" That's an employer's nightmare, but the founders of Glassdoor saw it as a business opportunity. In addition to salary information, the site has "reviews describing life on the inside" of almost 90,000 companies.

Consumer review and rating sites have a lot of power, have almost no accountability, and aren't always credible. How hard can it be, after all, to anonymously give your own restaurant a five-star review and fire a one-star blast at the bistro across the street at the same time? My own experience with Yelp is that small restaurants, where even a couple of reviews can have an impact, tend to show the biggest variations. I'm still trying to figure out how a new restaurant in my neighborhood—depending on whose review you read—can be both the best Italian restaurant this side of Tuscany and a roach-infested pit that I should avoid at all costs.

A recent study from Northwestern University and MIT shows that negative reviews may not even have a competitive rationale: they may come from "self-appointed brand managers" who are upset by a company's product when they may not even have bought it. For example, the study's authors note that many loyal Harley-Davidson customers were offended when the company introduced a perfume; it just didn't seem right to them. As one of the authors said, "For every thousand customers, only about 15 write these reviews— and one of them is writing negative reviews of products he hasn't bought."

Sometimes reviews are so blatantly fake that they make the news. There's nothing new about authors (this one excepted) posting good reviews of their own books on Amazon. But what about the Michael Jackson fans who organized a campaign against his biographer, all posting reviews that looked authentic but that added up to a coordinated attack on the book? Or the makers of a Kindle case who offered a steep discount with the strong hint that they expected a five-star review in return?

Manipulated reviews are ultimately bad for websites: over time, they'll damage a site's credibility. Review sites can fight the fakery by using linguistic analysis, looking for disparities between reviews and sales, or analyzing the place and time when reviews are posted. If a lot of reviews of a New York hotel are being posted at 3 a.m. New York time, when it's lunchtime in Bangalore, that may mean the hotel is outsourcing to a review mill in India.

In the fall of 2012, Yelp ran a sting operation to clean up its reviews. Yelp had noticed that businesses were advertising on Craig's List, offering to pay people to write positive reviews and giving them detailed instructions on how to do it. Yelp employees responded to several ads, figured out which companies were running them, and then outed those companies. They announced that Yelp would start putting a "Consumer Alert" icon next to companies that had been trying to pay for praise.

How many reviews are fake? One professional in the field says she believes the different estimates average out to about 5 percent. A Gartner study says the number is approaching 10 to 15 percent. Bing Liu, a professor of computer science at the University of Illinois at Chicago, has estimated that a third of all reviews are fake. In other words, no one really knows.

Fake reviews aside, different review sites tend to reflect different views of the world. Kristin Muhlner, CEO of the Washington, DC, market analysis firm newBrandAnalytics, walked me through the differences. "Generally speaking, people on Facebook are more positive than on other sites on the web," said Muhlner. "Yelpers talk more about service than other categories like pricing and value. We often see a disparity between Yelp star ratings and TripAdvisor star ratings, but that might be because of a certain demographic. Generally, women tend to be slightly more positive than men, but they often tend to have the most insightful feedback as well." Overall, across many industries, she said, about two-thirds of reviews are positive and one-third are negative.

When I met with Muhlner, I had just had an interesting experience that made me realize why analysts need to go into the actual text of reviews to learn anything meaningful, rather than just look at the star ratings and add up the numbers. I had stayed at a Georgetown hotel a few minutes' walk from newBrandAnalytics: great location, nice staff, beautiful room, tasty buffet breakfast, and the worst wi-fi I've found in a hotel in years. How would I rate it? Would I average these factors out and give it three or four stars? Would I give it only one star because the bad Internet service rules it out for me and most other business travelers? And if I did give it a one-star rating, would that be misleading for a family on vacation that doesn't need broadband—and might actually be happy to have the kids forced to spend family time instead of going online?

In the end, the only meaningful way for me to rate this hotel would be to rate each factor separately: five stars each for location, staff, room, and breakfast and one star (at most) for the wi-fi. That's essentially the information I'd convey in words if I wrote a descriptive review of the hotel. It turns out, Muhlner told me, that's how most people write reviews—and most people who go to review sites will intuitively focus on the write-ups more than the stars. They'll find a lot of information there: on average, a single review mentions about five different factors.

"One of the bits of research we've done has looked at reviews and how star ratings correlate with the actual content of the review itself," she said. "What we find is that 25 percent of five-star reviews contain something negative and 75 percent of one-star reviews contain something positive." That doesn't mean a numerical rating is meaningless or irrelevant; there's plenty of evidence that it affects a company's bottom line. But as Hamlet might have said if he were a marketing consultant, when a business is in trouble, the fault is not in the stars alone. The miniature narratives of consumer reviews also have a powerful effect on people's decisions.

For these reasons, social media analysts have to find ways to mine the full information that consumer reviews convey. And they can't just go to one or two review sites. To get a full view, they need to take insights from a range of different sources, either by scraping data from their websites or making arrangements with them or a data aggregator for data feeds.

You might think you could get around all these problems by looking to Twitter instead of consumer reviews. After all, Twitter is a massive data source—one billion tweets are now sent every three days—and that volume should include a lot of demographic groups and make it pretty hard to game the system. Twitter analytics, if you can call it that, is becoming a growing business. Twitter data has been used by the entertainment industry for several years and is now being used by other companies that want to gauge public opinion quickly.

Since the vast majority of tweets are public, it's all Open Data, at least in theory. Twitter does offer application programming interfaces (APIs) and data feeds for users who want to analyze them. But more extensive or sophisticated Twitter analysis may require additional help.

Two leading companies that function as data aggregators, Gnip and Datasift, can now put all that Twitter data in a manageable form and sell it to companies that want to use it. They analyze Twitter and other social media sources all in one place; Gnip has become known as "the Grand Central Station for the Social Web." While Gnip doesn't seem to post its prices online, Datasift advertises subscription services ranging from $3,000 to $15,000 a month.

It's not so clear, though, how much the "fire hose" of Twitter data is worth. Jonathan Taplin, director of the Annenberg Innovation Lab at the University of Southern California, did a study of a massive number of tweets about the 2012 election. He and his colleagues concluded, he said at a New York conference, that "Twitter has nothing to do with public opinion—it's a platform to see how snarky you can be. . . . If we're thinking about data, we have to separate data on what people do from data on what people say."

While political tweets may be especially nasty, other researchers also worry that relying heavily on Twitter is problematic: it may mostly tell them a lot about heavy Twitter users. Many now study Twitter simply because so many tweets are available to analyze. But some are having second thoughts. Helen Margetts, the political scientist who heads the Oxford Internet Institute at Oxford University, analyzes web and social media activity to study patterns of civic engagement—part of a new data-driven discipline that's being called "computational social science." "At a recent conference," she told me, "I noted that there's an awful lot of analysis in Twitter because it's easier to get Twitter data than it is to get anything else. I find that a bit worrying."

The Reputation-Improvement Business

It's a conundrum for any company. Reviews of products and services are influential, persistent, and seem to mean something. But they're largely uncontrolled, hard to analyze, and somewhat suspect. How do you manage the unmanageable and build your online reputation?

One solution is negotiation. I've been told that some hotel companies, for example, will monitor sites like TripAdvisor, find postings from unhappy customers, and then contact them to offer a bonus or deal that will make things right. In return, when the customer is satisfied, he or she will take down the damning post. While this strategy may work to a degree, some new companies are developing more systematic—and, they would claim, more effective—ways to manage a company's reputation online.

The most prominent is a California startup called Reputation. com, led by founder and CEO Michael Fertik. "You have to care about your reputation," Fertik explained when I met him in April 2013 in his Redwood City, California, office. "It will become increasingly possible to quantify and measure. And it's going to impact and influence every part of our lives."

Reputation.com is building a portfolio of services, including some I'll describe in a later chapter, but the core of the business, as the name implies, has been reputation management. "A lot of people want us to make sure that their Google results look pretty good," said Fertik, "making sure that the bad quarter that you had 10 years ago is not still the headline when you've had 10 years of uninterrupted growth since then. Increasingly, our customers care also about the review ecosystem."

Reputation.com helps companies improve their online images by using good reviews to drown out the bad. Fertik was clear that his company will not fabricate anything: "We will never create a review. We will never pretend to be our customer's customer. We will invite real customers, at least people we believe to be real customers, to provide real feedback, positive and negative. When it comes to search results, we will write content, but we will not say anything that is not 'Wikipedia approvable.' If you send us your resume, we'll write a short bio of you based on the resume; if you send us your LinkedIn profile, we'll basically rework it to turn it into a short file."

While this isn't unethical, you could argue that it's playing games with the system. But the counterargument is that the game is rigged to begin with. Anyone can say anything about you or your company online, and once they say it, it never goes away. Every potential employer or business partner, not to mention just about anyone you happen to meet, will Google you, find the bad stuff, and, human psychology being what it is, will probably believe it. Fertik said that his company will never ask posters to remove negative content from the web—it's not a good strategy, and it doesn't work anyway. So instead, they develop a larger volume of online content about you and make sure that much of that content is positive.

In the end, Fertik said, there's nothing sacred, or even necessarily good, about the natural state of the Internet and what it says about each of us. "Some people are very flippant in saying that the Internet is a source of truth," he said. "It's not. It's not a source of falsehood. It's just a source of half-truth, of incomplete truth. We just give you a fighting chance of explaining who you are."

Reputation.com is now working on a new product, the Reputation Score, that will synthesize reputational data in a clear and quantifiable way. "The Reputation Score, as we envision it, is intel on you— whether you're an individual professional or a large enterprise," Fertik wrote to me in a follow-up to our interview. "The idea of the score is to see how you're doing on an objective scale and relative to your competition. An individual attorney, for example, might be able to see how she's doing compared to others like her—and even possible projected career paths, based on her likely salary, career history, and educational background. In the future, if she interviews at a different firm, she might provide her Reputation Score as another proof point for making a favorable hiring decision. An automotive services company could see how it's doing, based on review volume, recentness, content, etc.—and understand how it stacks up to its closest competitors."

Realizing the Business Potential

Online reputation is now core to brand value. Any visible company needs a social media strategy that's not just about getting the word out about its products and services, but also getting information in about how the company is perceived. Review sites, blogs, and Twitter are all sources of information that become useful Open Data when you aggregate and analyze what they say about your company. One incident won't make or break your business—a smart company can recover quickly—but the reputation that builds up over time is either an important asset or an equally major liability. Paid advertising can't compensate for a visible online track record of unhappy customers, poor customer service, or disappointing quality. Businesses need to study what's on the web about them as closely as the most discriminating consumer will and respond quickly, intelligently, and continuously.

Learn How to Mine Social Media. Depending on the size of your business and your information needs, you may be able to do social media analysis in-house, or you may need more expert help. Twitter makes APIs available to help analyze the stream of tweets about your company. Some businesses may find that their most important input comes from tracking their reviews on sites like Yelp and TripAdvisor and responding to comments when necessary. For more extensive data collection, companies like Gnip and Datasift can provide their services.

Consider Using Reputation-Enhancing Services. Reputation.com is the clear market leader in this space. When I asked CEO Michael

Fertik why businesses should consider using his company, he wrote a response that could apply to any such service:

> *People trust what they find online as much as word of mouth. That's why companies need to be proactive when it comes to their online reputation. This can be a large-scale problem—and issues born in technology are most efficiently solved by technology. Services like Reputation.com make it possible for potential customers to find online results that reflect the offline reality of a business. We also help enterprise and small business customers to monitor, manage, and analyze their online reviews in real time. The service includes the ability to create customized outreach campaigns to ask a business's customers for their honest feedback (without providing incentives) on review sites. It's important to tap into the silent, satisfied majority who never think to write a review—because they will help build a review base that others can trust.*

Turn Complaints into Marketing Opportunities. Public complaints about a company's products or services can seem like a major headache, if not a nightmare. But their public nature can become an asset *if* they're handled well. Instead of handling negative comments by contacting individual customers, as is now often done, a better strategy may be to answer complaints in public, in ways that make it clear that a company is attentive, responsive, and fair.

This concept of social customer service—combining customer service and social media—is increasingly compelling. It's a way to respond to customers where they are, online and on social websites. It's more cost-effective than traditional call centers. And it's a way to display good customer service to the public and potential future customers as well.

When I interviewed Courtney Powell, the founder of the complaint website PublikDemand, I asked her what advice she would give if she were speaking to an audience of Fortune 500 executives. "If I were a Fortune 500 CEO," she answered, "I would be very keen to take advantage of the idea of social customer service and empower social customer service teams. Customer service and social media are melding into this one concept. It not only functions as customer service; it also functions as your marketing. People's ability to see the responses back and forth on Twitter means you are in the public eye and you will be judged on your response."

CHAPTER EIGHT

The Marketing Science
of Sentiment Analysis

THERE ARE TWO REASONS TO WATCH YOUR ONLINE REPUTA-
tion: one is to improve it, and one is to learn from it.
You can buy reviews outright (bad idea) or encourage authentically
positive reviews (better) to improve your company's online rep. But
that won't do anything to change the true level of customer satisfaction or make your company run better. To make smart changes
in business strategy and operations, you need to understand what
your customers are telling you through their tweets, reviews, and
blog posts.

A number of market analysts now use what's called *sentiment analysis* to get customer insights from social media. Sentiment analysis deals
with the potential biases of Twitter, blogs, and various review sites by
aggregating and analyzing Open Data from all of them, in the hope
that the combined data will be more representative and accurate. And
it goes way past the ratings star system to analyze the text of reviews
in detail.

To learn more about sentiment analysis, I went to Takoma Park, Maryland, to see Seth Grimes, founder of the consulting firm Alta Plana Corporation and a recognized industry guru on the subject. Up a flight of stairs between the storefronts for Mark's Kitchen and Middle East Cuisine I found his basic, functional office. The surroundings were unassuming, but the technology we talked about was cutting-edge.

Grimes has worked on the web since its early days and has been in and out of government and government-related organizations as a consultant and contractor. He worked for the Organization for Economic Cooperation and Development in the mid-1990s, helped the U.S. government with the 2000 census, and worked on other government projects in the United States and the United Kingdom. Around 2002, he became interested in text analysis, a decades-old field that was showing new potential. The possibilities of this technology led to his new career path and his current work.

The technology for text analysis dates back to the 1950s, Grimes explained, when it was developed both in academia and at research centers like IBM. It was important in an era when business transactions depended on paper documents and when analyzing the text in those documents electronically could be very valuable. But when IBM mainframes and other machines began to computerize business in the 1960s, paper documents became less important, and text analysis became less compelling. It took another 30 or 40 years before some visionaries began to see the commercial potential in text analysis and took a fresh look at that early research.

As Grimes and others have revisited this technology, they've brought a modern perspective to it. In the 1950s, he said, text analysis required "scanning documents and doing optical character recognition in order to get them into electronic form. Now, information is natively in electronic form, starting in the late 1990s in e-mail and on the web and starting five or six years ago with the social web. This huge volume of information being generated in electronic form has business value. The idea is to use computer software to do what people do, which is read text and make sense of it in some kind of situational framework."

Text analysis is now being used for a wide range of applications, both simple and profound. It's the basis for Summly, the app that 17-year-old Nick D'Aloisio developed to summarize newspaper articles and sold to Yahoo! for $30 million. At the other end of the spectrum, the Federal Reserve is using technology to monitor public opinion about the economy and understand what affects consumer confidence.

Text analysis has many profitable business applications. A pharmaceutical company, for example, might use text analysis to speed up the process of drug development. "There are many thousands of research articles from laboratory research created each year," said Grimes, "and repositories of millions of research articles. If you want to bring a new drug to market you want to find out what prior research has been done. You need to be able to not only search based on particular keywords, you need to be able to understand when a paper describes, for example, the interaction of two proteins or some kind of chemical substance." (A researcher familiar with biomedical science also flagged this for me as a major use of text analytics. She noted that Quertle, an ad-supported company, is now doing text analytics of several databases from the National Library of Medicine, while Compendia Bioscience and H3 Biomedicine have a collaboration to mine genomic data from the National Cancer Institute in a search for new cancer therapies.)

"If you're doing marketing," Grimes continued, "you want to do something similar. 'What do people have to say about my company's products? What are the particular flaws in the product? What do they really like? What do they think about the pricing, about the customer service, for not only my products but my competitors'?' There's a huge volume of information" in text that can be extracted and analyzed from the web. Doing that, and doing it well, is the essence of sentiment analysis.

IBM Meets Jane Austen

While sentiment analysis is promising, "the technologies are not mature by any means," said Grimes—and some companies that look into it may be disappointed by simplistic applications. "For a lot of people," he said, "sentiment analysis just means whether a particular tweet or review on TripAdvisor or article in the newspaper is positive or negative. To me that is a very stilted point of view. If you take the word *sentiment*, you might picture Jane Austen, and the word *sentiment* to someone like that is very broad. It encompasses emotion and mood and attitude and opinion."

Analytic tools that just look for positive or negative words can be entirely misleading if they miss important context. According to Grimes, "What's positive to you might be negative to me. If you're with Toyota and General Motors has a broad recall, then that's actually positive news for you. Or when a prominent figure dies—Whitney Houston was a great example—all over Twitter, you see people posting 'Oh, how sad I am about Whitney Houston's death.' Tools that are based on keywords see 'sad' as negative, but that's actually a positive tweet about Whitney Houston. The writer had a positive attitude toward her."

"A more sophisticated analysis," said Grimes, "will decompose a message or document into particular elements. Those elements could be the names of persons or places or companies or products or concepts or themes. More capable tools will extract those entities or concepts or themes, and they will analyze the sentiment attached to each element."

Grimes runs a twice-a-year conference on sentiment analysis, and I had a chance to go to the all-day event he held in New York in May 2013. The presentations showed the breadth of this work. Among other things, the speakers talked about using sentiment analysis to:

- Predict political unrest in Kashmir and the results of a national election in Pakistan
- Determine how effective antismoking scare ads are

- Find and fix problems with online payment systems
- Do text analysis of idiomatic Chinese
- Lay the data-based groundwork for campaigns to appeal to customers emotionally

Most applications of sentiment analysis are using a hybrid of machine and human work. Julie Wittes Schlack, the Senior VP of Innovation and Design at Communispace (who happens to be a high school friend of mine), describes machine analysis as a kind of "metal detector" that finds trends of interest to her company's consumer-focused clients. Human analysts can then use those clues, analyze the relevant social media messages in more depth, and feed their findings back to the computers to help improve their algorithms.

As sentiment analysis is refined, it will become a powerful tool for market research. A number of articles and blog posts over the last few years have talked about this potential, while also acknowledging that it's not yet fully realized.

Several examples have come from companies that have not used sentiment analysis to mine the web as a whole but have set up special websites for their products and analyzed what their customers tell them there. Unilever, for example, used sentiment analysis to study consumer opinions on websites it set up about its products. Communispace creates online communities for its corporate clients and helps them interpret the results.

Some of the most robust applications of sentiment analysis so far have been in the entertainment industry. In Cambridge, Massachusetts, Bluefin Labs monitors what 25 million people are saying about television via Twitter, Facebook, and other social media. Cofounder and chair Deb Roy says that they are "combing the entire landscape to find all the comments about TV" that they can analyze to create what they call the TV Genome, "essentially a huge dataset that quantifies and organizes all social media conversations about TV." Their system enables them to monitor reactions to commercials and shows in real time.

Sentiment analysis can also be used for competitive intelligence and strategy. One European consulting firm, for example, has done this kind of analysis for telecom companies. When negative comments about a competitor's service are spiking on social media, it may be an ideal time for a telecom company to run ads touting its own network's reliability.

New tools may make sentiment analysis more accurate in the years to come. Some companies are now figuring out how to analyze audio recordings not only for their words, but also for cues to emotional content like rapid speech, raised voices, or one speaker interrupting another. They're getting richer insights into communications as diverse as doctor-patient dialogues and customer service calls. At the same time, several startups are developing facial analysis technology to decode emotion from video feeds.

In a way, sentiment analysis is starting to come full circle. It began by deconstructing written documents to extract atoms of meaning from human communication. It may develop in the future by adding in the cues and signals that make our communication truly human.

What's Your Sentiment About City Government?

Less than 10 miles southwest of Seth Grimes's office, newBrand-Analytics is putting sentiment analysis to use in creative ways. This new company uses sentiment analysis to help major national chains improve their service and customer satisfaction. And in what seems to be a unique application, the company is also studying citizen satisfaction with the city of Washington, DC itself.

Kristin Muhlner, the CEO of newBrandAnalytics, came to the job with a background in enterprise software. When we met in 2013, she explained the unusual chain of events that led to the company's launch three years earlier. "The company was the brainchild of a couple of guys who had been serial technology entrepreneurs and ended up in the high-end salon business. They realized that what was impacting their salon business the most was what people were saying about them online. They started looking for tools to help them and nothing existed. That's how the idea for newBrandAnalytics was born."

Text analysis of online reviews and social media can do more than tell a business how its customers feel—it can show how to fix what's bothering them. Many clients of newBrandAnalytics are in the hospitality industry, including companies like Hyatt and Ruby Tuesday. newBrandAnalytics can help a hotel chain learn exactly how customers feel about the amenities at a specific location—the Grand Hyatt in Atlanta, say—and can direct attention to the details that matter most. Just as easily, newBrandAnalytics can analyze what a competitor's customers are saying about them. The company now monitors about 6,000 different businesses worldwide and roughly an equal number of their competitors.

What may be most unusual about newBrandAnalytics, however, is one unique client. In addition to studying hotel and restaurant chains, newBrandAnalytics monitors customer satisfaction for the city of Washington, DC. While this isn't a typical market research exercise, it's a sign of just how broad the applications of sentiment analysis are—and how governments can use market research in positive ways. Muhlner told me how the project came to be.

Mayor Vincent Gray was elected in 2010 and brought with him some new ideas about city government. "When the mayor came into office," said Muhlner, "he wanted to have an enormous amount of transparency. When he saw what we were doing, he became intrigued by the idea of applying it in a government setting. We'd never attempted it in a government application before. But as we started talking more, we realized, 'Well, it works in exactly the same way that it does when you walk into an Apple retail store or into a Five Guys,'" the hamburger chain that President Obama has been known to favor. Whether you're a customer at a burger joint or a "customer" waiting for service at the DMV, you're evaluating your experience as it happens and may write about it online.

The city started with five agencies in the pilot: the Department of Motor Vehicles, the Department of Transportation, Parks and Recreation, Public Works, and Consumer and Regulatory Affairs. The company analyzed Twitter, Facebook, blogs, and online forms the city agencies made available to people who used their services.

"We started gathering this data," Muhlner continues, "and did it for 60 days or so. We coded the sentiment on a five-point scale from very negative to very positive that translates pretty nicely into a letter grade. In the United States, at least, a letter grade has a strong emotional connotation to it." That turned out to be an understatement. In this first marking period, four of the five agencies were graded with a C-minus; Public Works was at the head of the class with a C-plus. And the agency directors reacted, predictably, a bit emotionally.

"We were in the first meeting, a standing monthly meeting with the mayor and all of his agency heads, and we delivered these grades. There was quite an uproar. Folks were very concerned about the implications, feeling very strongly that this didn't represent the local service that they were providing citizens. There were weeks of discussion. And at a certain point, the mayor's office said, 'Whether you like it or not, this is what people are saying about us publicly. So we need to stop talking about why it's wrong and we need to start talking about what we're going to do about it.' It was a phenomenal shift, and what you saw immediately was everyone agreeing and saying, 'We'll do this.'" The grades were made public in mid-2012 on a website the city built called Grade.DC.gov.

The agencies got to work improving their operations, and six months later, their new grades were much improved. At a one-year anniversary event for Grade.DC.gov, Mayor Gray praised the program and its impact on city agencies. "It's gotten competitive, which is good," the mayor told the *Washington Post*. "Because everybody wants to get an A, right?"

Other opinions about the program have been mixed. An earlier *Washington Post* piece critiqued Grade.DC.gov for posting grades that were at odds with other performance evaluations—for example, of DC's fire department—while the *Wall Street Journal* praised it as a civic innovation. In the end, the most significant innovation may simply be Washington's commitment to listening to its citizens, which could serve as a model for other cities.

No other city seems to have followed Washington's lead yet. Muhlner and her team are talking to some municipal governments, reminding them that they can choose whether or not to make their evaluations public. There are no takers yet, but she's hopeful. "This," she said, "is a very new concept for local governments."

Realizing the Business Potential

Sentiment analysis is an evolving field: it's tantalizing and useful but still imperfect. Watching its evolution reminds me of the way that speech recognition technology has changed over a decade and a half. I was introduced to Dragon Naturally Speaking by a friend, an early adopter, shortly after it was launched in 1997. I bought it, tried it out, discovered how long it would take to train the system to understand my voice, and quit. Today, every smartphone has Siri or its Google equivalent. These systems still make mistakes—often humorous ones—but they're vastly easier to use and more accurate than their predecessors.

Sentiment analysis, as nearly as I can tell, is somewhere between the early Dragon systems and the latest Siri incarnation in its ability to extract meaning from social media. Doing it well still requires a human-machine collaboration, and humans and computers both have their difficulties in coding text accurately. It's particularly vexing, for example, to try to figure out when a tweet is straightforward and when it's sarcastic. (Well, *that's* a big surprise!) Moreover, there is no standard accuracy measure for sentiment analysis—a gap that enables companies in the field, in Grimes's words, to "claim impossible accuracy numbers."

That said, sentiment analysis has the potential to turn social media into useful Open Data that can be analyzed for important marketing insights. While sentiment analysis is still an evolving science, it's attracting interest and experts in fields as diverse as linguistics, financial analysis, and artificial intelligence. One research driver is the fact that government agencies and academics are trying to use sentiment analysis for national security and to detect potential terrorist activity. We can expect this technology to move quickly in the years ahead, so it's worth learning about it and considering using it now.

Since the best results seem to come from a machine-human hybrid approach, this isn't a methodology you can just turn on and let run. But used with intelligence and care, sentiment analysis can be a powerful tool to help you understand your customers, your business environment, and your strengths and vulnerabilities. More than a simple overall report card, it can give insight into operational areas that are working well and those that need improvement.

For companies that are ready to explore sentiment analysis, there are consulting firms with growing expertise in text analytics and good information and perspective to offer. The twice-a-year conference that Seth Grimes runs on sentiment analysis brings together leaders in the field with diverse perspectives. You can find news about the conferences at sentimentsymposium.com. And Communispace, which sets up customized online communities for its clients, follows the field and related areas through a blog, Verbatim, at blog .communispace.com.

The most important thing, however, is to consider first whether sentiment analysis is right for your needs, and, if so, how you will use it. As one social media marketing newsletter pointed out, "Sentiment analysis mainly tracks the prevailing opinion of your brand, and it's most effective for larger brands, especially consumer brands. For smaller brands, there just aren't enough mentions of your brand to make sentiment analysis very insightful. For small brands, scouring specific websites, such as Yelp ... likely provides more insights regarding prevailing opinions about your brand."

When I e-mailed Seth Grimes to ask his advice for companies interested in sentiment analysis, he replied: "I advise potential users to start by determining business goals that could be reached by collecting and analyzing attitudinal data. Determine what data is most promising and the steps you'd need to collect, filter, and transform and analyze the data and the presentation interfaces you'd need in order to convey insights that are usable for decision making. The industry leaders to follow are the ones who are technology- and data-aware but who have expertise or experience in your business domain (e.g., hospitality, consumer electronics, public policy) or business function (e.g., market research, competitive intelligence, customer service, customer experience)." In other words, be sure you know why you're using sentiment analysis and how you'll use it before you dive in.

CHAPTER NINE

Tapping the Crowd for Fast Innovation

THE TERM *CROWDSOURCING* HAS BEEN USED TO DESCRIBE ALL kinds of ways to tap the knowledge and skills of large groups of people. But different "crowds" function very differently, and the term may be losing its value. (One recent paper counted 40 different definitions of crowdsourcing.) It's becoming common instead to refer to this way of working as "collective intelligence"—deriving data, knowledge, and insight from large groups connected online. While there are many varieties of collective intelligence, I think of it as encompassing three different approaches that use Open Data in different ways.

Open Innovation Through Collaboration. This is the model that may be most useful for scientific and medical research. Open innovation projects are like the world's largest research seminar. They engage a critical mass of experts in a field—maybe dozens, maybe even hundreds—to share data and insights with each other as they work to solve an important problem or set of problems. The classic example is the Human Genome Project, which established a commitment to data-sharing at a time when the web was just getting off the ground. In this model, research data becomes Open Data in a way that encourages intense real-time collaboration. This powerful approach is the subject of the next chapter.

Match.com for Research. This method searches for a small number of experts who have the unique skills to solve a particular difficult challenge. In these cases, someone with a problem to solve or data to analyze will try to reach as large a crowd as possible to find the few people who have the right experience, skills, and interests to help. These include contests like the ones on the government's Challenge.gov site that encourage new applications for federal Open Data, or the groundbreaking Peer-to-Patent project, described below, that opened up data from the U.S. Patent Office.

The Data Hive. This is the opposite of the Match.com model: instead of engaging a small number of experts in specialized work, it taps huge numbers of people to do routine work to analyze or improve Open Data. In the same way that tens of thousands of worker bees make up the hive that produces honey, many crowdsourcing projects engage thousands of ordinary people to contribute data, clean up datasets, or both. Each individual does small pieces of work that contribute to the solution, and together they make large-scale datasets more valuable. The Zooniverse "citizen science projects," which I'll describe later in this chapter, fit this model.

The Match.com Model: Experts and Projects Find Each Other

About a decade ago, some research centers began to realize that they could solve tough problems cost-effectively by offering incentives for outside experts to help them. InnoCentive, which bills itself as "the pioneer in open innovation, crowdsourcing, and prize competitions," was launched in 2001 and has worked with companies and organizations ranging from Eli Lilly to NASA. By offering prizes ranging from 500 dollars to over a million, InnoCentive taps a world of expertise.

Dwayne Spradlin, who now heads the Health Data Consortium that puts on the Health Datapalooza (see Chapter 2), was president and CEO of InnoCentive for five years. While the company has largely focused on scientific and technical problems, it runs contests around business, marketing, and social science questions as well. "InnoCentive is the concatenation of innovation and the word *incentive*," Spradlin told me. "We learned that if you understand a problem well enough to articulate it and structure it and indicate what is really needed and why, and you put the right inducements around the system, then innovators from all over the world can go to work and bring entirely new perspectives to the table."

Many InnoCentive challenges have involved data analysis and, in particular, predictive analytics. As Spradlin said, "In the world of Big Data, using the past to predict the future is increasingly important. These types of problems are extraordinarily well suited for competitions and crowdsourcing."

In these contests, solvers have tried to find the best algorithms for predicting such phenomena as disease outbreaks, adherence to drug regimens, solar flares, or the clinical course of patients with heart disease. To test the power of the algorithms, InnoCentive might give solvers a dataset from, say, 2010, and see how well they could predict the actual data from 2011. Interestingly, breakthrough solutions often "emerge from outside a given field," Spradlin said. "Often it's the new perspective and outside thinking that identify new patterns and correlations. Being an industry insider, in some cases, is actually a hindrance." While InnoCentive is largely focused on solving scientific research problems, the same approach could be used to predict the results of online promotions or marketing campaigns.

Other companies have set up their own specialized sites to recruit solvers for complex data problems. Kaggle presents challenges for data scientists that often center on predictive modeling: one contest sponsored by Amazon asked for help in predicting what level of IT access different employees would need based on their jobs, while another, from Yelp, challenged contestants to predict businesses' future ratings. Top-Coder, a similar "competitive community" for data problems, recently worked with Harvard Medical School to apply collective intelligence to a tough gene-sequencing problem and came up with solutions that were a thousandfold faster than anything designed before.

Scientists as well as entrepreneurs are just starting to see the benefits of tapping into online communities. In 2011, researchers at the University of Washington were stumped by a tough problem in AIDS research. They were trying to understand the structure of a monkey virus similar to HIV. They had collected years' worth of data from X-ray studies but couldn't make sense of it. So they tried something revolutionary: they released their data as Open Data on the puzzle site Foldit.com, made a game out of the problem, and invited users to help them solve the virus's protein structure. Within three weeks, a team of gamers had found the protein structure that had stumped scientists for over a decade. When the scientists published the results in *Nature*, they described it as "the first instance that we are aware of in which online gamers solved a long-standing scientific problem."

From Competition to Expert Networks

These kinds of contests have shown that collective intelligence can produce rapid, effective solutions to stand-alone problems. But others are working to develop more long-lasting "expert networks": ongoing systems to engage an expert crowd with critically important datasets. The first expert network built for government, and one that has become a model for developers in this field, was the Peer-to-Patent system developed by Beth Noveck.

Noveck has long been an Open Government pioneer promoting both citizen engagement and Open Data. Like many Open Data innovators, she came to the field from an eclectic background marked by intellectual energy and curiosity. She spent her undergraduate years at Harvard as a social studies major, went on to get a master's there in comparative literature, got her PhD in political science from the University of Innsbruck, where she wrote a dissertation on the writer Hugo Bettauer and the politics of 1920s Austria, and then got her JD at Yale Law School and became an expert in intellectual property.

After starting several projects on technology and innovation, Noveck was tapped by the Obama administration to become the first Deputy Chief Technology Officer of the United States and lead the administration's Open Government initiative. In addition to developing policies to promote "transparency, public participation, and engagement," she was instrumental in developing both Challenge.gov and Data.gov, the federal government's centralized resource for government data of all kinds. Today she leads the foundation-funded Governance Lab, or GovLab, at NYU, which studies new technology-enabled models of governance, trains students in these approaches, and helps put Open Government principles into practice. (Full disclosure: I'm now working full time as senior advisor to the Governance Lab.) The GovLab's guiding philosophy is that "greater engagement leads not only to more legitimate democratic governance, but also to better solutions for citizens."

The project that brought Noveck to President Obama's attention was her revolutionary approach to the patent process, which she developed at New York Law School. Peer-to-Patent, which Noveck chronicles in her book *Wiki Government*, was groundbreaking in two ways. First, it required the U.S. Patent and Trademark Office to release data about patent applications more openly than ever before. And second, it relied on an ad hoc network of self-identified experts to comment on and help vet those applications in an open forum. This approach to information development was already common for projects in the tech community, but using it to inform a government process was a radical idea.

Reviewing patent applications poses a unique data problem. Every application depends on a search for "prior art"—patent officers need to review any previous work that might have produced a similar invention and thus invalidate a patent claim. But with a backlog of hundreds of thousands of applications and little time to review them, it's easy for patent examiners to miss important precedents. Peer-to-Patent solves this problem by opening up the patent application system and inviting members of the public to submit examples of prior art that they are aware of. It treats the patent office's database of applications as Open Data and uses the work of volunteer reviewers to add new and valuable data efficiently.

Following Peer-to-Patent's lead, the United Kingdom, Japan, Korea, and Australia are now experimenting with similar systems. In his influential book *Future Perfect*, Steven Johnson summarizes the project's impact: "Just as Kickstarter widens the network of potential funders for creative work, Peer-to-Patent widens the network of discovery and interpretation, bringing in people who do not necessarily have the time or the talent to become full-time examiners but who have a specific form of expertise that makes them helpful to some patent cases."

In a recent conversation, Noveck reflected on the lessons of Peer-to-Patent and how they applied to her later work on Open Government and Open Data. "What was very instructive about this was, number one, that if you ask people online to help you by supplying useful information, they will do so—which ran contrary to previous assumptions. If you ask them a specific and hard question, they will give you a useful and meaningful response. Number two, the information that they will supply you, using the tools that software makes possible, can be used to make that information manageable. The typical experience with online engagement up to that point was that you would get 10,000 responses, and it would not be usable by decision makers. We could use the tools that are emerging today to organize engagement online and make it useful."

Other commercial enterprises have set up similar expert networks on an expanding range of subjects. Stack Exchange, which grew out of Stack Overflow, a Q&A site for programmers, now has more than a hundred different Q&A sites where experts can exchange information. Stack Exchange also now hosts Peer-to-Patent, currently called Ask Patent. While their business model isn't completely clear, Stack Exchange and Stack Overflow are based on free expert participation. By awarding points that increase community recognition, they motivate people to share their expertise without compensation.

That's also the model for CrunchBase, "the free database of technology companies, people, and investors that anyone can edit." Almost all of the information on CrunchBase comes from public contributions. Matt Kaufman, president of CrunchBase, told me that their data comes from "investors, entrepreneurs, journalists, fans," and other individuals. When I asked him what motivates them to contribute, he responded by e-mail: "In general, people are motivated to participate online by: (1) money, (2) sex, (3) recognition, (4) a means to establish identity, (5) a means to curate/build/nest. In a professional setting (e.g., CrunchBase), 3–5 are key."

It seems that expert networks need to inspire to succeed. Think of Wikipedia as the ultimate example. The online encyclopedia has been built with free labor; researchers have shown that contributors find satisfaction in the very act of contributing and becoming part of the community. But other projects have shown that you can't simply buy this kind of expert participation.

Perhaps the most striking failure of collective intelligence has been a company called InfoArmy, which planned to pay volunteers to develop reports on companies that it would then sell to other companies as business intelligence. The website promised to split the profits for each report with the researcher who created it. InfoArmy raised more than $19 million in venture capital and launched in June 2012. By the end of January 2013, InfoArmy announced that it had earned exactly $4,356 by selling individual reports and that it would no longer pay researchers for their work. The company said that it had been disappointed with the researchers' work and that the reports were not as saleable as it had hoped. InfoArmy is now developing a new business model, to be determined.

The Data Hive: 800,000 Worker Bees for Science

Not all projects need expert input. Some simply need to find thousands of volunteers to help them improve or manage their data. The "data hive" model engages volunteers to improve the quality of Open Data or process it. This model is being applied to government data and scientific data with some striking results.

In the federal government, NASA was a trailblazer in engaging volunteer help to analyze its massive amounts of data—for example, inviting people to help identify possible planetary systems in space telescope images. The National Archives and Records Administration (NARA) runs a Citizen Archivist program to engage ordinary people in tagging their records, with the goal of ultimately putting all of their records online. And the U.S. Agency for International Development used a group of volunteers to correct data on the locations of its loan grantees.

The National Archives has also done innovative work with the U.S. census. Records from each census are released publicly 72 years after the census is complete, apparently based on a calculation of average life expectancy that was done decades ago. But old records have had limited value: they were handwritten or typed on a manual typewriter and released on microfilm. To modernize the process, the National Archives decided to release the 1940 census online.

In early 2012, NARA was invited by the nonprofit website FamilySearch to join its 1940 Census Community Indexing Project. This project brought together archives, genealogy societies, historical societies, and genealogy companies to sponsor a collective-intelligence effort to index the 1940 census. NARA and FamilySearch together promoted the project through social media. And the index—which was not originally budgeted by NARA and could have cost millions of dollars—was completed in five months.

Outside of government (though sometimes working with government agencies), academics and other researchers are using "data hives" to work with massive amounts of Open Data and learn what it can tell us. These are the new "citizen science projects," where researchers rely on the kindness and geekiness of strangers to make their data useful. The website Zooniverse is a prime example: it's an international hub where anyone can help solve large-scale scientific puzzles.

At Oxford University I met with Robert Simpson, who is part of the team that runs the Zooniverse projects from there. He joined Oxford in 2010 with a PhD in star formation, got involved with the Zooniverse team to design a star formation project, and has become involved in all their projects since. When we met, he described how Zooniverse got started, how it has evolved, and what it's telling us about the potential of data-hive projects.

Zooniverse began at Oxford with a project called Galaxy Zoo that built on one of the world's most impressive sources of scientific Open Data—the Sloan Digital Sky Survey (SDSS), funded by the Sloan Foundation, which is a complete set of images of the entire night sky. Simpson recalled how SDSS led to the birth of Zooniverse in 2007:

> *An astronomer named Kevin Schawinski was working to go through lots, if not all, of the galaxies in the SDSS, which at the time was a catalogue of almost a million galaxies. . . . SDSS can't tell you what the galaxy looks like. It can't say whether it's a spiral galaxy or an elliptical galaxy. Computers can't do that, but people don't have a problem with it.*
>
> *Kevin and many PhD students before him had to go through these galaxies, looking for a specific, rare kind of galaxy. One week, Kevin went through 50,000 images: He spent his entire day for five days doing nothing but that task—and going mad by the end of it. So he and Chris Lintott came up with the idea that they should make a*

website. Galaxy Zoo was launched July 2007. The task it presented was to look at an image and say, is it a spiral, elliptical, or edge-on spiral galaxy or is it a star, an artifact, or more than one galaxy? That was it. There were six buttons.

People went nuts for it. It got on the radio here, it got on the TV, it was on BBC News Online, and people just loved it. Within days, we had more than 100,000 people clicking away, going through loads and loads of these galaxies. Within two days, we were doing 50,000 galaxies an hour. Every galaxy in the database can be looked at by multiple independent people so you don't have any bias.

Perhaps most surprisingly, the untrained amateurs who went onto Galaxy Zoo saw important things that the trained astronomers missed. "All astronomers were more likely to say that bluish-looking galaxies were spiral than elliptical," said Simpson, "because we were trained about what's true. For us astronomers, that's the nature of the galaxies, whereas the public doesn't have that bias. When you're looking for rare things like blue-elliptical galaxies, that's very useful."

While several Zooniverse projects still look to outer space, the program has also invited volunteers to look back in time. In one popular project, Old Weather, volunteers digitally transcribe records from the British Royal Navy around the time of World War I, capturing historical climate data from around the globe. In another project, Ancient Lives, volunteers catalog scraps of papyri from Oxford's Sackler Library that were dug up about 100 years ago from an ancient rubbish dump in Egypt.

Zooniverse, which has an open invitation for scientists to submit new challenges, has now posted its first biomedical project. Cell Slider uses online volunteers to help identify cancer cells. As Simpson pointed out, "A lot of medical research is all about visual pattern recognition. We hope this project will be useful." With its foray into biomedicine, Zooniverse has gone into a new area that may have huge economic and social potential (more on that in the next chapter).

Zooniverse now has more than 800,000 people registered, and even more have contributed to the site without going through registration. With numbers like that, the potential for drawing on the crowd is huge. Simpson quoted an often-cited calculation made by Clay Shirky, perhaps the most influential proponent of collective intelligence, in his book *Cognitive Surplus*. As Shirky points out, the whole of Wikipedia represents about 100 million hours of work—which is 1/20 of 1 percent of the time that U.S. adults spend watching TV each year. The "cognitive surplus" that we can all bring to bear by redirecting our spare time could accomplish a lot.

New organizations are taking the kind of approach that Zooniverse pioneered and applying it to other scientific, environmental, and social projects. CrowdCrafting.org presents a range of collective intelligence challenges in areas including basic science, linguistics, and the analysis of social media. An organization called SkyTruth uses the crowd to analyze Open Data in satellite images to keep a collective eye on the environmental impact of corporate activities. John Amos, the geologist who founded SkyTruth, analyzed these images himself in 2010 to show that the impact of the BP oil spill was far worse than the official estimates. In 2013, SkyTruth launched several projects on fracking including FrackFinder, which uses large numbers of volunteers to analyze images from areas of Pennsylvania where fracking is being done. It's all part of SkyTruth's mission: "If you can see it, you can change it."

In contrast to sites like these, which have the power to inspire participation, mass data-hive projects that pay people to participate in dull, routine tasks have had limited success. Research has shown that Mechanical Turk, an Amazon service that pays people to do these kinds of "human intelligence tasks," can attract more participants by paying more. But, significantly, higher payments don't help increase accuracy. The nature of the task, and of the community engaged in it, seems to determine dedication and performance.

Realizing the Business Potential

In his first book on crowdsourcing, *Here Comes Everybody*, Clay Shirky summarized the power of collective intelligence this way: "We are used to a world where little things happen for love and big things happen for money. Love motivates people to bake a cake and money motivates people to make an encyclopedia. Now, though, we can do big things for love."

This poses a conundrum for anyone using collective intelligence to build a business. Do you have to get people to love your project to get their best effort—and if you do, will they work for free? That approach has worked for the nonprofits Zooniverse and CrowdCrafting and for the companies StackExchange and CrunchBase. But are there other situations where you need to combine love and money to get the best result?

Apparently there are, and the federal government has helped develop the model for them. The Obama administration launched Challenge.gov as a website where "the public and government can solve problems together." In addition to the opportunity to help the government and gain recognition, Challenge.gov offers monetary prizes for the best solutions to questions from a wide range of agencies. The problems can be as diverse as helping the U.S. Mint design a coin celebrating baseball or developing mobile-tech approaches to help keep college students from binge drinking. Several challenges have focused on using government Open Data to create new apps to benefit businesses or consumers. Challenge.gov has sometimes served as a business incubator, launching new ventures with government data as a basis.

InnoCentive and data-focused companies like Kaggle and TopCoder have shown that there's tremendous knowledge and talent to be tapped for business needs—with the right combination of inspiration and payment. Posting a challenge to solve a tough research problem is win-win. It gives innovators a chance to be recognized and win some prize money, while it enables companies to find exactly the right talent to help them when they need it.

Dwayne Spradlin described what he'd learned about what makes InnoCentive so effective at finding new and innovative solutions to problems. As he told me, InnoCentive attracts bright, inventive, out-of-the-box problem solvers. "Our data-related challenges would attract thousands of technology-savvy solvers," he said, "often with mathematics and statistical backgrounds, often working in teams." Many InnoCentive competitions include a leader board showing each team's current score and rank, and showing which team's solutions are yielding the best results in real time. This approach, said Spradlin, creates powerful "competitive dynamics" that often produce breakthrough results. "It's adrenaline, IQ, and ego. High-performing problem solvers want to be at the top of the leader board."

Spradlin said that InnoCentive has been well studied by researchers who want to understand its success. Research, he says, has found that successful solvers are motivated by three factors: they want to take on projects that will have an impact, they want to be part of a group of elite problem solvers, and they want whatever inducement is being offered—either the intrinsic reward of seeing a solution put to use or extrinsic rewards like money and recognition.

Spradlin told me that InnoCentive found four different kinds of problem solvers with different skills and motivations: (1) students and academics, (2) active researchers, (3) retirees from related fields, and (4) tinkerers—the professional problem solvers. Groups 3 and 4, he said, are the most successful and appreciate being paid for their work (payment is a must for the tinkerers). Groups 1 and 2 are less successful at solving problems but are also less motivated by money and participate at a higher rate. Along the same lines, groups 1 and 2 are most attracted to do-good projects, big-idea challenges that will contribute to the public good, while 3 and 4 are best at coming up with specific, pragmatic solutions.

In general, Spradlin said, the research on InnoCentive shows that the desire to have an impact is a core motivator for everybody: a project has to be inspiring to attract much participation. But a monetary reward will help solvers choose one appealing project over another. And, finally, people are much more willing to work for little or no financial gain if they're taking on a challenge for, say, an international relief effort than if the challenge is sponsored by a pharmaceutical company. If you're posing a challenge that will help increase your company's profits, said Spradlin, "don't even think" about presenting it without putting money on the table.

CHAPTER TEN

The Open Research Lab: Innovating Through Open Collaboration

J AY BRADNER, MD, IS A RESEARCHER AT THE DANA-FARBER Cancer Institute in Boston. In 2010, he and his team discovered an important formula:

ClCl = CC = C(C2 = N[C@@H](CC(OC(C)(C)C) = O)C3 = NN = C(C)N3C4 = C2C(C) = C(C)S4C = C1

Then he decided to give it away.

At a TEDx talk in Boston in June 2011, Bradner described the unusual journey that led from a series of lab experiments to what he called a social experiment: opening up the results of his cancer research early on for the world to see. Bradner is a member of the scientific establishment in very good standing. He directs a lab at one of the most prestigious cancer research centers in the world. Yet as he talks about his work on the TEDx video, he comes across as a kind of "Dr. Smith Goes to Boston"—a still-young, clearly idealistic scientist who, more than anything else, wants to see rapid progress in lifesaving treatments.

Like many in the field, Bradner was motivated by personal experience. His father was diagnosed with pancreatic cancer, a particularly deadly form of cancer that was essentially untreatable. As he reflected on his own family tragedy, Bradner was struck by the gap between the explosion of data about the human genome and cancer on one hand and medicine's reliance on primitive anticancer drugs like arsenic and thalidomide on the other. Already a physician, Bradner went back for further study in chemistry with the goal of developing targeted drugs that can disable cancer cells' growth at the molecular level.

From the beginning, Bradner saw the potential to draw on the wisdom of his colleagues by sharing research as Open Data. Back in the lab, he began work on a compound that could interfere with malignant cells in a rare kind of cancer called midline carcinoma. He shared research data with other labs, got some particularly helpful insights from Oxford, and soon showed that the compound, which they called JQ1, could stop the growth of midline carcinoma in mice and save their lives.

"We started to wonder," Bradner said in his talk, "what would a drug company do at this point? Well, they probably would keep this a secret until they turned a prototype drug into an active pharmaceutical substance. And so we did just the opposite. We published a paper that described this finding at the earliest prototype stage." (It appeared in *Nature* in September 2010.) "We gave the world the chemical identity of this molecule, typically a secret in our discipline"—it's the string of letters, symbols, and parentheses shown above. "We told people exactly how to make it. We gave them our e-mail address, suggesting that, if they write us, we'll send them a free molecule."

While Bradner's experiment was born out of idealism, it may turn out to be smart from a business perspective as well. What Bradner shared was research that was still many steps away from an approved,

patentable drug. A startup called Tensha Therapeutics, in which Bradner says he has a small stake, is now working with his lab to develop
this compound, as well as a few others from their work, into drugs
they can then take through clinical trials. Pharmaceutical companies
as well as academic labs have shown great interest in his lab's discovery. The result may be a number of lifesaving and commercially viable
drugs beyond what Bradner's own lab could have envisioned.

In the short time since Bradner's lab did its bold experiment in
the sociology of science, the Open Data approach to research has
gathered momentum. Science and research no longer take place just
behind closed laboratory doors. Labs, foundations, and government
agencies are rapidly sharing their findings as Open Data in a new
research model, often called *open innovation*, where colleagues collaborate online to solve the toughest problems. The shift may change the
way science is done in some fundamental ways. And it will challenge
drug companies, engineering firms, and others to find ways to make
open research work with new business models.

There's a compelling scientific case for Open Data in medicine.
Collaborative work across different labs, often in different countries,
may be the fastest way to find causes and cures for major diseases. A
classic example, described in the book *The Wisdom of Crowds*, was the
race to fight the SARS outbreak of 2002 and 2003. A few months after
the first case was reported, the World Health Organization contacted
11 research labs in 10 countries and asked them to collaborate to find
the cause. Working at the same time on the same samples, the scientists first identified the virus within about a week and had a definitive
ID a month after they'd started.

Michael Nielsen, a physicist and writer in Toronto, describes these
and other kinds of open innovation in his book *Reinventing Discovery:
The New Era of Networked Science*. Nielsen is an evangelist for opening
up research using Open Data. "I believe the reinvention of discovery
is one of the great changes of our time," his book begins. "To histori-
ans looking back a hundred years from now, there will be two eras of

science: prenetwork science and networked science. . . . But it's going to be a bumpy transition."

For academics in a publish-or-perish world, data can be the key to a successful career, and it may seem almost perverse to share data before it's been peer reviewed and officially published. For drug companies spending millions on drug development, releasing Open Data may seem like a commercial risk. But on the other side of the argument, data sharing may accelerate the pace of research so effectively that it's hard to justify holding data back. And the funders of research, from disease-focused foundations to the federal government, are pushing for a new research process that speeds innovation and finds answers more quickly.

Open Data for Open Innovation

For scientists to solve problems as a virtual team, they need two things: access to data and a network for collaboration. While the idea of Open Data in science seems new, it's an approach that actually goes back a couple of decades. Here's how Nielsen describes the historic Bermuda Agreement on gene research, crafted at a 1996 conference "attended by many of the world's leading biologists, including several leaders of the government-sponsored Human Genome Project":

> *Although many attendees weren't willing to unilaterally make the first move to share all their genetic data in advance of publication, everyone could see that science as a whole would benefit enormously if open sharing of data became common practice. So they sat and talked the issue over for days, eventually coming to a joint agreement—now known as the Bermuda Agreement—that all human genetic data should be immediately shared online. The agreement wasn't just empty rhetoric. The biologists in the room had enough clout that they convinced several major scientific grant agencies to make immediate data sharing a mandatory requirement of working on the human genome. Scientists*

who refused to share data would get no grant money to do research. This changed the game.

Rufus Pollock, who is cofounder and director of the Open Knowledge Foundation, notes that the Human Genome Project "was Open Data before there was Open Data" as a general concept. While the project developed well-thought-out protocols for sharing data openly, it was competing with companies who kept more data to themselves. Pollock cites a recent MIT study that gives the advantage to openness. "The competition was between Celera and the open genome project," he said. "Celera got patents in some areas where they did the sequence first. The MIT study did a comparison, and the evidence showed that their having the patents reduced follow-on innovation or usage in those areas by 30 percent." Establishing openness as the general standard for genomic research, he said, was "a massive, massive win."

Despite its success, the Human Genome Project did not rewrite the rules for scientific research or even for large collaborative projects. When President Obama announced a $100 million brain research initiative in 2013, there was no commitment to sharing data as it was developed, although the Open Knowledge Foundation pushed to make it an Open Data program. But the Open Data movement in science has been growing for years and may be reaching a tipping point.

Recently, an international effort with government support has been started to make data accessible and usable across borders. The Research Data Alliance was started by the European Commission, the Australian government, and the National Science Foundation in the United States "to accelerate and facilitate research data sharing and exchange." The Alliance works through about 20 special-interest working groups on areas including agriculture, astronomy, oceans, and genomics. Other organizations focused on scientific data sharing include the Committee on Data for Science and Technology (CODATA) and the Yale University Open Data Access Project (YODA). May the force be with them.

Some foundations are starting to require Open Data sharing as a condition of funding. Medical research foundations see Open Data as a way to accelerate treatments and cures and don't want anything to stand in the way of rapid progress. The Michael J. Fox Foundation, for example, has been running a major project to find biological markers for Parkinson's disease, called the Parkinson's Progression Markers Initiative (PPMI), as an Open Data undertaking. (It was modeled on an earlier project on brain imaging for Alzheimer's disease.)

Through the PPMI, scientists at two dozen clinical sites publish their findings on blood markers for the disease with "full, open access" for other scientists. As the Fox Foundation describes it, "All PPMI clinical data and characterized biosamples are available in real time, providing researchers around the world with an unprecedented resource to help speed and unify disparate biomarker validation studies. To date, 460 scientists from academia and industry have downloaded PPMI data more than 50,000 times in over 30 countries worldwide, and 21 applications have been made for use of PPMI biospecimens in biomarker research."

The pressure to publish data openly is coming not only from funders, but also from patients themselves. One remarkable patient-turned-foundation-head is Kathy Giusti. An MBA who had been an executive at both Merck and G.D. Searle, Giusti was diagnosed with multiple myeloma in 1998 at age 37 and was appalled to learn that there was no research being done on multiple myeloma drugs. So she started the Multiple Myeloma Research Foundation with a commitment to releasing Open Data from the research the foundation supports. Thanks largely to the foundation's efforts, survival rates for patients with multiple myeloma have doubled over the last decade.

Giusti is now a cancer survivor and a strong advocate for a new way of conducting science. "The number-one problem is that data is kept within the walls of the academic centers and within companies," she recently said in a *Fast Company* interview. "If patients knew this, they would be beside themselves. The system and the incentives are really, really broken."

Some patients are helping research on their own through an influential website, PatientsLikeMe. On PatientsLikeMe, individuals share details about their diseases, the drugs they're taking, the side effects, and other information about their treatment. The company is a for-profit venture with an altruistic mission: helping people voluntarily share data that would otherwise be inaccessible for privacy reasons. As the website says, "We believe sharing your healthcare experiences and outcomes is good. Why? Because when patients share real-world data, collaboration on a global scale becomes possible. New treatments become possible. Most importantly, change becomes possible. At PatientsLikeMe, we are passionate about bringing people together for a greater purpose: speeding up the pace of research and fixing a broken healthcare system."

The toughest challenge in opening scientific data may not be academic, foundation-funded research but the commercial research done by drug companies. To say that pharmaceutical research is closely guarded would be an understatement. Drug companies not only secure their data while studies are under way but carefully control which studies will be published after they're completed. Studies that show a positive clinical result with few side effects are likely to see the light of day; studies that show the opposite generally don't. The result is a scientific literature that tends to show new drugs in a positive and profitable light until the side effects become clear after they're on the market.

A British-based advocacy group called AllTrials has been formed by a coalition of funders, medical organizations, and activists to correct the system. They simply want "all trials registered/all results reported," so that the true pros and cons of new drugs will be clear to everyone. In early 2013, AllTrials scored a big win when the pharmaceutical giant GlaxoSmithKline agreed to make all its clinical trials public.

Prior to that decision, GSK had a public relations problem on its hands: the company had just paid a $3 billion fine for the inappropriate marketing of two antidepressants, Paxil and Wellbutrin. Without FDA approval, the company had promoted Paxil for use in children and Wellbutrin as a treatment for sexual dysfunction and an aid to weight loss (what some called the "happy, horny, skinny pill"). Agreeing to release its clinical trials may have been a strategy to get some good publicity when the company needed it most.

Whatever GSK's motivation, however, opening its clinical trial data could help start an overdue and much-needed trend. Since GSK's announcement, there have been reports and leaked memos about the pharmaceutical industry's plans to fight to keep clinical trials private. But the AllTrials campaign makes such scientific sense and could have such significant public benefit that it has the feel of an Open Data campaign that will be successful.

Open Access: Transforming Scientific Publishing

The growth of Open Data online and the rise of a tech-savvy population open up unprecedented opportunities for scientific research and development. But the most basic scientific and technical information sharing is still done through published articles. There's now a growing movement to make published research data free to all and accessible online in ways that would allow researchers to search across different but related articles to analyze their findings together.

In the research community, the push to Open Data has been known as Open Access—a movement to share data from all kinds of research more freely. The Open Access movement had been building for several years, but it was only a few years ago that several different efforts converged. As a result, we're now moving in a direction where not only the results of research, but also the data behind the findings may become more rapidly available than ever before. The result will be new opportunities for open innovation, accelerated R&D, new publishing opportunities, and a more transparent scientific process.

The tragic hero of this movement was Aaron Swartz. For a week or two in January 2013, even people who only use the web for e-mail and shopping were engrossed in the story of this young Internet pioneer. Since 2011, the Department of Justice had been pursuing a case against Swartz for computer fraud and related charges. On January 11, 2013, Swartz hanged himself rather than face the risk of prosecution and imprisonment. The case sparked outrage against the Department of Justice and a call for new rules on access to data.

The story became a symbol not only of government overreach, but also of the contradictory and confusing rules that have determined how we define and regulate public data. When Swartz figured out how to make government legal documents available free of charge, his idea was validated and turned into an ongoing university-based project. When he tried to do the same thing for scientific research, he was prosecuted by the Department of Justice.

Back in 2008, Swartz, who already had a national reputation as both a web entrepreneur and Open Data activist, had decided to liberate data from PACER—the database run by the Administrative Office of the United States Courts that provides Public Access to Court Electronic Records. Swartz took advantage of PACER's free trial to download 19,856,160 pages of documents, which reportedly would have cost him $1.5 million. He reposted them on a website he called RECAP (PACER spelled backwards). Perhaps predictably, PACER quickly discontinued its free trial policy. But RECAP went on to find a home at Princeton, which set up an easy-to-use website at www.recapthelaw.org.

Lawyers can use RECAP to make publicly available the documents that they've purchased through PACER. This is legal because PACER's records, like all U.S. government documents, are free from copyright restrictions. (Government documents in the United Kingdom and some other countries, in contrast, are copyrighted.) PACER had charged users for the administrative costs of making records available; if the people who used them reposted the documents online, there was no additional cost to the government.

What got Swartz into trouble was not liberating documents from PACER but his next big project: taking steps to liberate articles from copyrighted academic journals. At the end of 2010, Swartz used the MIT computer system to download a large number of articles from JSTOR, a digital system that covers some 1,700 publications. While Swartz may have intended to redistribute those articles for free, which would be a copyright violation, it's not clear exactly what was wrong with what he actually did. Swartz had access to JSTOR as a research fellow at Harvard; he agreed after his arrest not to distribute the articles he had downloaded, and JSTOR did not press charges. Nevertheless, the U.S. Department of Justice prosecuted Swartz, ultimately bringing 13 felony counts against him, including five of computer fraud and one of "unlawfully obtaining information from a protected computer."

If Swartz was a victim of overzealous prosecution, JSTOR was arguably an unlikely target for activism. The organization is a nonprofit that charges libraries fees to cover its operating costs. The bigger concern for the Open Access movement has been the for-profit publishers of scientific journals who make a large profit by charging high prices for information. Elsevier, the largest scientific publisher, recently reported an annual profit of more than $1.1 billion, roughly a 35 percent profit margin. That's especially striking when you consider that the publisher doesn't pay the authors and reviewers of the papers it publishes. What makes this particularly galling to scientists and activists is that so much of the research is supported by public funds to begin with. (JSTOR's website points out that its journals focus on the humanities, social sciences, and field sciences, which get less government support than biomedical research.)

The Revolt of the Academic Spring

At the same time that the Aaron Swartz case was raising awareness of the issue, Open Access was being promoted by a combination of academics and librarians. The Open Access movement reached a peak in 2012 with what came to be called the Academic Spring. In January of that year, a Cambridge mathematician named Timothy Gowers called for a boycott of Elsevier, motivated by the publisher's support for a Congressional bill that would have made copyright restrictions on federally funded research even stricter than they already were. By midyear, more than 12,000 academics had signed on to the boycott.

A new group called Access2Research, supported by a coalition of activist research librarians, formed in May 2012 to advocate on the issue. The group decided to use a tool of Open Government to push for Open Access: they started a campaign on We the People, the new federal website for citizen petitions, asking the government to "require free access over the Internet to scientific journal articles arising from taxpayer-funded research." Under the petition website's rules at the time, they had to garner 25,000 signatures within 30 days to merit a response from the administration. They reached that level in two weeks and went on to get a total of 65,000 signatures.

In February 2013, John Holdren, head of the White House Office of Science and Technology Policy (OSTP), responded to the petition in a positive way. Noting that OSTP had been discussing this issue for some time, he wrote on the petition website that "the Obama administration agrees that citizens deserve easy access to the results of research their tax dollars have paid for. . . . The logic behind enhanced public access is plain. . . . the Obama Administration is committed to ensuring that the results of federally-funded scientific research are made available to and useful for the public, industry, and the scientific community. . . . Americans should have easy access to the results of research they help support."

On the day he wrote this, Holdren issued a memo instructing every federal agency that funds more than $100 million in R&D to figure out how to make the published results of the research they support available for free within a year of publication. As he noted, this new policy mirrored a policy the National Institutes of Health had instituted in 2008 with much success.

His memo also instructed agencies to develop plans for making federally funded research available as Open Data. To help encourage open thinking, the White House announced a "Champions of Change" contest to recognize people who had helped make scientific information more accessible. The winners, announced in June 2013, were people who had made an impact by "providing free access to data or publications generated from scientific research; or, leading research that uses publically available scientific data." In the Obama administration's view, scientific publishing and Open Data are clearly linked.

While the new government policy was generally welcomed, it may not go far enough. Waiting a year for free access is a long time in the world of research. A week before Holdren's announcement, a bill known as FASTR—the Fair Access to Science and Technology Research Act—was introduced in the House and Senate. Under the FASTR Act, research articles would be made available online in a usable form within 6 months of publication, not 12.

Some top researchers haven't waited for the new policies to take effect: they're developing new publishing models that make information available for free or for a low price. In the year 2000, three well-respected academic biologists founded the Public Library of Science (PLoS), a nonprofit that makes peer-reviewed research available for free and open for reuse through several online journals. The organization was founded by Patrick Brown of the Stanford University School of Medicine and the Howard Hughes Medical Institute, Michael Eisen, a geneticist at the University of California, Berkeley, and Harold Varmus, a Nobel Prize winner who had been head of the National Institutes of Health and later became head of the National Cancer Institute.

The Open Access movement has been fueled by both a professional desire to see science flourish and by a personal sense of outrage at the current system. Jonathan Eisen, the brother of PLoS cofounder Michael Eisen and the academic editor-in-chief of *PLoS*

Biology, described his epiphany in an excellent animated video about Open Access:

> *Even with my brother starting the Public Library of Science, I wasn't convinced. I didn't understand why this was a big deal. And then we had a family medical emergency, and I was up at three in the middle of the night in a hospital, next to my wife in the hospital room, surfing the web on the crappy wireless hospital Internet. I was trying to find out information about a particular medical treatment, and I couldn't get access to the damn papers. Our doctors didn't know the answers to these particular questions, and we needed to decide what to do with this medical treatment. Here I was, a trained scientist with the ability to read and interpret and understand many of these papers, and I couldn't get them.*
>
> *That was the moment for me. I was like, "You've got to be kidding me."* . . .
>
> *[While] In the hospital room, I bought dozens of articles. The problem is that you don't know which article is relevant until after you pay for it* . . . . *Are you going to spend $1,200 to just find out if possibly they're relevant?* . . . *Nobody is saying that publishing is free. What people are saying is that we need to work on models.* . . . *In the end, taxpayers and the government are paying for this, so why can't we do it in a way where the knowledge is distributed broadly, as opposed to knowledge is restricted?*

There are signs that scientific publishing is already moving toward Open Access, with some benefits for the scientists involved. A recent study done for the European Union found that about half of all scientific papers published in 2011 were available online for free. Another study found that genetics papers that published their findings as Open Data were cited more often than those that didn't, a difference that lasted at least five years. (This paper was published in an Open Access journal itself.)

For the next generation of scientists, raised on the Internet, the current publishing system may simply be unacceptably archaic. Jack

Andraka, a teenager young enough to be Harold Varmus's grand-son, is the whiz kid from Maryland who won the top prize at the Intel International Science and Engineering Fair in 2012. He's been compared to a young Thomas Edison, and with good reason. As one science writer described it, his achievement was "developing a novel paper sensor that detects pancreatic, ovarian, and lung cancers in five minutes and costs as little as three cents. The rapid diagnostic test is 168 times faster, 26,000 times less expensive, and more than 400 times more sensitive than the current test." While his system is in early testing and still far from clinical use, it's not a bad start for a scientist in his midteens.

To develop this potential breakthrough, Andraka had to work around the scientific publishing system. He used Open Access sources when he could find them. He did a lot of research using Google and Wikipedia. And he borrowed some of the more expensive journals from a mentor who happened to subscribe to them. What does he say he wants to do today? Keep working on new biomedical projects and do some public speaking about the importance of Open Access.

As persuasive as Open Access sounds, it's not a no-brainer, even for the academic institutions that pay for scientific journal subscriptions. If a new model requires academic institutions to pay for their research to be published, they could potentially end up paying more than they do now to subscribe even to high-priced journals.

Writing in the *New England Journal of Medicine*, the Executive Director of the American Physiological Society estimated that "Har-vard Medical School would have to pay $13.5 million (at $1,350 per article) to publish the 10,000 articles authored by its faculty in 2010—considerably more than the $3.75 million that was in its serials-acquisition budget that year. Research-intensive institutions will thus bear the burden of funding free access to the research lit-erature, subsidizing access for less-research-intensive institutions, including pharmaceutical companies." The debate on Open Access is well under way.

Realizing the Business Potential

Open innovation poses a challenge: how to balance the benefits of making scientific knowledge available as Open Data, which helps the research community and society as a whole against the need to cover the costs of the research that produces the data. Rufus Pollock, who holds a PhD in economics from Cambridge University, cofounded the Open Knowledge Foundation in 2004 to open up the way that information of all kinds can be used. For Pollock and his colleagues, the goal is for people to share information and data in the interest of collaboration.

Pollock described to me why the economics of collaboration work better around information and knowledge than around goods in the physical world. "You don't get the maximum benefit of a piece of land by everyone having a part of it," he said. "But for knowledge it makes more sense. When it's shared, we get the maximum benefit to society. As Jefferson said, 'He who gets the idea from me is like somebody who lights a candle from mine. He gains light without darkening me.'"

The problem, however, is how to pay for creating that knowledge in the first place. A classic approach is to protect intellectual property for a period of time, as patent law does—but that approach can delay the open release of scientific data. And, says Pollock, "it's far from the only option. For example, you can have up-front funding by governments, philanthropic institutions or 'crowdfunding,' you can have voluntary creation, you can have complementary goods (CDs are free but you sell access to the concerts), et cetera."

"The key point is that every time we restrict access to knowledge and data we are losing something. Let's take scientific research as an example. The vast amount of it is publicly funded and yet at the moment we lose an immense amount of value by much of it being closed. It means that we don't get lifesaving treatments when we misspend that money or spend it on less efficient research. That is a fundamental cost to our society. Instead of restricting access to knowledge, letting data get locked up in proprietary database or journals, we should be making it open."

The Alfred P. Sloan Foundation has helped launch large scale data-sharing projects ranging from an economics project at the Open Knowledge Foundation to Wikipedia. Daniel Goroff, Sloan's vice president and program director, analyzes the economics of Open Data using the concept of a "public good." Technically speaking, a public good is a type of commodity that is "nonrival" and "nonexclusive." It's "nonrival" because one person's use of a public good doesn't make it harder for other people to use it as well, and it's "nonexclusive" because, in general, anyone can use it.

Classic examples of public goods include lighthouses, parks, ideas, and national defense, as well as Open Data. But public goods are notoriously difficult to finance. As Goroff says, "there could be many possible ways to design fees, business models, or cross-subsidy schemes that can serve the public interest even better than simply declaring openness and leaving it at that. For example, it may sometimes make sense to charge for value-added services or for special collections in order to keep the basic data current, accurate, comprehensive, and useful."

In the wide realm of open innovation, there are a few immediate opportunities to put this kind of theory into practice. One important commitment to Open Data, which all drug companies should consider, is to participate in the AllTrials campaign. The AllTrials campaign makes a strong case for publishing clinical trial data and the movement may gain momentum. With a continuing stream of news stories about drugs that turn out to be ineffective, dangerous, or both, it's hard to defend a system that only shows the public and medical scientists the research results that drug companies want them to see. Drug manufacturers that accept the concept of open clinical trials now will have a chance to be seen as industry leaders.

Another opportunity: create new business models for research publishing. The Open Access movement recognizes that there's a role for publishers but believes, reasonably enough, that there has to be an approach somewhere between making everything free and publishing journals that cost thousands of dollars a year. A new publishing company called PeerJ, cofounded by leading tech publisher Tim O'Reilly, is publishing articles with different levels of peer review using a model in which researchers themselves pay a modest amount for publication. Some research funders, such as the Wellcome Trust, have indicated that they would be willing to pay publication costs if doing so makes research results more freely available. Scientific publishing is a significant industry and one that's now wide open for innovation.

The largest question is whether Open Data and open innovation can transform the biotechnology and pharmaceutical industries in a positive way. When Jay Bradner shared the formula for a potential cancer drug, he did what most drug companies would consider unthinkable. But an early proto-drug is not the same as a market-ready pharmaceutical, and there's still business opportunity in developing this and other potential treatments from Bradner's lab.

In fact, there may be a stronger business case for scientific Open Data than there seems to be at first look. In their influential book *Wikinomics*, Don Tapscott and Anthony Williams make the case by looking back to one of the most apparently idealistic examples of open innovation: the Human Genome Project.

"The Human Genome Project represents a watershed moment, when a number of pharmaceutical firms abandoned their proprietary human genome projects to back open collaborations," they write. "So what exactly were these firms up to? We call it 'precompetitive knowledge commons' . . . a new, collaborative approach to research and development where like-minded companies (and sometimes competitors) create common pools of industry knowledge and processes upon which new innovations and industries build."

According to Tapscott and Williams, drug companies saw an advantage in sharing knowledge in a "precompetitive" state at a time when it was still basic research data that was not yet ready for commercial application. This was particularly true in the mid-1990s when small biotech firms were patenting their discoveries, raising the prospect that large drug companies would need to pay a high price to use them later on.

"One company," Tapscott and Williams write, "saw another option that could rewrite the rules completely." Merck Pharmaceuticals and the Washington University School of Medicine launched the Merck Gene Index, a public database of gene sequencing. By 1998, they had published over 800,000 gene sequences. "But why would Merck make this investment, which, according to one estimate, cost them several million dollars? . . . Like many pharmaceutical firms, Merck sees gene sequences as inputs rather than end products. Their business is developing and marketing drugs, not hawking genetic data and research tools. By placing gene sequences in the public domain, Merck preempted the ability of biotech firms to encumber one of its key inputs with licensing fees and transaction costs. Fortunately for Merck, other pharmaceutical firms shared its concern over patents on upstream genetic information."

The research that Jay Bradner has now published as Open Data—and research that could come out of similar labs—could play the same role as open gene sequences, giving pharmaceutical companies tools they can all develop without hindering their ability to make competitive drugs. When I talked to Bradner in August 2013, he was seeing evidence that this was true.

While making it clear that "this isn't a business experiment, it's an experiment in public health," Bradner was pleased to see the impact his work was having and its business potential. Since he released his formula, he said, "The volume, velocity, quality, and reproducibility of data has been stunning. There's no question that this accelerates innovation." In addition, he's seen several biotech and drug companies "jumping on it. They recognize that data of this quality that's free to them is a real opportunity."

A real test, said Bradner, is whether his experiment in open innovation will spark new kinds of applications beyond those that he and his lab could have envisioned. The answer seems to be yes. Bradner has surveyed the labs he sent his data to, and an initial look at more than a hundred responses showed that most of them had not worked with chemical compounds in this class before. Now they're finding new uses for his formula. Bradner's work, he said, turns out to be "applicable to human papilloma virus, HIV, and heart failure. These opportunities are well beyond the scope of where we began."

Bradner noted the success of putting biological research data into the public domain—genetic data being the prime example—and said that he hopes his "experiment" can begin to do the same for chemical research. The day before I talked to him, he had given a presentation at one of the prestigious Gordon Research Conferences. His audience, he said, had been "a roomful of career medicinal chemists—senior drug hunters—who collectively must have more than a thousand patents. They were tremendously excited by the possibility that their work in chemistry could go to biological application more quickly." The discussion continued over dinner, with general agreement, Bradner says, that his approach could work.

Some major drug companies have experimented with open innovation. Eli Lilly runs an Open Innovation Drug Discovery program designed to "connect external investigators to Lilly science to find compounds that may become medicines." GSK, Novartis, AstraZeneca, and others have released Open Data related to drugs for malaria, tuberculosis, and other diseases of the developing world. As the authors of *Wikinomics* point out, "They may not stand to make any profits, but they can at least enhance their corporate images while taking advantage of a low-risk, low-cost route to getting established in developing-country markets."

So far, though, major drug companies haven't embraced the same Open Data approach to basic research connected to more profitable kinds of drugs. It's time for someone to see whether a "precompetitive knowledge commons" for drug research could accelerate innovation while preserving profits.

PART TWO

The Business Environment: New Trends in Open Data

CHAPTER ELEVEN

Privacy, Security, and the Value of Personal Data

Back in 1999, SUN Microsystems CEO Scott McNealy famously told a tech-savvy audience, "You have no privacy anyway. Get over it." But as Mark Twain might have said, the death of privacy may have been exaggerated. However much privacy we do or don't have today, no one is "getting over" this issue any time soon.

As I'm writing this, the United States is embroiled in a debate about privacy and personal data. Americans are trying to figure out exactly what the National Security Agency knows about us from both online and phone records, how they know it, and how worried all of us should be. By the time this book is published, there will probably be several books out about this subject, not to mention a continuing stream of articles, blog posts, and commentary.

The NSA saga isn't really about Open Data, because the NSA never intended its data or even the nature of its work to be public.

Edward Snowden's revelations don't count as Open Data either: to be truly open, data must be released intentionally by someone who has the authority to do so and for a clear public purpose. But the shockwaves from the NSA could bring us to a tipping point in the way that personal data is treated in general and how the law protects privacy. The result may include private-sector solutions that actually provide new Open Data opportunities for both businesses and individuals, under new and better rules.

The NSA's PRISM program is just the latest topic, though the most disturbing, in a series of debates about personal data and how open it should be. Congress and the Federal Trade Commission have been looking at data brokers—those companies that gather data from hundreds of sources and resell it to businesses that use it to market their products to consumers. Parents of schoolchildren have raised alarms about a company that's collecting data about kids' school records, even though the goal is to help the kids do better in school. Gun owners are worried by public databases that show who's armed and where they live, and the right to keep gun ownership secret is now being debated along with the scope of the Second Amendment. And every day, untold numbers of people try one more time to figure out Facebook's privacy settings and wonder exactly what Facebook knows about them anyway. Most people have had only one concern about their personal information: they want to keep as much of it as they can as private as possible.

Now a number of innovators, from tech entrepreneurs to researchers for the World Economic Forum, believe that we're ready for a paradigm shift. As data analysts, entrepreneurs, and policy makers have realized the value of personal data, a new kind of solution has emerged. Instead of trying to keep all this data secret, the new thinking goes, let's set it free—but only when an individual wants to, and only in a way that he or she approves.

In the new world they envision, consumers will control their own information through "personal data vaults" that keep facts about their lives, their buying habits, and their preferences secure. Individuals will then have the option to release data about themselves as a kind of Open Data to get better deals, job offers, or other benefits. Paradoxically, helping people control their own data could give us a world with more, not less, Open Data about individuals. And that Open Data could both improve public health and welfare and transform consumer markets.

This visionary idea began with some of the world's top computer scientists, has been developed by the World Economic Forum, and is now fueling some prominent startups. While promising, it's far from being realized. The companies that pose the biggest privacy concerns haven't jumped to support this solution; Google and Facebook, for example, aren't making personal data vaults part of their privacy strategy. But some implications of the new paradigm are already clear:

- The current "accept/don't accept" format for privacy agreements is antiquated and needs to change. It doesn't give consumers any real control and doesn't reflect how data is used and disseminated today.

- At the same time, new kinds of tools can make it possible for individuals to control how their own data is used. Personal data vaults, also called personal data "stores" or "lockers," can both put power in the hands of consumers and open new business opportunities. While this idea has been around for years, the ability to store data in the cloud may finally make it more achievable. In addition to offering privacy protection, personal data vaults can enable consumers to profit from selling access to their own data, create opportunities for tech companies, and give consumer-facing companies new marketing strategies.

- Any organization that releases data that has ever had personal information in it will have to be extremely careful. Simple methods of stripping out that personally identifiable information, or PII, don't work. But new technical solutions will make it possible to mine data about populations without revealing data about individuals.

- The concept of "privacy by design"—embedding privacy protections into the technical fabric of data management—will be an important part of the solution.

What Protections Do Consumers Have Now?

Privacy law is confusing and complex. The European Union has an evolving, unified system of privacy protections that American companies operating internationally are starting to deal with. In the United States, in contrast, we have a patchwork system that's less clear and less effective.

The United States does have a number of regulations that protect certain kinds of personal data. The Fair Credit Reporting Act, for example, gives individuals the right to see financial data about themselves and correct it if needed. Other laws give U.S. citizens the right to confidentiality of health and educational data and the right to see what information the government holds about them. In some ways, private companies have more leeway to share individuals' data—for example by buying and selling mailing lists—than the government does, and there are no clear rules about how individuals' data can be used online.

The Obama administration has now laid out a blueprint for across-the-board consumer privacy protections that could take the United States closer to the European model. In February 2012, the White House released a report titled "Consumer Data Privacy in a Networked World," which called on Congress to pass a "consumer privacy bill of rights." Significantly, as the *New York Times* put it, "The White House initiative broadened the historical American view of privacy as 'the right to be left alone' . . . to a more modern concept of privacy as the right to commercial data control."

The White House report stated, "Consumers have a right to access and correct personal data in usable formats, in a manner that is appropriate to the sensitivity of the data and the risk of adverse consequences to consumers if the data is inaccurate." That statement not only stressed the consumers' right to correct mistakes in data records, but also implied that consumers should be able to download their personal data in the kinds of ways described in Chapter 3. At this writing, however, Congress has not acted on these proposals.

Part of our confusion about data privacy could stem from the law lagging behind technology. That's the view of Jim Dempsey, who is Vice President for Public Policy at the Center for Democracy & Technology, which works on digital privacy, among other issues. We talked a few months before the NSA story broke. "One of our major projects," he said, "is to extend Fourth Amendment principles—the protections around search and seizure—to data online."

As Dempsey explained it, the Fourth Amendment has historically been interpreted to cover new kinds of communication technologies, but only years after they were developed:

In the 1870s, a case came up to the Supreme Court where the government said that they had the right to open postal mail in the course of a criminal investigation. The government claimed that the defendant had given up his right to shield the letter from search and seizure because he had surrendered it to a government agency when he mailed it. The Supreme Court ruled that mail was protected by the Fourth Amendment, and that the government could not open it without a warrant.

Fast forward 50 years to 1928, when a case of the government wiretapping telephones came up to the Supreme Court. The government said that you voluntarily surrender your rights when you make a telephone call. This time, the Supreme Court agreed. It wasn't until 1967 that the Supreme Court finally ruled that Fourth Amendment protection applied to telephone calls as well. Thereafter, Congress passed the Wiretap Act and set up a set of procedures required to get court warrants to intercept telephone calls.

Now, what about your e-mail? Everybody pretty much assumes today that e-mail is protected when it is transmitted through the Internet, or when a copy is stored in your computer or printed out and kept in your desk. But after the transmission, the e-mail remains stored with a third party, and there's been some debate about whether it's also protected in that form. We're taking the position that storing a communication with a third party does not remove the Fourth Amendment protection, any more than mailing a letter or making a telephone call does.

We also believe the same logic applies to any documents or data stored in the cloud. We're saying that for all of the private communications and documents, drafts, private photographs, everything that now we've stored through cloud-based services it's time to do what the Supreme Court has done before and say that data in the hands of a third party still retains that protection.

Against this background, the government's commitment to releasing more Open Data and the benefits of Open Data I've argued for throughout this book add new privacy challenges to a system that's already shaky. The new federal Open Data Policy, mentioned in Chapter 2 and described more fully in Chapter 13, will need to be implemented with close attention to data privacy.

As agencies release more and more Open Data, they need to be careful not to trigger the so-called mosaic effect, where releasing separate pieces of data, each innocuous on its own, can give hackers the material to put together a picture of an individual's activities and identity. Nick Sinai, U.S. Deputy Chief Technology Officer and a key member of the policy team, told me the policy is "explicit about the need to protect private information and . . . explicit about the mosaic effect. . . . So there's a set of guidelines and requirements around the checks that agencies have to go through when they're taking that kind of data and delivering it to the public. . . . There's a variety of different techniques, whether it's masking, or even introducing slight error into certain records, or other statistical techniques to make sure that folks can't be reidentified."

A Unified Theory of Personal Data

There's a central paradox here. Releasing personal data as Open Data can benefit society and help the individual. But if the data is not controlled carefully, having it out in the open will damage individual privacy and outweigh the benefit. A possible way out of this paradox is emerging in what you could call a new unified theory of personal Open Data.

One of the leading theoreticians is computer scientist Alex "Sandy" Pentland, who directs MIT's Human Dynamics Laboratory and the MIT Media Lab Entrepreneurship Program and co-leads the World Economic Forum Big Data and Personal Data initiatives. He's done cutting-edge work analyzing the "data exhaust" of modern society. Pentland has shown that analyzing cell-phone records—done securely and with appropriate permissions—can give clues to everything from crime rates to the physical health of an individual or a community.

The bulk of the datasets that Pentland and his colleagues use in their research are privately held. But he's made the case that it would benefit us all to make more of our personal data publicly available. And he's helped create a model for doing that safely.

First, why would anyone want their personal data to be public? Some reasons are altruistic. Pentland has shown that tracking individuals' behavior and movements through their cell phones, with their permission, could reveal population-wide patterns that help predict when a flu epidemic is about to start or help design cities that manage their traffic in ways that save energy and help fight global warming.

A less lofty but more immediate application is already here. A company called TrueCar, cited by the World Economic Forum as an example of applying personal data, has made the true cost of buying a car transparent to consumers. The company gets data on individual car transactions from "well-known data aggregators in the automotive space," its website says, and analyzes the data to give an accurate picture of local car prices and help shoppers learn what other people are paying for the car they want. The company, founded in 2005, claims to have saved consumers close to $2 billion off of the manufacturer's suggested retail price through its network of cooperative dealers.

For the full benefits of personal data to be realized, people have to be willing to make their data open voluntarily, securely, and selectively. That's why Pentland proposed a solution he called the "New Deal on Data." This formulation, which built on legal discussions that had been going on for some time, would establish a clear ownership right to personal data that doesn't exist today. As he described it in an article written for the World Economic Forum in 2009, the proposal was elegant in its simplicity. Here's the whole thing:

> *The first step toward open information markets is to give people ownership of their data. The simplest approach to defining what it means to "own your own data" is to go back to Old English Common Law for the three basic tenets of ownership, which are the rights of possession, use, and disposal:*
>
> 1. *You have a right to possess your data. Companies should adopt the role of a Swiss bank account for your data. You open an account (anonymously, if possible), and you can remove your data whenever you'd like.*
>
> 2. *You, the data owner, must have full control over the use of your data. If you're not happy with the way a company uses your data, you can remove it. All of it. Everything must be opt-in, and not only clearly explained in plain language, but with regular reminders that you have the option to opt out.*
>
> 3. *You have a right to dispose of or distribute your data. If you want to destroy it or remove it and redeploy it elsewhere, it is your call.*

This simple but radical proposal influenced thinking about data privacy in the U.S. government, the European Union, and in the World Economic Forum, which is running a multiyear project to rethink the use of personal data today. The World Economic Forum has produced several reports, with the latest, "Unlocking the Value of Personal Data," published in February 2013. That report concluded that personal data has both social importance and significant economic value. And it set out a framework for managing the use of data in a way that would make it possible to realize this value.

The World Economic Forum began by challenging the usefulness of "binary" user agreements—either "accept" or "don't accept"—as an effective way to get individuals' consent. Put aside for a minute the fact that individuals don't have a real choice; those agreements are what lawyers call contracts of adhesion, giving people a take-it-or-leave-it option completely on the seller's terms. And put aside the fact that there's not even a pretense that these are true agreements any more. (For one thing, it's estimated that if an average Internet user were to read every policy he or she "accepts," it would take 30 days out of every year.) Even if the current privacy agreements were meaningful, they wouldn't allow for the kind of control that will make personal data both secure and useful.

The World Economic Forum report notes that, "Organizations need to engage and empower individuals more effectively and efficiently. Rather than merely providing a binary yes-or-no consent at the initial point of collection, individuals need new ways to exercise choice and control, especially where data uses most affect them. They need a better understanding of the overall value exchange so that they can make truly informed choices."

That logic supported a closer look at the concept of personal data vaults. As the figure that follows (taken from the report) shows, these data vaults will make it possible for individuals to store their own data, gathering it from retailers, service providers, and the government, and release it selectively to businesses that want to use it. People will be able to turn their own data into Open Data, but on their own terms.

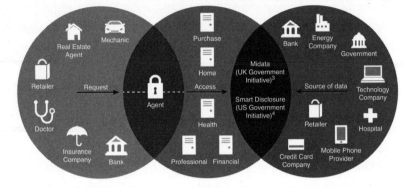

This might sound like a futuristic view, but as with so much in digital technology, the future is already here. The World Economic Forum report defines personal data vaults as "secure, private clouds that individuals can access via web and mobile apps . . . they empower individuals with their data, allowing them to aggregate, store, find, securely share and get value from data about them and their lives." These tools already exist, and they're starting to transform the way that technologists, consumers, and businesses think about all kinds of transactions.

Consumers Controlling Their Data for Fun and Profit

Putting individuals in charge of their data is a big idea that could upend conventional marketing strategy. Doc Searls, author of *The Intention Economy*, has written that Customer Relationship Management—CRM—could soon be joined by VRM, Vendor Relationship Management. In this new world, consumers control the data about themselves that tells companies whether they're likely customers. Companies can then reach out to the best prospects and pay them for the privilege of marketing to them. For millions of consumers, this would be the ultimate revenge on telemarketers. For businesses, it would make for a marketplace that is consumer-friendly and efficient—*and* protects individual privacy.

Searls believes that personal data vaults are key to making this happen, and his book frequently mentions Washington-based Personal. com, one of the first companies to develop data vaults for consumer use. This company helps you set up an individual, secure data vault to store a wide range of personal data that can only be accessed with your permission. The company promises to help you keep "all life's details in one secure place," reducing the hassle of managing multiple passwords and credit card numbers, among many other digital artifacts that we keep losing or forgetting. The Personal.com mobile app has ingeniously designed "gems" for all different kinds of personal data that you can keep secure, share with your family, or share more broadly. Personal.com also supports the principles of "privacy by design"—building privacy protections into the way data is handled from the beginning—and is the first online consumer-facing company to be named a "Privacy by Design Ambassador" by Ann Cavoukian, Information and Privacy Commissioner for the province of Ontario, who developed the concept.

In an interview with *The Economist*, Personal.com's president and CEO Shane Green estimated that consumers could ultimately earn a thousand dollars a year in benefits and savings by sharing their personal data with retailers, who would pay to have access to desirable customers. While Personal.com initially offered its service for free, the company announced in June 2013 that it will begin charging $29.99 a year for a personal data vault. Its plan is generally not to charge consumers directly, but rather to charge institutions such as banks, insurance companies, or schools that could then offer the service to their customers as a benefit.

This life management tool is just the introduction to a larger vision of how personal data control can help business and improve society. Personal.com has developed an app called Fill It that enables people to fill out all kinds of forms automatically by uploading the data from their vaults with password protection. Personal.com began by testing Fill It with government forms, such as the ones used by the Washington, DC, Department of Motor Vehicles, and found that it helped ease the often onerous and repetitive process of filling out those forms. Consumers can use the same app to fill out forms for companies that partner with Personal.com to offer data vaults to their customers.

Personal.com is now working with the U.S. Department of Education to enable students with federal loans to upload their application data to their vaults. That way, they can reuse it when they redo their federal aid forms every year, or they can use it on other forms as they wish. More than 20 million people benefit from federal student aid, and the government estimates that completing these long, detailed forms takes up more than 30 million hours each year. Using data stored in personal vaults will also help make the forms more accurate and may help students get loans more effectively.

Personal.com is also working with the World Economic Forum's Global Agenda Council on Data and its partners to make automated form filling a widely used application. In its February 2013 report, the World Economic Forum estimates that this could "save the world 10 billion hours [a year] and improve the delivery of public and private sector services. . . . Automated form filling could [allow] far more efficient online, mobile, and in-person interactions; unlock new permission-based, data-driven services from both public and private organizations . . . drive major new economic benefits for both individuals and businesses and improve the delivery of government services; potentially save hundreds of millions (if not billions) of dollars in reduced security breaches." The word *potentially* is significant here—but still, the promise is great.

Turning the Internet on its Head

Another new company, Reputation.com—whose work on online reputation is described in Chapter 7—is also working to help individuals

188

get data about themselves under control. When I met with Michael Fertik, Reputation.com's founder and CEO, we talked about the future of data privacy. Fertik is a long-haired, high-energy entrepreneur who doesn't look like a typical Harvard Law School graduate, but he has both the legal training and the business skills to set high goals for his high-profile startup. He doesn't lack ambition: as he told me simply, "I want to turn the Internet's basic business model on its head."

"If you look at the first, say, trillion dollars of wealth that's been created on the Internet, to take an arbitrary number," he said, "and you set aside hardware companies and Internet service providers, the great majority of what's left is advertising. That means that Silicon Valley is very good at funding entrepreneurs who are very good at creating things that they give to you to use free, and then they collect your data and sell your data. I don't think this is an evil proposition, you know. But the basic trade is that you as a user are giving up all sense of control, all avenues of defining yourself and controlling your data flow. And users do not know that. I went to Harvard Law School and I cannot make head or tails of almost any terms of service."

He went on to say, "The basic business model that a company runs is based on the obfuscation of what they do with your data. And fundamentally, as a matter of basic law and economics, you cannot have this as the center of the value proposition and then care deeply about a customer's privacy. It's impossible to do both. What I've decided to do about it is to try to put the user at the middle of the Internet again."

Fertik believes that the economic value of controlling and using personal data, through the tools that his company and others provide, can be in the trillions of dollars. Here's how he calculates it: "First, imagine if you completely cut the advertising business off at the knees, replace it, turn it on its head, and put you in the middle of every transaction. Next, think about every brokerage business in the world that's reliant on data. If you are valued at $2,000 a year to a data broker times, let's say, 100 million guys who look enough like you, then that's a pretty good business."

Reputation.com, said Fertik, can enable you to use your data for your own benefit in four distinct ways. "Number one is an offer. An offer is usually going to look like a discount but it could also be an offer for employment" if you're posting searchable data about yourself that helps potential employers find you.

"Number two is status." Perks like frequent-flyer mileage should be easy to keep if you change cities or other circumstances, but it's often difficult. Making your personal data visible would make it easier for airlines or other companies that offer personalized benefits to find you and keep your perks current.

"Third would be cash. If someone comes in for a test drive, it's worth $2,000 in nominal value to a luxury car maker. That $2,000 is a property of two things; one, you have the right person who could afford the car—a self-selected demographic—and two, intentionality. If you have brought yourself to the car lot, you're probably ready to buy a car." Given the value of bringing in good prospects, said Fertik, "You might be able to offer $100 to a large number of people, say, people who have graduated college, people who have graduated college in the last ten years, people who have gone to a certain set of colleges, people who have graduated graduate school, whatever it is."

The fourth benefit of data control is the most obvious: "Privacy. You get to surf the web and purchase things and you're fully anonymous. So you go to Amazon, you buy something, they'll never find out anything actually about you except that you exist and that you have an address and you're able to pay. Your address is obfuscated, and it goes through some third party that actually gets the purchase to your house."

This last and most basic benefit is the foundation for the other three. The vision is that data becomes more valuable when it becomes a scarcer resource that is under the consumer's control. In a world where more people are storing their data in secure vaults, companies may offer better deals, special customer service, or even cash incentives to people who intentionally share data to make themselves findable.

The business model is intriguing, but it's unproven: as of the end of 2012, Reputation.com had received $67 million in venture funding and had yet to turn a profit. And it's a sure bet that a trillion-dollar-plus online advertising industry will not give up without a fight.

Plenty of marketers are skeptical of Reputation.com's model. Peter Fader, a marketing expert and professor at the Wharton School of Business, told *Technology Review* that, "Despite the ways that companies delude themselves, demographics and other personal descriptors are rarely useful." He emphasizes that data on consumer behavior, which marketers already collect, is more important. Moreover, Fader believes that consumers will be resistant: "The effort required to manage your personal data will be seen as greater than the benefits that arise from doing so."

In a recent blog post entitled "Adventures in the Open Data Market," Katrina Lerman, senior researcher at Communispace, told the tongue-in-cheek story of one consumer who decided to put in the effort. She described an experiment by "Federico Zannier, a graduate student and former business consultant. . . . Since February [2013], he has been meticulously recording ALL of his online activity, including HTML pages, screenshots, webcam images, GPS location, and an app log; he even mapped his mouse pointer position. Then he launched a Kickstarter project called 'A Bite of Me,' offering his data starting at $2 a day. Not only did he quickly meet his $500 goal, but at the end of a month, he had raised almost $3,000, including three backers who paid $200 for his entire 7GB data trove. . . . Could Zannier be the first of a new breed of professional data generators?" Probably not.

But even if personal data vaults don't become a revolutionary marketing idea overnight, they're likely to take hold for, well, personal reasons. Doc Searls, author of *The Intention Economy*, has written about this issue, including a comprehensive blog post early in 2012. There he points out that:

> *Brokering personal data is far from the only business model for Personal [or] what Connect.me, Singly, MyDex, Azigo, Qiy, Glome, Kynetx, the Locker Project, or any of the other VRM (Vendor Relationship Management) companies and development projects . . . exist to do. . . . Mostly they exist to give individuals more control over their lives and their relationships with organizations, with each other, and with themselves. . . .*
>
> *[W]hat are marketers willing to pay to individuals directly for personal data? . . . In fact, there never has been a market where people sell their personal data. What we do know for sure is that personal data has **use value**. . . . Think about all the personal data in your life that can be digitized and stored: photos, videos, letters, texts, e-mails, contact information for yourself and others, school and business records, bills received and paid, medical and fitness data, calendar entries. . . .*
>
> *All the VRM developers . . . are in the business of helping individuals understand and empower themselves, as independent and autonomous actors in the marketplace. Not just as better "targets" for marketing messages. The movement of which they are a part—VRM, for Vendor Relationship Management—is toward giving individuals tools for both independence and engagement. . . . For example, we are working on terms of service that individual customers can assert: ones that say, for example, "don't track me outside your website," and "share back with me all the data you collect about me, in the form I specify." That has nothing to do with what anything sells for. It's about relationship, not transaction.*

For an entirely new kind of marketing to emerge, we would need to reach a tipping point where so many people are using personal data vaults that the data in them can drive the new marketing model. It's possible that data vaults will become so popular because of their other uses—and because of increased concern over personal privacy—that the transition will happen sometime soon. In the meantime, at the least, personal data vaults give individuals a new form of control and open new possibilities in an increasingly disquieting digital world.

Realizing the Business Potential

The new focus on personal data holds several lessons for businesses. Here are some basic strategies to consider.

Respect Your Customers' Privacy. This is the most basic lesson of current trends. We've all seen the articles about companies—and not just Google and Facebook—that use their customers' data in ways the customers don't want. Expect the concern about privacy to become a drumbeat. Congress may never take comprehensive action, but even holding repeated hearings on data brokers, Internet privacy, and related issues can raise public awareness. Companies that promise to protect consumers' privacy and follow through will have a well-earned edge in attracting and keeping customers.

Give Your Customers Access to Their Own Data and Help Them Control It. The idea that people should have a right to their own data is being widely accepted. The concept is key to Smart Disclosure, to the concept of personal data vaults, and to the emerging approach to consumer data and privacy. Consumers will come to expect access to their own customer data; forward-thinking companies should give it to them. More than that, consumers may come to question the contracts they "accept" with online companies that give those companies control of their data. They may start demanding to see what kinds of information the data brokers hold about them as well.

Experiment With Customer-Driven Marketing. In the wake of new privacy concerns, we can expect that more consumers will use websites and applications to store, record, and analyze data about their finances, purchases, and preferences. Businesses can give consumers an incentive to share this information with them as Open Data and help consumers match their own needs to the companies' offerings. By doing so, they can reach consumers as more than passive recipients of ads and promotions. The greatest opportunity is in high-end markets where the value of a purchase is greatest, such as cars, electronics, travel, and real estate.

Explore the Privacy Business. Personal data protection may become a significant business driver, as some entrepreneurs now believe. If it does, there will be many business opportunities to help consumers protect their data through personal data vaults, software solutions, and applications. By using data vaults to ensure privacy, companies can develop more direct relationships with their customers where sensitive data is involved.

In an e-mail to me, Josh Galper, chief policy officer and general counsel of Personal.com, wrote about the ways that businesses are starting to use his company's services. "A primary way we're working with businesses and other entities is to partner with them to provide co-branded data vaults to their customers/members prepopulated with information associated with their accounts that the customer can then share and reuse, whether to access it from any device, securely share it with a loved one, or auto-complete forms with data through Fill It. Not only does this empower people with their own information and help to break down the silos that currently hold it, this two-way exchange of data and documents also radically improves front-office solutions for connecting and exchanging information between the customer and the company. It's a win-win for businesses and individuals." Galper says that Personal.com has worked in this way primarily with the insurance, education, and financial sectors.

"We are also working," he said, "with partners that sell co-branded vaults to their customers that contain 'BYOD' [Bring Your Own Data] apps geared toward specific use cases that they value, such as a digital wallet, a password vault, or for important files like wills and financial documents. Again, the rules of ownership and control by the individual alone dictate how these vaults function technically and practically."

"Finally," Galper added, "businesses can register for Personal.com as Owners as well, allowing colleagues at work to securely share important data and files with one another, such as passwords, the FedEx account, sensitive files they'd prefer to have encrypted and shared through the vault instead of email, etc. In addition, a business would be able to auto-complete forms using data from its vault through Fill It, whether for government or other forms."

CHAPTER TWELVE

Doing Business in a See-Through Society

OPEN DATA HAS BEEN A BOON TO JOURNALISTS AND ACTIVists—and a sobering reality for the governments and businesses they choose to investigate. As more and more public data has become available, a growing number of reporters and advocacy organizations have figured out how to use it. They analyze data on government contracts, political contributions, healthcare companies, and corporations of all kinds. Their mission is to use data to equalize the balance of power between government and corporate entities on the one hand and the public on the other. Their success has a message: it's harder than ever to hide.

This new breed of data detectives uses technology both to analyze data and to get their results to the public. The Sunlight Foundation, a leader in promoting transparency, runs an in-house tech lab with almost 20 developers whose goal is to bring transparency to government activities and to government's relationship with business. Global Witness analyzes corporate and financial records to expose money-laundering schemes. The Project on Government Oversight

197

analyzes federal contracts and contractors. MySociety in the United Kingdom, founded and directed by Tom Steinberg, publishes data obtained through the Freedom of Information Act, among other activities. Journalistic organizations like ProPublica and the Center for Public Integrity dive deep into data on healthcare providers. And at the same time that these organizations use data that is already public, they pressure government agencies to release still more data, going to court if they have to and often winning.

The data detectives provide a kind of third-party oversight on government and businesses. Thanks to their work, companies and governments alike now operate in a world where secrets are harder to keep. It's now part of risk management to run your operations with the assumption that anything you do may eventually be found out.

The Birth of Computer-Assisted Reporting

The modern era of data-driven journalism goes back to 1973. It was a banner year for investigative reporting. In May of that year, Bob Woodward and Carl Bernstein won the Pulitzer Prize for their *Washington Post* coverage of the Watergate scandal. The year had begun with the conviction and resignation of several top Nixon aides. It ended with Nixon declaring "I am not a crook" as he headed inevitably toward his own resignation the following year. While history allows various interpretations, it's fair to say that investigative reporting brought down the president.

But perhaps the most significant event in journalism that year was a turning point that went almost unnoticed. In 1973, Indiana University Press published the first edition of a book called *Precision Journalism: A Reporter's Introduction to Social Science Methods* by a Knight Ridder reporter named Phil Meyer. While Watergate made a generation of reporters want to become the next Woodward or Bernstein, Meyer's book began to give them the tools for a new, data-driven approach to investigative reporting. Where Woodward and

Bernstein set up late-night meetings in parking garages with their sources, Meyer used quantitative methods and mainframe computers to get at the truth.

Meyer began to develop what would become known as computer-assisted reporting on a Nieman journalism fellowship at Harvard. He then applied the concept in 1967, when he was flown in to Detroit to help the staff of the *Free Press* cover the urban riots of that year. In that overwrought newsroom, theories were flying about exactly who the rioters were educationally and demographically. Meyer came up with the radical idea of doing a survey to find out. The survey, done in collaboration with the University of Michigan, had some surprising findings, including the fact that many college-educated people had participated in the riots. The *Free Press* won a Pulitzer. And Meyer realized that he was on to something.

As he was writing his book, a colleague suggested calling Meyer's methods "precision journalism" as a contrast to what was then called the "new journalism," a subjective approach that put the reporter and his or her opinions right in the middle of the action. The new journalism seems pretty old these days—anyone read *The Electric Kool-Aid Acid Test* lately?—but Meyer's work couldn't be more contemporary. His book is still in print, now in its fourth edition, and has been updated repeatedly to keep up with new technology.

Computer-assisted reporting, which is now used by watchdog organizations as well as by reporters, has evolved into one of the most important uses of Open Data. Over the last four decades, journalists have learned how to analyze data to detect fraud, reveal government spending patterns, track demographic trends, and more. A number of nonprofits now use the same methods to fuel their data-driven policy analysis and advocacy.

The result of all this delving into data is that businesses, governments, public institutions, and large nonprofit organizations are all living in proverbial glass houses, with an army of experts around the world who know how to probe their secrets. As more information is released as Open Data, the data detectives will all have more to work with. Newspapers may be in decline across the country, but the investigative techniques that reporters have developed are actually growing in impact.

Old-School Reporting, New Techniques

Chuck Lewis has lived through three great careers, as a reporter, a nonprofit leader, and now as a professor at American University. The wall of his office in the School of Communication where I interviewed him sports a few caricatures and spoofs that were gifts from colleagues and friends. There's a mockup of him on the cover of the long-gone political magazine *George* and one showing him as The Godfather—of nonprofit investigative reporting, not of Don Corleone's empire. But in contrast to Brando's threatening character, Lewis was professorial and cheerful as he described his life's work.

"I've been doing investigative reporting now for a little over 30 years," he told me. He had worked at ABC News in Washington and *60 Minutes* in New York when he was inspired to launch an organization called the Center for Public Integrity. Lewis launched the Center out of his house in 1989, grew it into a powerful journalistic force, and worked there for 15 years, leading the Center's award-winning investigative work on 300 reports and 14 books. "I have two political science degrees," he said, "and our general approach was to try to combine the best elements of political science and journalism. I wanted to do thorough research that's more relevant and accessible than most political science and do a form of reporting that was more in depth than anything you generally see."

The Center's strategy, said Lewis, has been to focus on "public data that no one ever reads." Among other scoops, the Center published details on Halliburton's government contracts in the Iraq and Afghanistan wars. As the web took off in the 1990s, so did investigative reporters, who used the Internet to get new access to data and documents.

"In the early 1990s the National Institute for Computer-Assisted Reporting was started as part of Investigative Reporters and Editors," said Lewis. "NICAR's most recent conference had 600 people, and it's increasing. The exciting part of that is they're increasingly in their 20s and early 30s."

Investigative reporting has kept pace with technology, and Lewis's old organization has been in the forefront. The Center for Public Integrity, he notes proudly, "just did the biggest project in the history of computer-assisted reporting." The Center pushed to make critical government information about healthcare available as Open Data and then used it in a revolutionary way.

The Center had decided to take a close look at Medicare, which, Lewis observes, is "a sprawling, elaborate, massively complex morass of programs." The Center's researchers became interested in investigating Medicare fraud and realized that the records they needed were not publicly available. Together with Dow Jones, publisher of the *Wall Street Journal*, they asked for the records from the Department of Health and Human Services, which would not release them. "They filed in U.S. District Court," said Lewis. "Finally, HHS gave them the records begrudgingly. The Center and the *Wall Street Journal* together ended up paying about $12,000."

"Now they were looking at hundreds of millions of records," he told me. "They were able to show that in 24-hour emergency centers and small clinics, a person would go in for one problem, and next thing you know, the billing would have multiple categories added. And suddenly, instead of Medicare paying $100, it was paying $700."

According to Lewis, the Center was "able to identify somewhere in the range of $11 billion in fraud. It's a huge number. Within two months of that report coming out, the inspector general for the department announced they were going to conduct an investigation into the fraud that the Center had uncovered. A newspaper and a nonprofit had been able to initiate this project, pull down the datasets, and then mesh those gears and figure it out."

This was a victory for both journalism and good government, but it was still incomplete. A court injunction from 1979 prevented the journalists from linking the records of suspect charges to individual doctors. Then, in May 2013, the U.S. District Court in Jacksonville, Florida, vacated that earlier decision on the grounds that interpretation of privacy law had changed in the intervening 33 years. That decision means that the investigation won't just affect Medicare as a whole: it may have real repercussions for specific healthcare providers and their practices.

While no one else may have matched the scope of the Medicare investigation, many other investigative reports have put some heat on the healthcare industry. The most consistently effective data-driven investigations are now probably done by ProPublica, a nonprofit organization launched in 2008 that has about 40 staffers.

Like the Medicare investigative team, ProPublica sometimes finds itself fighting to get data released as Open Data. A few years ago, ProPublica decided to do an investigation of dialysis treatment in the United States. To do their work, they asked for data under the Freedom of Information Act but were only able to get it after protracted negotiations. Once they had the data, ProPublica was able to show serious cost and safety problems with the dialysis system. The group developed a Dialysis Facility Tracker to help patients find the best care. That was in 2010. The following year, under questioning from Senator Charles Grassley (R-IA), the Centers for Medicare and Medicaid Services announced steps to make its data on dialysis centers more available to the public. "More scrutiny and transparency are good for consumers," the senator said, but he added that "it shouldn't take an investigative media exposé and pressure from Congress to make those improvements happen."

While ProPublica tracks data on a number of public-interest issues, including government bailouts and nonprofit finances, the organization has had some of its greatest impact with healthcare investigations using Open Data. Its Prescriber Checkup project makes it possible to compare individual prescribing patterns for doctors under the Medicare drug benefit. Dollars for Doctors tracks the payments that drug companies make to doctors and other healthcare professionals to encourage them to prescribe their products. And Nursing Home Inspect makes it possible to identify low-quality nursing homes in any state based on regulators' reports.

Other enterprising journalists across the country and around the world are finding Open Data that they can analyze to great effect. Lewis points to the *Atlanta Journal-Constitution*'s investigation of high school test scores throughout the state, which showed a suspicious number of high scores. The paper did a probabilistic analysis that showed persuasively that school administrators were cooking the numbers. The story had an impact: the retired district superintendent and 34 other educators were indicted on charges including racketeering and theft.

Newspapers and other news organizations are also taking a creative approach to investigative work by engaging their readers in gathering, analyzing, and improving Open Data. ProPublica, for example, invited the public to help develop a database on campaign ad funding during the 2012 election. But the likely world champion at journalistic crowdsourcing is *The Guardian* in the United Kingdom. Beginning in 2009, *The Guardian* obtained detailed expense reports on Ministers of Parliament and invited their readers to help by going through the reports line by line. In what appears to have become sort of a national pastime, *The Guardian*'s readers were happy to help find out exactly what their representatives had been spending their money on, and the paper has covered the results as an ongoing series. Since they began, a lot more MPs have been taking the tube instead of a cab.

The Business Drivers for Business Transparency

Historically, investigative reporters were on their own, working to dig up information despite their targets' efforts to hide it. The financial dealings of large corporations were especially hard to untangle. But some recent changes are bringing greater transparency to the financial sector and to corporate operations, both in the public interest and in the interest of the economy's health.

To understand why, just think back a few years. The scariest movie of our time, to my mind, wasn't a zombie epic or an apocalyptic dystopian fantasy. It was the HBO adaptation of Andrew Ross Sorkin's book *Too Big to Fail*, the story of the 2008 financial crisis.

When HBO released *Too Big to Fail*, viewers were treated to scenes that played like a classic disaster movie. Here was Hank Paulson (played by William Hurt) leaving a meeting to throw up from the stress. There was Timothy Geithner (Billy Crudup) cursing nonstop into his cell phone. The mood was like one of those asteroid movies from the late '90s where a chunk of the asteroid has already wiped out Paris and the bigger chunk is heading for New York and Washington. Except here, Paris was Lehman Brothers, which collapsed in September 2008, and New York and Washington, with their fate hanging in the balance, were AIG and Bear Stearns.

At a screening of *Too Big to Fail* in 2011, covered by *The Daily Beast*, Timothy Geithner acknowledged in an onstage interview that the country's financial leaders had been as panicked as they looked. "Things were falling apart," he said. "We had no playbook and no tools.... Life's about choices. We had no good choices.... We allowed this huge financial system to emerge without any meaningful constraints."

The meltdown had several causes, but one was a failure of transparency—that is, a failure of data. In its aftermath, the financial crisis has become one of the most compelling arguments for more Open Data about corporations and financial institutions and the ways they operate. A new drive to better data is being led by an unusual combination of advocates, entrepreneurs, investors, regulators, and businesses. This new transparency will help journalists and data detectives of all kinds, but it will also ultimately help investors as well.

One of the most troubling things we learned from the crisis is that no one truly knows how major financial institutions are structured—perhaps including the institutions themselves. Consider this: an international banking study done after the collapse of Lehman Brothers found that "The Lehman Brothers group consisted of 2,985 legal entities that operated in some 50 countries. . . . a complicated mix of both regulated and unregulated entities. . . . [A] trade performed in one company could be booked in another." Even if regulators had been suspicious of Lehman Brothers, they would have found it almost impossible to see through the 3,000 faces of Lehman and take action before the company failed.

What was true of Lehman Brothers is true of most major financial institutions and many large corporations. Corporate entities in the United States and other countries have developed remarkably complex structures of ownership, subsidiaries, and board governance—sometimes for tax reasons, sometimes for operational reasons, and sometimes apparently because they've grown through accretion. There's a growing demand for Open Data that can help make these complex companies more understandable and accountable in a meaningful way.

The Dodd-Frank Act of 2010, passed as a response to the financial crisis, mandates transparency in many areas. The first stated goal of the act is "to promote the financial stability of the United States by improving accountability and transparency in the financial system." Its Title VII, on Wall Street Transparency and Accountability, requires greater transparency about credit default swaps and credit derivatives. Title IX, which covers Investor Protections, authorizes the SEC to issue "point-of-sale" disclosure rules for financial products and services and requires periodic shareholder approval of executive compensation. Title X establishes the Consumer Financial Protection Bureau (CFPB), which has the power to improve transparency and disclosure for a number of financial products.

While government mandates like these are being implemented, private companies are also bringing new levels of transparency to corporations and financial institutions. Open Corporates, one of the companies being incubated at London's Open Data Institute, has developed in-depth analyses of corporate structures and mapped those structures to make them visible.

Open Corporates CEO Chris Taggart described the result for Goldman Sachs, which has 1,475 subsidiaries registered in the United States and 739 in the Cayman Islands. "By visualizing it by country, [the searchable map] shows particularly in the cases of Goldman Sachs and Morgan Stanley, just how critical the Cayman Islands is to those networks," Taggart told the tech news service GigaOm. "That's the sort of thing you could have done as an academic study based on this data, but maybe half a dozen people would have read it. This is an almost automatic byproduct of putting this into a single open dataset." (While Open Corporates releases all its findings for free as Open Data under an open license, its business model includes offering additional paid services.)

If you think that efforts like these are driven by anticorporate radicals, British Prime Minister David Cameron would like a word with you. In January 2013, the Conservative Prime Minister attended the World Economic Forum in Davos, Switzerland. The United Kingdom had assumed the presidency of the G8, and Cameron was there to outline his priorities. Speaking about "trade, tax, and transparency," and the relationship between the three, he laid out the case for Open Data as a business imperative. Here's an excerpt:

> *We need more transparency on how governments and, yes, companies operate. . . . [D]oesn't this sound like an antibusiness, bash the rich, tax success agenda? Absolutely not. This is a resolutely probusiness agenda. I'm about the most probusiness leader you can find. . . . But I also passionately believe that if you want open economies, low taxes, and free enterprise then you need to lay down the rules of the game and you need to be prepared to enforce them. . . . This is a vision of proper companies, proper taxes, proper rules. A vision of open societies, open economies, and open government.*

Shining Sunlight on Government

Data-driven research has not only transformed investigative reporting, it's also created a new breed of public-interest nonprofits. They're using the same kind of investigative data analysis that reporters do to probe the workings of government, corporations, and the relationships between the two.

The aptly named Sunlight Foundation, launched in 2006, may be the most influential and most technically sophisticated of these groups. It was founded by Ellen Miller, who had run two other nonprofits focused on money and politics and continues to lead the Sunlight Foundation today. "The original founding insight for Sunlight came from journalists," she told me when we met in the spring of 2013. "It was that if data was more easily accessible about money, power, and influence and what that money buys and how it affects government, then it would be easier for them to write convincing, compelling stories that would drive discussion and debate about unaccountable government."

Early on, Sunlight brilliantly took a cue from Google and set up the Sunlight Labs as a center of innovation. (The first lab director was Greg Elin, whom I later worked with when he was chief data officer for the FCC.) The labs, which now have close to 20 people, came up with one creative app after another. Several of them have exposed the relationship between public officials and private money. For the 2012 election, for example, Sunlight developed a smartphone app called Ad Hawk: you could point it at your TV, have it "listen" to a political ad, and then read about who actually paid for the ad on your smartphone's screen. The tool, Sunlight said, was designed to help voters who were being "bombarded by ads from super PACs and other groups with innocent-sounding names like Americans for Puppies."

One of the most widely used Sunlight apps is Influence Explorer, which combines 10 different datasets on money, politics, and influence. Miller described how Influence Explorer can show that a major company is one of the biggest spenders on lobbying and campaign contributions, show how many executives it has on federal advisory committees and how much it receives in federal grants and contracts, and show how many times it's been cited by the EPA. As Miller said, "the idea is to be able to scroll down a page and see a profile of a labor union, a corporation, a corporate executive, or any entity and what their influence profile looks like, at the state or federal level."

Federal contractors should now be prepared for increasing scrutiny. The Project on Government Oversight (POGO) has focused for years on increasing transparency for government contracts. The new movement to Open Data in government will probably result in the release of more detailed, readable information on contracts over time. If you're doing business with the federal government, your business may become more public than it's been in the past. On the other hand, if you're a potential government contractor, you'll get greater insight into existing vendors, which may help you compete.

State government contractors should also be prepared to answer some questions, particularly if they've benefited from state subsidies. The organization Good Jobs First has built up data on how governments subsidize companies to persuade them to do business in their states. Their data was one of the main sources used in a *New York Times* series, "The United States of Subsidies," that documented and criticized this practice. There's even an iPhone app, BizVizz, that can instantly give anyone information on corporate subsidies. At a time when state budgets are tight, state workers are being laid off, and unemployment is high, these subsidies may come in for increasing public criticism.

Realizing the Business Potential

For many businesses, the see-through society seems to present more of a challenge than an opportunity. Still, it's worth noting that the same government Open Data that reporters can use is also accessible to businesses. It's telling that businesses are the most frequent users of the Freedom of Information Act. Although business intelligence wasn't the FOIA's original purpose, it's turned out to be a significant by-product of open information laws. (More on that in the next chapter.) Every business should know how the FOIA works and how to use it as a business intelligence tool.

On the defensive side, businesses need to be aware that they're operating in more of a glass-house environment—glass boardrooms, perhaps?—than at any time in the past. Journalists and watchdog groups are getting better than ever at probing the workings of large companies and governments and the relationship between the two. They're setting the tone for public concerns about federal spending, government contracts, corporate transparency, lobbying, and campaign finance—all issues of real civic importance that can affect businesses and their investors.

The organizations mentioned in this chapter are doing influential work that citizens and companies alike should follow. They include:

- The Center for Public Integrity
- Global Witness
- Good Jobs First
- MySociety
- Open Corporates
- Project on Government Oversight
- ProPublica
- The Sunlight Foundation

The see-through society doesn't just apply to large corporations. Individuals whose business dealings are tracked in government systems, such as healthcare providers reimbursed by government programs, could find their business practices suddenly made public as Open Data.

The recent court decision to identify Medicare providers in government records could turn out to be a benchmark decision, a sign that records with the names of business or service providers may become more open than in the past. The court's decision was based on interpreting privacy law in light of current practices and the public interest. It's not yet clear how broadly this reasoning will apply, how it will be challenged, or how it will be implemented. At this writing, the Department of Health and Human Services has not yet determined how it will find the right balance in protecting privacy while releasing the data the court has now said must be made public.

In general, it's prudent to expect that more operational data about businesses large and small will become public as Open Data. The implications are straightforward. Do business in a way that you think the public would find fair and ethical—not to mention legal—and be prepared to defend yourself if you don't.

All of this may sound like the familiar concept of corporate accountability, which has never been too popular with corporations themselves. The very words, after all, imply that large companies are hiding something they need to account for—not only in their financial dealings, but also in their labor practices, their safety records, or who knows what else. But a number of converging trends have created a new kind of demand for Open Data on business. All at the same time:

- The near-collapse of the world financial markets has led to public pressure, and some legislation, to require greater transparency in financial institutions.
- Government agencies have mandated financial and operational transparency in a wide range of industries.
- Public interest groups and journalists have honed their data-mining expertise to learn more about the private sector than they could before.
- Perhaps most important, investors, business analysts, and corporations themselves are demanding greater transparency from the companies they invest in or do business with.

There's an opportunity here to go beyond defensive approaches and create what I'd call a new era of *corporate credibility*. It's not just about simple transparency and accountability any more—it's about disclosing Open Data to engender confidence and trust. Companies that are wary of this trend should know two things: it's inevitable, and it will ultimately be good for business. There is too much data out there already for companies to hide what they don't want the world to know. As companies become more open, many will adopt better operating practices, grow their business, and attract new investment.

CHAPTER THIRTEEN

Government and Data: Setting the Rules for an Open World

O N May 9, 2013, the *New York Times* and the *Wall Street Journal* gave top coverage to Congressional testimony about the Benghazi terrorist attack. *USA Today* focused on new developments in the kidnapping and sexual abuse saga in Cleveland. Most of the media continued to cover the Obama administration's IRS scandal. Except for a short piece in the *Washington Post*, just about everybody missed one of the most important tech stories of the year—and one that could affect technology, business, and government for decades to come.

On that day, on a trip to a technology center in Austin, Texas, President Obama announced the release of an Executive Order and official Open Data Policy that have revolutionary potential for business, for government, and for the American public. Through this policy, the president promised that "we're making even more government data available, and we're making it easier for people to find and to use. And that's going to help launch more startups. It's going to help launch more businesses. . . . It's going to help more entrepreneurs come up with products and services that we haven't even imagined yet."

The technology press, bloggers, and long-time advocates of Open Data and Open Government celebrated the news as a milestone. The next week, the policy got some extensive play on *Slate*, thanks to a piece by Alex Howard, who covered Open Government for several years for O'Reilly Media, the leading technology publisher. Howard's story billed the announcement as "The Best Thing Obama's Done This Month." Not that it was a great month for the president, but still—accurate enough. As Howard wrote, "This is perhaps the biggest step forward to date in making government data—that information your tax dollars pay for—accessible for citizens, entrepreneurs, politicians, and others."

Long-time Open Data advocates had high praise for the new Open Data Policy. They greeted its announcement with statements like, "This memorandum is the most significant advance in information policies by the federal government since the passage of the Freedom of Information Act" (and that was in 1966). "Open Data, as the White House has defined it, will transform our government." "We're thrilled that the President (and some very dedicated staff) have been listening and are aggressively pursuing a strong vision for what Open Data should mean."

The policy isn't just good news for proponents of Open Government. It's also going to help any company in the country that needs to use government Open Data in its business. The Open Data Policy did something unusual for a government memo: it combined a broad, ambitious vision with highly specific guidance. "We wanted to make sure we operationalized this," Nick Sinai, Deputy U.S. Chief Technology Officer, told me. "This is not just a check-the-box policy exercise. It's something that should really become part of the core DNA of agencies, where they see Open Data as valuable to achieving their mission objectives."

To appreciate what the new policy means, you have to appreciate what a mess the federal data system (if it can be called a system) has been. Each of the more than 100 federal agencies has had its own rules for gathering data; its own data management systems, which are often different for different bureaus within a single agency; and its own rules for what data it will and won't release. By one well-informed estimate, there are 10,000 different information systems used in the federal government, many of them two or three decades old, and most of them incompatible with each other. People who are trying to change the system compare it to that warehouse full of endless crates at the end of *Raiders of the Lost Ark*—except you need to visualize those crates labeled in different languages, from Middle English, perhaps, to ancient hieroglyphics.

The directives in the Executive Order and the Open Data Policy will ultimately enable businesses, organizations, and individuals to access government data (unless it's sensitive or confidential), enable them to analyze it, and enable them to combine the data from one source with data from another. The policy will make government data machine-readable, meaning that it will be in a form computers can ingest and process—the difference, say, between a downloadable Excel spreadsheet of budget data (machine-readable) and a handwritten list of the same numbers (not).

The Open Data Policy sets out seven key criteria for government Open Data. It states that Open Data released by the government must be:

- *Public*, with agencies adopting a "presumption of openness" unless there are privacy, confidentiality, security, or other constraints on a particular dataset
- *Accessible*, so that it can be conveniently retrieved, downloaded, indexed, and searched
- *Described* in ways that help users apply the data
- *Reusable* under an open license for unrestricted use

215

- *Complete*, releasing the primary data in the way it was collected as much as possible
- *Timely*, made available as quickly as is practical
- *Managed postrelease*, meaning that there must be a point of contact to help people use each dataset after it has been released to the public

The policy also instructs agencies to pay attention to data quality and to get input from the people who use their data. This is the clearest invitation yet for businesses to connect with the federal government and make their data needs known.

The Open Data policy is part of a larger set of government initiatives, not only from the U.S. federal government, but also from state and local governments and leadership in other countries. This chapter describes how the Open Government movement is making more Open Data available, what opportunities it creates, what it means for business, and what next steps government should take.

Geeks, Wonks, Liberators, and Government Open Data

The government's strong commitment to Open Data began on President Obama's first day in office. On January 21, 2009, the president released a memorandum on transparency and open government calling for "a system of transparency, public participation, and collaboration." "My administration," he wrote, "is committed to creating an unprecedented level of openness in government." He described federal data as a "national asset" and said that "agencies should harness new technologies to put information about their operations and decisions online and readily available to the public." A number of government appointments and memos soon followed. The administration launched Data.gov, a new centralized platform for government Open Data. Later, U.S. Chief Technology Officer Todd Park and Chief Information Officer Steve VanRoekel announced a new

Digital Government Strategy to modernize how the government handles data.

Where did the push for government Open Data begin? By the time President Obama took office, the Open Data movement was already being driven by an odd-couple collaboration between two groups with very different skills, vocabularies, and areas of expertise: the Geeks and the Wonks. The Geeks, or computer science experts, have developed the tools to analyze ever larger sets of data in ever more illuminating ways. The Wonks, on the policy side, have come up with creative ways to use this computing power for better government, smarter business policy, and faster innovation. Put them together and you have usable, open datasets that can have a powerful impact for the public good and economic growth.

The Open Data movement has been accelerated by a third group, the Liberators. This diverse group, both inside and outside of government, has been dedicated to making data widely accessible—not only to people in computer labs and think tanks, but to any application developer, journalist, policy analyst, entrepreneur, or concerned citizen who wants to use it. They have been motivated by a passion for what technology can do to drive progress in the areas they care about. The Liberators are dedicated to what some have called "data democracy" and believe it can have a social as well as a business impact.

The Obama administration's commitment to Open Data grew out of a broad, small-d democratic vision for Open Government that includes both releasing Open Data and engaging citizens in the process of governance. When those two elements come together, Open Government is especially powerful. The participatory budgeting movement, for example, has developed systems to share budget data with a city's residents and then enable them to help decide how a portion of the budget should be spent. The movement began in the city of Porto Alegre, Brazil, and has spread to about 1,500 cities worldwide.

The philosophy of Open Government and a corresponding commitment to Open Data have now become an international movement.

British Prime Minister David Cameron has echoed President Obama's call for transparency—he has said that "transparency is at the heart of our agenda for government"—and together, the two countries have led an international effort. About 60 countries have joined the Open Government Partnership, which is committed to releasing government data as Open Data.

In the United Kingdom, the government stewards of Open Data have started a national data dialogue with their constituents. Paul Maltby, who became the U.K. Cabinet Office Director for Transparency and Open Data at the start of 2013, is committed to increasing citizen engagement. I met with him when he was three months into the job and was developing an approach to Open Data that takes both business needs and the public interest into account.

In contrast to the U.S. version of Data.gov, where government agencies have generally posted whatever they want to in their own way, Data.gov.uk has been "cocreated" with the people who use it. "We've got an Open Data User Group," Maltby told me, "and it's a broad range of people including big business, small entrepreneurs, and campaigning organizations. With my team, they work out what the users want, what is the top list of stuff that's seen as valuable that they really want available—they create a list of priorities." Today, said Maltby, "this is a user-driven agenda as much as it is a central government one."

Recently, analysts have tried to estimate the potential value of "public sector data" in Europe and the United Kingdom. This is data that's publicly available but is not yet truly Open Data because it may require a fee or have restrictions on reuse. One study, done by the consulting firm Deloitte, estimated that such data is worth between about $3 billion and $9 billion in U.S. dollars for the United Kingdom, while another, done by Graham Vickery, gave a value of about 30 to 140 billion euros for data across the European Union. Each of those estimates shows the range of possible use for that public sector data, from direct uses of the data, for example in new informational websites and apps, to the larger value that could come from indirect benefits, such as creating a market for data-analysis technology or making government more efficient.

Seeing this economic potential, the European Union has adopted an Open Data policy that, as in the United Kingdom, will make public sector data open by default over time. In other words, government data will be released as Open Data unless there is a compelling reason not to do so. Based on Vickery's study, the EU estimates that this change will add about 40 billion euros annually to the value of public sector information in Europe. With the United Kingdom's leadership, the G8 has now adopted a similar policy.

Back in the United States, as in many other countries, there are three major kinds of Open Data where federal policy is having a major impact:

- Scientific data collected or created (via funding) by the government, such as weather data or government-sponsored medical research. This kind of data is a public resource for further research, analysis, and business development. I've discussed this kind of data in previous chapters.
- Data about the workings of government, for example, government spending or the operations of government programs. This data is important for government's accountability to citizens and may also reveal business opportunities for potential government contractors and others.
- Data about regulated industries that is either collected by the government or made available by industries themselves under government mandate. The required release of this data is an increasingly common form of regulation with a direct impact on business.

Government Transparency: Data About How Government Works

Since 2007, the website USASpending.gov has summarized government expenses for the public. It was launched as a result of legislation sponsored by then-Senator Barack Obama and Republican Senator Tom Coburn of Oklahoma. The site was one of the first major government efforts to release Open Data to increase government transparency and came after years of advocacy by good-government groups.

USASpending.gov, however, has been far from the final word on federal spending. It doesn't give a line-by-line breakdown of payments to government contractors or subcontractors. It doesn't include salaries for government employees. About two-thirds of federal programs send no data to the website, report data that's inconsistent with other programs, or submit data that's missing some key information. And, not surprisingly, USASpending.gov is inaccurate, to the tune of $1.55 trillion in the most recent analysis by the nonprofit Sunlight Foundation (described in Chapter 12).

While the problems with USASpending.gov have become all too obvious, another government program—the American Recovery and Reinvestment Act (ARRA)—has shown that better data is possible. When the Recovery Act was passed in 2009, it came with strict requirements that the more than $800 billion stimulus spending it authorized would be tracked impeccably. The Recovery Accountability and Transparency Board, which was set up to monitor stimulus spending, required direct reporting on the use of stimulus funds in standardized data formats. The Board published the data online, together with the zip codes of the companies that received funds, so that the public could help hold companies accountable. This system made it possible to look at spending by all agencies in one place for the first time, and helped prevent tens of millions of dollars in waste and fraud.

Inspired by ARRA, some legislators are trying to hold the rest of the federal budget to the same standard. The most significant bill on the table is what's become known as the DATA Act, described briefly in Chapter 4. Sponsored in the House by Darrell Issa (R-CA) and Elijah Cummings (D-MD), chair and ranking member, respectively, of the Committee on Oversight & Government Reform, and by Senators Mark Warner (D-VA) and Rob Portman (R-OH) in the Senate, the DATA Act would require the federal government to standardize and publish all its spending data in detail.

Hudson Hollister, who leads the Data Transparency Coalition, which is pushing for the DATA Act, sees the act as essential to help realize the promise of the Open Data Policy. While the policy sets out goals and definitions for Open Data, he told me, "The federal government's systems of reports and databases that track its own spending and operations don't currently meet that definition. We need the DATA Act to transform the government's spending and operations from chaotic, inaccessible documents into Open Data for true accountability."

With the DATA Act, said Hollister, "We would be able to avoid disagreements over the fiscal consequences of a particular law because we would be able to map those all out automatically. It would be possible to trace a particular dollar through all of the different stages of government spending," he said, "from that first decision by Congress to the final disposition of the funds. We could automatically check every grant and every contract for the common indicators of fraud." Finally, "It would be possible to automatically coordinate the amount spent on a particular program with that program's performance."

The move to open up government data is likely to survive this administration whether the next president is a Republican or Democrat. In a sharply partisan country, it may be one of the rare initiatives that can be truly bipartisan. The DATA Act has strong support from both parties in both the House and Senate. Open Data about government has a kind of libertarian appeal: it gives citizens the information they need to make their own decisions and helps them keep an eye on their government at the same time.

Freedom of Information—for Businesses, Too

Another, longstanding tool for government transparency—the Freedom of Information Act (FOIA)—is proving to be helpful to business as well as the public good. The FOIA was passed in 1966; it was the first such law in the world except for Sweden's, which predates it by two centuries. In 2009, the Office of Government Information Services (OGIS) was launched within the National Archives and Records Administration to make FOIA more effective. The OGIS serves as a kind of FOIA ombudsman to work with federal agencies that implement the FOIA and to mediate disputes between requesters and requestees. "FOIA is pretty simple in concept," Miriam Nisbet, the head of the OGIS, told me. "You can ask anybody and you can ask for anything."

While people often think of the FOIA as a tool for enterprising journalists, it turns out that journalists are responsible for only 6 percent of federal requests. In contrast, a large number of federal FOIA requests now come from companies that want to find out about other companies and their dealings with the government. The FOIA can help them do competitive analysis, assess potential partners, and gauge investment risk.

FOIA is now most helpful to businesses that have the resources to make full use of the system. In a recent investigation, *The Wall Street Journal* reviewed more than 100,000 Freedom of Information Act requests over five years and found that a large number came from investment firms and hedge funds. In what one portfolio manager called "an information arms race," these firms are asking government agencies involved in health, energy, and other areas to give them information about companies and products that fall under the agency's jurisdiction. For example, the U.S. Food and Drug Administration receives many requests for "adverse event reports" on different drugs—a potential sign that the drug is problematic and that its manufacturer's stock may be due for a fall.

In theory, any business could use the results of other companies' FOIA requests. Once an agency releases information under FOIA, it's considered public information that anyone has a right to see.

The problem, though, is that FOIA data is so decentralized that it's hard to make the best use of the results. About 100 federal departments and agencies, and several bureaus in each of those, handle the

650,000 FOIA requests that come to the government each year. That doesn't count people asking for their own records from, say, the Social Security Administration, or those who think the FBI is after them and want to see their files. Different agencies handle FOIA requests differently and have had no formal way to coordinate responses to related requests.

The FOIA system could provide a huge amount of useful information efficiently if only it provided it in searchable, downloadable electronic form—that is, if it provided it as Open Data. A plan to do that is now in the works. The OGIS has worked with the Environmental Protection Agency and others to create FOIA Online, an electronic system that can organize FOIA requests and documents across agencies for the first time. "The concept," said Nisbet, "is to have a one-stop shop for making requests, finding out what is happening to your request, but also to see who else is making requests and what has been released."

Unfortunately, there is no requirement for agencies to use FOIA Online, and only a few have signed on so far. It may take programs outside of government to make the FOIA a more effective source of Open Data more quickly. In addition to a FOIA website called WhatDoTheyKnow launched by MySociety in the United Kingdom and several other countries, a New Jersey–based nonprofit called MuckRock provides online forms that make it easier for individuals to navigate the FOIA system. Congress is also discussing possible FOIA reforms that could make the system more efficient and effective for both those who use it and those who run it.

Open Data as a Regulatory Tool

Under the Obama administration, federal agencies have tried to do what some call "light-touch" regulation: they're finding ways to improve the industries they regulate without actually telling them what to do. Transparency through Open Data is an effective form of light-touch regulation. By mandating better disclosure, as the Consumer Financial Protection Bureau is doing for financial products under the Dodd-Frank Act, government agencies can help consumers make choices that reward the most consumer-friendly companies and improve the marketplace. For their part, businesses may embrace transparency as a way to comply with existing regulations and avoid the risk of more burdensome ones.

The basic philosophy behind much of Dodd-Frank—that Open Data can change businesses and markets—has driven a wide range of regulatory policies. Cass Sunstein followed this philosophy when he was head of the Office of Information and Regulatory Affairs (OIRA), the office that oversees regulatory policy across the federal government. He's now written about it in his recent book, *Simpler*. The Transparency Policy Project at Harvard's Kennedy School, headed by Archon Fung, Mary Graham, and David Weil, has described this approach as "targeted transparency": the use of government-mandated transparency to achieve a regulatory end.

The classic example is the Toxics Release Inventory (TRI), which was mandated by an act of Congress after the chemical catastrophe at a pesticide plant in Bhopal, India, in 1984. Under the TRI, thousands of manufacturing and other facilities have to report their chemical emissions in air and water to the Environmental Protection Agency every year. Using TRI data, local newspapers have publicized some of the worst polluters, and the companies have generally been quick to clean up their act.

Sean Moulton, director of open government policy at the Center for Effective Government, recalls the Center's early work with the TRI (under the Center's original name, OMB Watch). The Center began working with TRI data at the end of the 1980s, years before the web, when it developed something called the Right to Know Network and made it available through dial-up services. Unwieldy though it was, this form of transparency worked.

"The simple act of making this information available to the public created enormous pressure to get these toxic emissions down," said Moulton. "There was no legal requirement on these companies to make any reductions whatsoever, and yet over the years since the late eighties we've seen a 60 or 70 percent reduction in these toxic releases. Over the years, the EPA has added new chemicals and new industry sectors. Same pattern: very high levels initially being tracked, and then they come down." In many cases, he said, companies didn't know how high their emissions were—especially large, decentralized chemical companies—until they saw the numbers.

While the companies involved could hardly have been thrilled with this kind of Open Data, their business operations improved as a result. In his thorough study of the TRI, *Regulation Through Revelation*, public policy professor James Hamilton notes that "the TRI changed decisions and debates. Quantitative studies show that the toxics information brought news to investors, reporters, and residents." And, in addition, "case studies reveal how the TRI alerted some managers to environmental releases they did not previously know about and led many to undertake actions to reduce their TRI figures."

Despite the antiregulatory climate in Washington, it's a fair bet that we'll see more transparency requirements like those of the TRI. While it's hard to pass regulations that actively tell companies how to operate, it's also hard to argue against the basic idea that regulators, investors, and the public should know what those companies are doing. In addition, federal agencies have a fair amount of leeway to pass regulations that require transparency and to release information as Open Data. For example, while Congress has been unable to pass cap-and-trade legislation—to the deep frustration of environmental advocates—that hasn't stopped the Environmental Protection Agency from launching a website that shows greenhouse gas emissions across the United States.

Public Data and Public Safety

The federal government and some state and local governments have been especially active in making safety data available to the public. With leadership from the Consumer Product Safety Commission, several government agencies have worked together to create Safer-Products.gov, which makes it easy to report product safety issues, and Recalls.gov, which is a hub for recall alerts. One problem with recalls is that six different agencies handle them, ranging from the Environmental Protection Agency to the U.S. Coast Guard. These agencies have now put their data on a common platform that makes it all accessible in one place.

The Recalls.gov website and mobile app let consumers search for recalls without worrying about which agency has what jurisdiction over which products. The mobile version is especially useful for consumers shopping for secondhand items at a thrift store or yard sale—venues that recalls never reach. Nongovernmental organizations such as the websites SaferKidsAndHomes and WeMakeItSafer also use this information and help get it to the public.

The website Foodsafety.gov, launched in the fall of 2009, came out of a collaboration between the Centers for Disease Control and Prevention, the Food and Drug Administration, and the USDA. These agencies share responsibility for food safety under a set of arcane rules, making it hard for consumers to know where to find information. The website pulls it all together so consumers can find alerts on bad hamburger or contaminated cheese without having to study the federal bureaucracy.

Highway safety is also getting new attention. In 2012, the Department of Transportation released a SaferBus mobile app (buses carry 750 million passengers a year in the United States). And in 2013, the DOT teamed up with the National Highway Traffic Safety Administration (NHTSA) to release the SaferCar app. This comprehensive app "allows users to search [NHTSA's] Safety Ratings for vehicles by make and model, locate car seat installation help, file a vehicle safety complaint, find recall information, and subscribe to automatic notices about vehicle recalls."

SaferCar draws on work that NHTSA has done for years. The agency has databases of vehicle crash statistics, available as Open Data, and has a "safety complaints search engine" to search complaints filed with the agency based on make, model, and year. These resources have probably been underutilized. For example, they might have helped uncover the Toyota brake problem that led to massive recalls in 2009.

One of the best-known auto information sites, CARFAX, provides safety information and more about used cars by tapping a wide variety of government and other data sources. According to the company's website, "CARFAX receives data from more than 34,000 different sources including every U.S. and Canadian provincial motor vehicle agency plus many police and fire departments, collision repair facilities, auto auctions, and more. The CARFAX database is the most comprehensive vehicle history database in North America, containing over 6 billion records."

Consumer organizations are also using government Open Data on safety issues in new ways. *Consumer Reports* has taken data from the federal website Hospital Compare, added other information such as state data, and come up with safety ratings for more than 2,000 hospitals and additional information on another 2,000. It's one of the strongest examples yet of government Open Data fueling Smart Disclosure to help consumers make a critically important choice.

Kevin Merritt of Socrata, which provides platforms for federal, state, and local data (see Chapter 4), points to the ways in which local governments are providing safety data in cities like New York and San Francisco, both Socrata clients. "For example, with restaurant inspection data in a machine-readable and rapidly updated format on New York City's Open Data platform, Yelp now informs customers on the cleanliness of their favorite restaurants," he told me. "Furthermore, Trulia and Appalicious help to inform prospective renters and homeowners about the safety of their buildings with housing data provided by DataSF, San Francisco's Open Data platform."

Open Government Goes Local

Beyond safety data, there's now a growing movement to make all kinds of state and local data more available, useful, and visible. The city of San Francisco was an early pioneer, as former Mayor Gavin Newsom describes in his book *Citizenville*. Open Data also helps municipal governments understand the cities they're trying to run. Chicago has a data nerve center at metrochicagodata.org, established under Mayor Rahm Emanuel, that was one of the first to integrate city data of all kinds.

In New York City, Mayor Michael Bloomberg has launched a "geek squad"—officially known as the Office of Policy and Strategic Planning—that develops new insights from city data on an almost daily basis. The Office has analyzed data to identify restaurants that dump grease into the city's sewers, schedule counseling appointments for low-income residents, and calculate the average time for city police to respond to a crime in progress (nine minutes and six seconds). "What we're really running here," Analytics Director Michael Flowers told the *New York Times*, "is an office of New Yorkology."

At the same time, New York State has launched Data.NY.gov, a central hub that serves as a resource for both businesses and ordinary citizens. It includes a site-within-a-site of resources for businesses operating in the state, job notices for the state government, and data on the state budget, as well as a guide to New York's best fishing spots and a random-number generator for playing the state lottery. And Kansas is developing a new online hub for businesses to submit data to the state government and use data from it.

The Center for Technology in Government, a public-private partnership at the University at Albany, works with both national and city governments around the world to "foster public sector innovation, enhance capability, generate public value, and support good governance." As its work has shown, the potential for Open Data to help city and state governments globally is just beginning to be tapped.

"Cities large and small have embraced the principles and potential of Open Data," Theresa Pardo, the Center's director, told me in an e-mail. "We're seeing this from Beijing to Binghamton and from Albany to Abuja. City leaders are working to create the necessary conditions for government-wide Open Data programs, but the challenges facing their cities are not all alike. Some have robust infrastructures while others are just beginning to modernize. The hardest work isn't always the technical challenge. It begins when leaders take steps to disrupt internal policies and practices to ensure that government data is born, not just digital, but open as well."

Using Data for Development

In developing countries, where cell phones and smartphones are becoming ubiquitous, national governments are sponsoring Open Data projects to help their citizens by using the mobile web. They can help turn sprawling urban areas into "smart cities" that use data to manage their growth in sustainable ways. During disasters, people can use their cell phones to get data back to government relief workers instantly. The software program Ushahidi ("testimony" in Swahili) was developed to help the government of Kenya monitor reports of postelection violence and later helped Haiti coordinate relief efforts after the 2010 earthquake.

The World Bank sees Open Data as a tool for economic development and is funding a number of projects around the globe. World Bank projects have supported some basic mapping of urban areas, from the Kibera slum in Kenya to the streets of Dar es Salaam in Tanzania. The World Bank supports the Open Development Technology Alliance and maintains a website for its Striking Poverty program to use innovation and Open Data to fight poverty worldwide.

These efforts don't always work, at least not right away. Huduma, an African project to gather data about city problems so local governments can fix them, attracted only a handful of participants in its first year. Apparently people didn't believe that anyone would really fix the potholes they reported.

What works best? A project called Exploring the Emerging Impacts of Open Data in Developing Countries (ODDC) is trying to answer that question. The project's website presents case studies and serves as a forum for research on Open Data and development. And in June 2013, several civil society groups announced that they were launching the Global Open Data Initiative to encourage Open Data and transparency worldwide.

In many countries, a particular kind of Open Data, generated through collective intelligence, has become a significant tool to report corruption, uncover government influence, and fight unfair pricing schemes. These platforms for citizen investigation are important both to improve democratic governance and to create a more open business environment. For example:

- The Indian website IPaidABribe invites people to anonymously report the bribes they had to pay to get government officials to help them, creating data on "the market price of corruption" and helping people learn how to get government help bribe-free.
- In Russia, RosPil, a crowdsourced anticorruption organization that's been studied by Harvard Business School, has had large-scale success. By the end of 2011, RosPil had prevented $1.3 billion in dubious contracts from being given to companies that had promised kickbacks in return for getting the business.
- In a successful collaboration between an NGO, national governments, and citizens, the Southern African Regional Programme on Access to Medicines and Diagnostics (SARPAM)

won price concessions from multinational drug companies. SARPAM recruited patients to use their smartphones to report the prices they paid for different drugs. When they found major differences for the same drug between, say, Angola and Zimbabwe, SARPAM would take the evidence to the government, which would use it to negotiate effectively for a lower price.

- In Chile, a new web platform called Poderopedia has been launched to show profiles of and connections between key players in business and politics in an effort to make circles of influence more apparent. It relies on both public sources and crowdsourced contributions for its data.

Realizing the Business Potential

This chapter takes us back to where this book began: to the critical, driving role that governments have in making Open Data available for public and business use. To discuss the full range of steps that governments can take, both to release Open Data and to promote Open Government, would take several books. Here are some recommendations, focused on what the U.S. federal government can do, that will have the most leverage in the areas of greatest importance to business.

Maintain Central Open Data Resources. The government has steadily made Data.gov, the central repository of federal Open Data, more accessible and useful and is planning to improve it further. As part of implementing the Open Data Policy, the government has also set up Project Open Data on GitHub, the world's largest community for open-source software. These resources will be invaluable for anyone working with Open Data either inside or outside of government. State and local governments, too, can set up central Open Data hubs, as New York City and New York State, the state of Kansas, the city of Chicago, and others have done.

Pass Bipartisan Legislation to Govern Open Data. In a country that has almost given up on the ability of Congress to get anything done, legislation on Open Data and privacy could still be passed as practical, business-friendly bills with bipartisan support. Three immediate opportunities are to:

- *Pass the DATA Act.* The DATA Act has widespread support; there's near-universal agreement that federal spending must be more transparent. Congress should move forward and pass the DATA Act as the logical next step in the work that the Obama administration's Open Data Policy has begun.

- *Establish a Consumer Privacy Bill of Rights.* The White House report recommending a Consumer Privacy Bill of Rights (described in Chapter 11) was the right first step. Now we need legislation to make it effective. In considering a privacy bill of rights, the United States may be able to learn from the European Union's data protection policies. Both the United States and the European Union will need to figure out how any privacy bill of rights can be technically enforced, given the ease with which data can be copied and distributed.

- *Reform the FOIA.* Since it was passed in 1966, the federal Freedom of Information Act has gone through two major revisions, both of which strengthened it. Many people both inside and outside of government now believe that another revision is due. Current legislative proposals would, among other things, establish a centralized web portal for all federal FOIA requests, strengthen the FOIA ombudsman's office, and require agencies to post more high-interest information online before they receive formal requests for it. These changes could make much more information from FOIA requests available as Open Data.

Use Government Technology Dollars More Effectively. Federal, state, and city governments manage critical information with legacy systems that wouldn't pass muster if they were being built today, and sometimes spend more for worse technology than the private sector would allow. The system that now governs federal technology contracting, described in Chapter 4, is a major impediment that needs to be changed. Cities and states may have more flexibility to experiment with new technology and should use it. As one positive example, New York City invested $1 million (less than 1/500 of 1 percent of the city's total budget) and recruited a small army of young, enthusiastic tech geniuses to start extracting meaning from mountains of city data.

Improve Data Quality. As federal agencies begin to release more Open Data and follow the policy guidance to release information about data quality, we can expect a lot of embarrassing moments. It's an open secret that a lot of government data is incomplete, inaccurate, or almost unusable. The $1.55 trillion error in USASpending.gov is just one egregious example. Some agencies, for instance, have pervasive problems in the geographic data they collect: if you try to map the factories the EPA regulates, you'll see several pop up in China, the Pacific Ocean, or the middle of Boston Harbor. Government agencies may have to do some cleanup themselves, demand better data from the businesses they regulate, or use creative solutions like turning to crowdsourcing for help.

Engage Stakeholders in a Genuine Way. Up to now, the federal government's release of Open Data has largely been a one-way affair. Typically, an agency decides to make a certain dataset available; it posts the data on Data.gov or another website; and it hopes that people will use it. In our work on the Task Force on Smart Disclosure, we saw several instances where entrepreneurs found that the government data they wanted to use was not available or wasn't available in a suitable form. In my view, the government has too often released data with a supply-side approach. I came up with the term "demand-driven data disclosure" to describe a more inclusive process that would engage all the relevant stakeholders, as in the figure below.

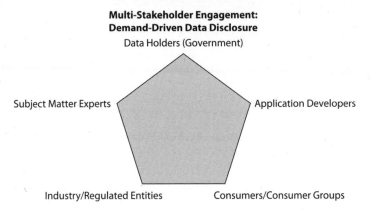

Multi-Stakeholder Engagement:
Demand-Driven Data Disclosure

Data Holders (Government)

Subject Matter Experts

Application Developers

Industry/Regulated Entities

Consumers/Consumer Groups

It's good to see that the Open Data Policy specifically calls on agencies to solicit input on their Open Data plans. That directive should be taken seriously and implemented in a way that truly involves the stakeholders that have the greatest interest in using Open Data.

Keep Using Federal Challenges to Encourage Innovation. The federal website Challenge.gov applies the best principles of collective intelligence and agencies should continue to use it. In particular, they should pose challenges that invite people to use the government's Open Data resources to solve business, social, or scientific problems. Other approaches to citizen engagement, including federally sponsored hackathons and the White House Champions of Change program, can play a similar role.

Make Government-Funded Research Data as Open as Possible. The new federal policy on making research papers free and the proposed FASTR legislation described in Chapter 10 are timely. These Open Access policies still need to be developed and implemented. It's important that the new federal policy requires most federally funded scientific research to be made available as true Open Data, not just in articles that summarize it. It's time for the U.S. government to promote full, free access to the results of the research it funds.

CHAPTER FOURTEEN

The Open Data Future

T HIS BOOK HAS DESCRIBED A WIDE RANGE OF BUSINESSES, government agencies, and innovators that are finding new ways to put Open Data to use. Writing the book has been inspiring and challenging—inspiring because so much creative, exciting work is under way and challenging, among other reasons, because the field is changing so rapidly that it's hard to keep up. As I was finishing this manuscript, I was still coming across new companies using Open Data in ways that seem entirely unique. For example:

- The Swiss-headquartered company Zurich Insurance now sells a tool for global businesses called the Zurich Risk Room. Using a simulated three-dimensional display, the Risk Room is a multidimensional graph that shows where different countries fall on different measures of risk, including environmental, political, social, and other factors. Think of it as looking into a virtual room where one corner is Nirvana, another corner is Armageddon, and most countries fall in between. As Zurich describes it, this sophisticated application "uses publically available data, on risks as varied as water shortages, energy price fluctuations, or political unrest . . . and shows the complex interactions between many different types of risks." Special bonus: you can download it onto your iPad.

- Relationship Science has been called "a Rolodex for the 1 percent," an oddly retro but accurate metaphor for this high-tech business. Founded with $60 million in venture capital and powered by a staff of 800, mostly working in India, Relationship Science is the ultimate network for reaching the world's most influential people. The company boasts a network of more than 2 million power brokers, including personal and social information, that bankers can use to connect with them if they pay a hefty annual fee. It's sort of like a super LinkedIn, but it is different in that it doesn't rely on people to sign up: the network is built with public Open Data.

- Food Genius, based in Chicago, has compiled a database of over 100,000 menus from independent and chain restaurants, including data on price, ingredients, and preparation for each dish. The company has figured out how to analyze those dishes using descriptors of 14,000 ingredients, techniques, and concepts and can use the data to spot trends of great value to the food industry. "The big food companies take it on faith that innovation starts in independent kitchens," CEO Justin Mass told the tech news site *GigaOM*. "The problem is the lifecycle of product development at a company like Kraft is two years. Meanwhile, in an independent restaurant, a new dish could be conceived and executed in 30 minutes."

The Open Data revolution, which few people even saw coming a few years ago, will bring us more innovations like these that no one can accurately predict. Still, it's a good bet that the trends described in this book will continue to build. We can expect to see more businesses large and small grow by using Open Data; more high-value datasets released by governments at all levels; more ways to analyze the data for market insights, brand management, and predicting trends; and more research of all kinds using open innovation. With that background, here's a short summary of some core advice for established businesses and for entrepreneurs—followed by a look at what the Open Data future could be.

Advice for Entrepreneurs

Open Data is an abundant, free resource that has fueled a wide range of startups, including consumer-focused websites, business-to-business services, data-management tech firms, and more. The following approaches can be used by Open Data startups of all kinds.

Use Open Data as a New Resource for Business Development. We're seeing an inversion of the value proposition for data. It used to be that whoever owned the data—particularly Big Data—had greater opportunities than those who didn't. While this is still true in many areas, it's also clear that successful businesses can be built on free Open Data that anyone can use. They add value to the data in the analytical tools, expertise, and interpretation that's brought to bear.

Focus on Big Opportunities: Health, Finance, Energy, Education. As the stories above show, a business can be built on just about any kind of Open Data. But the greatest startup opportunities will likely be in the four big areas where government, at least the federal government, is focused on Open Data release.

Explore Choice Engines and Smart Disclosure Apps. Smart Disclosure is a powerful tool for consumer choice and should be the basis for a new sector of online startups. No one, it seems, has quite figured out how to make this form of Open Data work best. The United Kingdom now has choice engines with large scale but low customer satisfaction; the United States has had some general choice engines, like BillShrink, that were popular with users but couldn't get to scale. Business opportunities await anyone who can find the right model for these much-needed consumer services.

Help Consumers Tap the Value of Personal Data. In a privacy-conscious society, more people will likely be interested in controlling their personal data and sharing it selectively for their own benefit. The value of personal data is just being recognized, and opportunities remain to be developed. While one kind of business is setting up and providing personal data vaults, there's a whole other business opportunity in applying the many ways they can be used.

Provide New Data Solutions to Government and Business. It's surprising to see how badly government datasets have been managed at the federal, state, and local level. The good news, such as it is, is that these governments are now realizing that they need help. If governments can successfully change their contracting processes, data management for government is likely to be a growing industry with more opportunities for new contractors than we've seen in the past.

Look for Unusual Open Data Opportunities. Building a successful business by gathering data on restaurant menus and recipes is not an obvious route to success. But it's working for Food Genius, whose founders showed a kind of genius in tapping an opportunity others had missed. While the big areas for Open Data are becoming clear, there are countless opportunities to build more niche businesses that can still be highly successful. If you have expertise in an area and see a customer need, there's an increasingly good chance that the Open Data to help meet that need is somewhere to be found.

Advice for Established Companies

For established companies, Open Data provides an opportunity to improve current operations, assess new partnerships, and manage investments more effectively. It can also be a tool to connect with customers and increase customer loyalty.

Use Open Data to Evaluate Business Partners and Potential Investments. Between increased SEC reporting, new digital investment services, and websites like Open Corporates and Duedil, more data than ever is available on public and private companies, and it's in more usable forms. Any business or financial firm considering a company as a partner or investment prospect should use these new sources as part of due diligence.

Release and Use Environmental, Social, and Governance Data. So many companies now release ESG data that a failure to do so may raise questions. Investors, shareholders, and consumers are demanding it. By releasing ESG data and, more important, by following sustainable business practices to begin with, companies can attract investment capital, top talent, and consumer goodwill.

Build Customer Loyalty by Giving Customers Their Data. There's ample evidence that consumers are interested in data about themselves, whether it's their medical records, cell-phone bills, or shopping history. In the United Kingdom, major energy companies, telecom companies, and at least one major retailer have given data back to their customers as a loyalty-building strategy. Some American utilities are doing the same thing, and businesses in all consumer sectors have an opportunity to use this approach.

Use the Social Web and Practice Social Customer Service. Review sites, blogs, and Twitter can tell you more about your company's reputation, good and bad, than most focus groups can. Monitoring the social web and the Open Data derived from it can be a primary source of marketing intelligence. At the same time, using social media to reply to customers' concerns through social customer service—not just using the web for promotions or branding messages—can be an effective brand-building strategy.

Experiment with Open Innovation. Sharing scientific research data early on may not just be idealistic: it may be good business. By releasing early results as Open Data before they've pointed a clear way to marketable products, drug companies may be able to accelerate R&D significantly. The benefits to public health are clear; the potential business benefits are still to be determined.

Learn to Operate in a See-Through World. Truly proprietary information—a company's analysis of its customers, its business strategies, or its internal R&D—should never become Open Data, and no one is proposing that. But the aspects of business operations that affect the wider world—a company's environmental record, its labor history, its political contributions, its adherence to regulations—are rapidly becoming an open book. In these areas, expect more government mandates to release data and more experts who are adept at interpreting it.

Look for Public/Private Partnership Opportunities. Federal agencies may be able to partner with companies that can make government data more available and useful, both as a public service and because those companies want to analyze the data themselves. The government's Open Data Policy focuses on setting rules for data management rather than detailing what should happen to the masses of data that have already been collected. The private sector can help put that voluminous resource to use. In perhaps the best example, since 2010, Google has worked with the U.S. Patent and Trademark Office at no charge to distribute the agency's data to the public for free. Google has now made patent and trademark data dating back to the year 1790 available in an easily searchable format.

A Preview of the Open Data Future

This advice is all based on what we can see today—the Open Data opportunities that exist here and now. But think about how Open

Data could change things by the next decade. This book has described many Open Data trends, some near certain, some more speculative. There is a wide range of possibilities ahead of us.

If Open Data reaches its full potential, we'll see real changes in innovation, business, and even daily life. Here's how the world could look in the mid-2020s:

Computable data on just about any subject, with the exception of personal or protected data, is now available as Open Data online. In-depth, usable data on healthcare, real estate, financial trends, scientific advances, education, and more is as accessible as the *New York Times* on your 3-D iPad. It all comes from thousands of free federal datasets, and even more sources of city and state data, that are now easy to download and use in standard formats.

High school students and some precocious middle schoolers now take AP Data Science courses where they routinely do projects that would have stumped data analysts a decade earlier. (Analytic software has kept pace with the Open Data explosion.) Stock market projects are especially popular. Some of the best students put themselves through college with investments they choose by analyzing the SEC's XBRL data, using predictive analytics, and throwing in some sentiment analysis to boot.

These students' parents—or, in some cases, their older siblings—are building new business ventures in a data-fueled economy. Just about every tech startup uses Open Data in some way; it's simply part of the toolkit, as natural as having wi-fi access be part of your laptop. We've stopped counting the startups that use Open Data because the ones that don't are the exceptions.

Because all important datasets are now interoperable, many new companies are based on creative data mashups. A website called City-Chooser.com, popular with new college graduates and retirees alike, helps you pick an ideal place to move to based on up to 20 different factors. In addition to familiar variables like education, safety, and commuting time, CityChooser includes data on types of cultural activities, neighborhood psychographics (based on opinions from community residents), restaurant quality, predicted changes in property values, and predicted weather over the next 10, 20, or 30 years, taking climate change into account.

While hot startups get the most publicity, established businesses also have Open Data success stories. A wide range of consumer-facing companies have become more efficient, more customer-focused, and smarter at marketing, increasing their operating margins significantly. Many companies have built strong customer loyalty by using Open Data to understand and serve their customers better.

Consumers now routinely expect and get healthcare and financial services that are personally tailored to their needs. Applying for a mortgage, for example, no longer takes months of frustration. People keep all the relevant data that lenders need in personal data vaults, where it can easily be uploaded with their permission. Choice engines use that data to find which mortgages an applicant will qualify for and the one of those that offers the best terms. The applicant then sends his or her data to the lender digitally; the required forms are filled out automatically; and 95 percent of home buyers are approved within a week.

Consumer satisfaction scores are on the rise for previously unpopular industries. Wireless companies, airlines, banks, and other consumer-facing companies have learned how to work with their customers quickly and effectively to resolve any problems. The turning point came when Bloomberg developed its Consumer Complaint Index, rating companies based on sentiment analysis of their customers' online comments. Some of the most sought-after business consultants are the experts in social customer service who teach companies how to keep their customers happy and their online reputations positive.

Small and medium-sized businesses have found new investors willing to lend them the capital they need. By releasing more data about their operations in ways that can easily be analyzed, these companies quickly show themselves to be worthy of investment—or not. Some fail more quickly than they would have in the past. But in this form of natural selection, the successful ones grow at a rapid rate.

Several serious brain diseases can now be managed effectively, prevented, or even cured. Once scientists agreed to make the 10-year BRAIN Initiative an open-innovation project, the pace of discovery accelerated dramatically. By the time the initiative wrapped up in 2023, effective drugs had been developed for Alzheimer's disease and early diagnosis and intervention prevented many cases of autism. In other biomedical areas, several major pharmaceutical companies began large-scale open innovation projects using a new business model.

Some of society's most intractable problems are on the way to being solved. Urban transportation has been transformed by Open Data analyses that route buses more efficiently and control traffic by rerouting cars in real time. (The rapid adoption of Google's self-driving cars was helpful here.) World hunger is on the decline thanks to new "precision agriculture" programs that help farmers plant crops more successfully using weather and soil data. The federal budget is now balanced every year. After the DATA Act passed, federal spending became so transparent that even a partisan Congress was forced to agree on new cuts and revenue sources, under pressure from good-government advocates that used the data to rally the public.

Most important, Open Data has helped slow the rate of climate change and may even help to stop it. After severe droughts in the South, floods in the Midwest, and hurricanes in the Northeast all hit in one year, the United States began to focus on climate change as a matter of urgency. While Congress never passed a carbon tax, the possibility that it could finally happen led investors to focus on carbon emissions as a risk factor. The SEC declared sustainability a material factor that all public companies had to report as Open Data using a simplified version of the Global Reporting Initiative framework. Once the data was public, companies worked quickly to improve their sustainability practices.

At the same time, Open Data fueled major engineering projects that helped fight global warming while generating substantial profits. The smart grid, which used Open Data to help consumers control their use of electricity, dramatically increased energy efficiency nationwide. New, advanced analysis of weather data helped wind-energy companies build in areas where changing wind patterns would favor them. And in an especially encouraging development, an international open innovation project found a way to make artificial photosynthesis viable at a competitive price, using collaboration to solve a problem that had stymied individual labs for years. With a new source of energy that actually removes carbon dioxide from the atmosphere, the prospect of stopping climate change is real for the first time.

Of course—coming back to the present—there's no way to know how many of these benefits we'll get to see. But if even some of this comes to pass, we'll be living in a better world with new sources of economic growth. Open Data is a positive, disruptive force that offers great opportunities for business, society, and consumers alike. Whoever understands Open Data and knows how to use it will be best prepared for the future.

Welcome to the Open Data world—and safe travels on the road ahead.

Selected Bibliography

AUTHOR'S NOTE: THE WORLD OF OPEN DATA CHANGES VERY rapidly. This list includes some of the most important print resources as of October 2013. For ongoing news and information about Open Data, see my website, OpenDataNow.com.

Books

Ayres, Ian. *Super Crunchers*. New York: Bantam Dell, 2008.

Brabham, Daren C. *Crowdsourcing*. Cambridge, MA: MIT Press, 2013.

Duval, Jared. *Next Generation Democracy: What the Open-Source Revolution Means for Power, Politics, and Change*. New York: Bloomsbury, 2010.

Eccles, Robert G., and Michael P. Krzus. *One Report: Integrated Reporting for a Sustainable Strategy*. Hoboken, NJ: John Wiley & Sons, 2010.

Eggers, William D., and Paul MacMillan. *The Solution Revolution: How Business, Government, and Social Enterprises Are Teaming Up to Solve*

Society's Toughest Problems. Boston: Harvard Business Review Press, 2013.

Esty, Daniel C., and Andrew S. Winston. *Green to Gold: How Smart Companies Use Environmental Strategy to Innovate, Create Value, and Build Competitive Advantage*. Hoboken, NJ: John Wiley & Sons, 2009. (First published by Yale University Press, 2006.)

Fung, Archon, Mary Graham, and David Weil. *Full Disclosure: The Perils and Promise of Transparency*. New York: Cambridge University Press, 2007.

Garfield, Bob, and Doug Levy. *Can't Buy Me Like: How Authentic Customer Connections Drive Superior Results*. New York: Portfolio/Penguin, 2013, NOOK e-book edition.

Goldstein, Brett (ed.) with Lauren Dyson. *Beyond Transparency: Open Data and the Future of Civic Innovation*. San Francisco: Code for America Press, 2013.

Goleman, Daniel. *Ecological Intelligence: How Knowing the Hidden Impacts of What We Buy Can Change Everything*. New York: Broadway Books, 2009.

Hamilton, James T. *Regulation Through Revelation: The Origin, Politics, and Impacts of the Toxics Release Inventory Program*. Cambridge, UK: Cambridge University Press, 2005.

Johnson, Steven. *Future Perfect: The Case for Progress in a Networked Age*. New York: Riverhead Books, 2012, NOOK e-book edition.

Lathrop, Daniel, and Laurel Ruma (eds.) *Open Government: Collaboration, Transparency, and Participation in Practice*. Sebastopol, CA: O'Reilly Media, 2010, NOOK e-book edition.

Mayer-Schönberger, Viktor, and Kenneth Cukier. *Big Data: A Revolution That Will Transform How We Live, Work, and Think*. New York: Houghton Mifflin Harcourt, 2013.

Newsom, Gavin, with Lisa Dickey. *Citizenville: How to Take the Town Square Digital and Reinvent Government*. New York: Penguin, 2013, NOOK e-book edition.

Nielsen, Michael. *Reinventing Discovery: The New Era of Networked Science*. Princeton, NJ: Princeton University Press, 2012.

Noveck, Beth Simone. *Wiki Government: How Technology Can Make Government Better, Democracy Stronger, and Citizens More Powerful*. Washington, DC: Brookings Institution Press, 2009.

Savitz, Andrew W., with Karl Weber. *The Triple Bottom Line: How Today's Best-Run Companies Are Achieving Economic, Social, and Environmental Success—and How You Can Too*. San Francisco: Jossey-Bass/John Wiley & Sons, 2006.

Searls, Doc. *The Intention Economy: When Customers Take Charge*. Boston: Harvard Business Review Press, 2012, NOOK e-book edition.

Shirky, Clay. *Here Comes Everybody: The Power of Organizing Without Organizations*. New York: Penguin, 2008.

Shirky, Clay. *Cognitive Surplus: Creativity and Generosity in a Connected Age*. New York: Penguin, 2010, NOOK e-book edition.

Sifry, Micah L. *Wikileaks and the Age of Transparency*. New York: OR Books, 2011, NOOK e-book edition.

Smolan, Rick, and Jennifer Erwitt (eds.) *The Human Face of Big Data*. Sausalito, CA: Against All Odds Productions, 2012.

Soyka, Peter A. *Creating a Sustainable Organization: Approaches for Enhancing Corporate Value Though Sustainability*. Upper Saddle River, NJ: FT Press, 2012, NOOK e-book edition.

Sunstein, Cass R. *Simpler: The Future of Government*. New York: Simon & Schuster, 2013, NOOK e-book edition.

Surowiecki, James. *The Wisdom of Crowds*. New York: Anchor Books, 2005.

Tapscott, Don, and Anthony D. Williams. *Wikinomics: How Mass Collaboration Changes Everything*. New York: Penguin, 2006.

Tauberer, Joshua. *The Principles and Practices of Open Government Data* (self-published), Edition 1.1a, June 2012, http://opengovdata.io.

Thaler, Richard H., and Cass R. Sunstein. *Nudge: Improving Decisions About Health, Wealth, and Happiness*. New York: Penguin, 2009. First published 2008 by Yale University Press.

Government Documents (U.S., U.K., European Union, and G8, listed chronologically)

Obama, Barack. Memorandum for the Heads of Executive Departments and Agencies, "Transparency and Open Government," January 21, 2009, http://www.whitehouse.gov/the_press_office/transparencyandopengovernment

Orszag, Peter R. Memorandum for the Heads of Executive Departments and Agencies, "Open Government Directive," December 8, 2009, http://www.whitehouse.gov/sites/default/files/omb/assets/memoranda_2010/m10-06.pdf.

Sunstein, Cass R. Memorandum for the Heads of Executive Departments and Agencies, "Informing Consumers Through Smart Disclosure," September 8, 2011, http://www.whitehouse.gov/sites/default/files/omb/inforeg/for-agencies/informing-consumers-through-smart-disclosure.pdf.

The White House. "The Open Government Partnership: National Action Plan for the United States of America," September 20, 2011, http://www.whitehouse.gov/sites/default/files/us_national_action_plan_final_2.pdf.

The White House. "Consumer Data Privacy in a Networked World: A Framework for Protecting Privacy and Promoting Innovation in the Global Digital Economy," February 23, 2012, http://www.whitehouse.gov/sites/default/files/privacy-final.pdf.

U.K. Cabinet Office & Department for Business Innovation and Skills. "Better Choices: Better Deals—Consumers Powering Growth," April 13, 2012, http://www.bis.gov.uk/assets/biscore/consumer-issues/docs/b/11-749-better-choices-better-deals-consumers-powering-growth.pdf.

U.K. Cabinet Office. "Open Data White Paper: Unleashing the Potential," June 28, 2012, http://www.gov.uk/government/publications/open-data-white-paper-unleashing-the-potential.

Holdren, John P. Memorandum for the Heads of Executive Departments and Agencies, "Increasing Access to the Results of Federally

Funded Scientific Research," February 22, 2013, http://www. whitehouse.gov/sites/default/files/microsites/ostp/ostp_public_ access_memo_2013.pdf.

Obama, Barack. Executive Order, "Making Open and Machine Readable the New Default for Government Information," May 9, 2013, http://www.whitehouse.gov/the-press-office/2013/05/09/executive-order-making-open-and-machine-readable-new-default-government-.

Burwell, Sylvia M., Steven VanRoekel, Todd Park, and Dominic J. Mancini. Memorandum for the Heads of Executive Departments and Agencies, "Open Data Policy—Managing Information as an Asset," May 9, 2013, http://www.whitehouse.gov/sites/default/files/omb/memoranda/2013/m-13-13.pdf.

National Science and Technology Council. "Smart Disclosure and Consumer Decision Making: Report of the Task Force on Smart Disclosure," May 2013, http://www.whitehouse.gov/sites/default/files/microsites/ostp/report_of_the_task_force_on_smart_disclosure.pdf.

U.K. Cabinet Office. "Policy Paper: G8 Open Data Charter and Technical Annex," June 18, 2013, https://www.gov.uk/government/publications/open-data-charter/g8-open-data-charter-and-technical-annex.

Reports (in chronological order)

Vickery, Graham. "Review of Recent Studies on PSI [Public Sector Information] Re-Use and Related Market Developments." For the European Commission, 2011, http://www.umic.pt/images/stories/publicacoes6/psi_final_version_formatted-1.pdf.

McKinsey Global Institute (James Manyika, Michael Chui, Brad Brown, Jacques Bughin, Richard Dobbs, Charles Roxburgh, Angela Hung Byers). "Big Data: The Next Frontier for Innovation, Competition, and Productivity." McKinsey & Company, May 2011,

www.mckinsey.com/insights/business_technology/big_data_the_
next_frontier_for_innovation.

Deloitte Analytics. "Open Growth: Stimulating the Demand for Open Data in the U.K." Deloitte, 2012, www.deloitte.com/assets/ Dcom-UnitedKingdom/Local%20Assets/Documents/Market%20 insights/Deloitte%20Analytics/uk-da-open-growth.pdf.

McKinsey Center for U.S. Health System Reform (Peter Groves, Basel Kayyali, David Knott, Steve Van Kuiken). "The 'Big Data' Revolution in Health Care: Accelerating Value and Innovation." McKinsey & Company, January 2013, www.mckinsey.com/ insights/health_systems_and_services/the_big-data_revolution_ in_us_health_care.

World Economic Forum. "Unlocking the Value of Personal Data: From Collection to Usage." World Economic Forum, February 2013, http://www3.weforum.org/docs/WEF_IT_Unlocking ValuePersonalData_CollectionUsage_Report_2013.pdf.

Deloitte. "Market Assessment of Public Sector Information." For the Department for Business Innovation & Skills (U.K.), May 2013, https://www.gov.uk/government/uploads/system/uploads/attach-ment_data/file/198905/bis-13-743-market-assessment-of-public-sector-information.pdf.

McKinsey Global Institute, McKinsey Center for Government, and McKinsey Business Technology Office (James Manyika, Michael Chui, Peter Groves, Diana Farrell, Steve Van Kuiken, Elizabeth Almasi Doshi). "Open Data: Unlocking Innovation and Performance With Liquid Information," McKinsey & Company, October 2013, http://www.mckinsey.com/insights/business_technology/ open_data_unlocking_innovation_and_performance_with_liq-uid_information.

APPENDIX A

Using OpenDataNow.com

AUTHOR'S NOTE: THE WEBSITE THAT I'VE LAUNCHED TO COVER Open Data, OpenDataNow.com, is more than an accompaniment to this book. I hope it will serve as an ongoing resource for information, discussion, and news about the growing field of Open Data. In that context, readers may be especially interested to know that the website includes numerous interviews and articles about the people and organizations discussed in this book. Here is a list of relevant posts as of the time of publication and the chapters where the subjects of the posts first appear, in order of appearance.

Chapter 1: Gavin Starks, Open Data Institute

Chapter 2: David Friedberg, The Climate Corporation; Todd Park and other leaders at the Health Datapalooza; Sir Nigel Shadbolt and leaders of the companies at the Open Data Institute "incubator"

Chapter 3: Bill Jackson, GreatSchools

Chapter 4: Hudson Hollister, Data Transparency Coalition; Jeremy Bronfman, Enigma.io

Chapter 6: Dara O'Rourke, GoodGuide

Chapter 7: Courtney Powell and A. T. Fouty, PublikDemand; Kristin Muhlner, newBrandAnalytics; Michael Fertik, Reputation.com; Helen Margetts, Oxford Internet Institute

Chapter 8: Seth Grimes, Alta Plana Corporation

Chapter 9: Beth Noveck, The Governance Lab; Robert Simpson, Zooniverse

Chapter 10: White House Champions of Change for Open Science

Chapter 11: Nick Sinai, U.S. Deputy Chief Technology Officer

Chapter 12: Ellen Miller, Sunlight Foundation; Tom Steinberg, MySociety

Chapter 13: Paul Maltby, U.K. Cabinet Office

APPENDIX B

Defining Data Categories

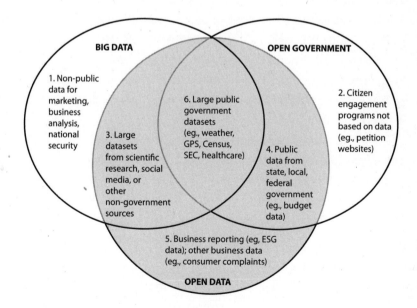

BIG DATA, OPEN GOVERNMENT, AND OPEN DATA ARE CLOSELY related, but they're not the same. The Venn diagram on the previous page is my attempt to map how they relate to each other.

The definitions for Big Data and Open Government aren't crystal clear. Big Data essentially describes very large datasets, but that's a somewhat subjective judgment and depends on technology: today's Big Data may not seem so big in a few years when data analysis and computing technology improve. Open Government is a combination of ideas: it includes collaborative strategies to engage citizens in government; government releasing data about its own operations, like federal spending data; and government releasing data that it collects on issues of public interest, such as health, environment, and different industries.

For this book, I've chosen a simple and expansive definition of Open Data: it's *accessible public data that people, companies, and organizations can use to launch new ventures, analyze patterns and trends, make data-driven decisions, and solve complex problems.* Others have defined Open Data in more detail. All definitions of Open Data include two basic features: the data must be publicly available for anyone to use, and it must be licensed in a way that allows for its reuse. Open Data should also be in a form that makes it relatively easy to use and analyze, although here there are gradations of "openness." And there's general agreement that Open Data should be free of charge or cost just a minimal amount.

Starting with those basic definitions, the intersection of these three concepts defines the six subtypes of data shown on the diagram. (There's no separate category for the intersection of Big Data and Open Government—anything in that category is also Open Data.) Here are characteristic examples of each, referring to the numbers in the figure.

1. *Big Data that's not Open Data.* A lot of Big Data falls in this category, including some Big Data that has great commercial value. All of the data that large retailers hold on customers'

buying habits, that hospitals hold about their patients, or that banks hold about their credit card holders falls here. It's information that the data holders own and can use for commercial advantage. National security data, such as the data collected by the NSA, is also in this category.

2. *Open Government work that's not Open Data.* This includes the part of Open Government that focuses purely on citizen engagement. For instance, the White House has started a petition website, called We the People, to open itself to citizen input. While the site makes its data available, publishing Open Data—beyond numbers of signatures—is not its main purpose.

3. *Big, Open, nongovernmental Data.* Here we find the kinds of scientific data-sharing and citizen science projects described in Chapters 9 and 10. Big data from astronomical observations, from large biomedical projects like the Human Genome Project, or from other sources realizes its greatest value through an open, shared approach. While some of this research may be government funded, it's not "government data," because it's not generally held, maintained, or analyzed by government agencies. This category also includes data that can be analyzed from Twitter and other forms of social media.

4. *Open Government data that's not Big Data.* Government data doesn't have to be Big Data to be valuable. Modest amounts of data from states, cities, and the federal government can have a major impact when it's released. This kind of data fuels the participatory budgeting movement, where cities around the world are inviting their residents to look at the city budget and help decide how to spend it. It's also the fuel for apps that help people use city services like public buses or health clinics.

5. *Open Data—not Big, not from government.* This includes the private-sector data that companies choose to share for their own purposes—for example, to satisfy their potential investors or to enhance their reputations. Environmental, social, and

governance (ESG) metrics fall here. In addition, reputational data, such as data from consumer complaints, can have a big impact on businesses.

6. *Big, Open, government Data (the trifecta).* These datasets may have the most impact of any category. Government agencies have the capacity and funds to gather very large amounts of data, and making those datasets open can have major economic benefits. National weather data and GPS data are the most often-cited examples. U.S. census data and data collected by the Securities and Exchange Commission and the Department of Health and Human Services are others. With the new Open Data Policy, described in Chapter 13, this category will likely become larger, more robust, and even more significant.

Glossary

AUTHOR'S NOTE: FOR THIS GLOSSARY, I'VE DRAWN ON A NUMber of sources listed in the Selected Bibliography and some additional ones cited here. In several cases, I've drawn on multiple sources to define terms in my own words. My goal has not been to give the most technically precise definition possible or to reconcile all the various definitions of every term, but to give readers a basic understanding that will help demystify the world of Open Data.

Anonymization. "Anonymization refers to stripping out from **datasets** any personal identifiers, such as name, address, credit card number, date of birth, or Social Security number. The resulting data can then be analyzed and shared without compromising anyone's privacy" (Mayer-Schönberger and Cukier, *Big Data*, 154). While the process is meant to protect privacy, it isn't foolproof; see **mosaic effect**.

API (application programming interface). An API, or application programming interface, allows an application or website to talk to another one and use its software and data. An API provided by a federal agency, for example, can enable outside programmers to retrieve some of the agency's software and process some of its data to develop new applications that can involve other data and software as well.

Big Data. Big Data has been described in various ways. This description from the McKinsey Global Institute is helpful: "'Big data' refers to datasets whose size is beyond the ability of typical **database** software tools to capture, store, manage, and analyze. This definition is intentionally subjective and incorporates a moving definition of how big a dataset needs to be in order to be considered big data. . . . We assume that, as technology advances over time, the size of **datasets** that qualify as big data will increase." The report also notes that an amount of data that would be considered "big" by one industry may not be so big for a different industry that has more powerful analytic tools (McKinsey Global Institute, "Big Data," 6). Other definitions also add "velocity," the speed at which data changes, and "variety," the increasing kinds of data available, to the "volume" of data, thus referring to the "three Vs" of Big Data.

Choice engine. An interactive website or app that uses data about products and services to help consumers choose the option that best meets their needs. Current examples include travel sites that are used to book airline flights or hotels. Choice engines may be designed to implement **Smart Disclosure.**

Collective intelligence. *Wikipedia* defines collective intelligence as "shared or group intelligence that emerges from the collaboration and competition of many individuals and appears in consensus decision making." In a somewhat different description, the *Financial Times Lexicon* online says that "Collective intelligence—or crowdsourcing—refers to harnessing the power of a large number of people to solve a difficult problem as a group. The idea is that a group of people can solve problems efficiently and offer greater insight and a better answer than any one individual could provide." In general, the term is used to cover the different kinds of group-enabled problem solving described in Chapters 9 and 10.

Computational social science. The use of large **datasets** to do research on issues such as public health, social trends, or political activity. Examples include the analysis of responses to online petitions or the use of cell-phone records to predict trends in public safety or crime.

Computer-assisted reporting. "Computer-assisted reporting describes the use of computers to gather and analyze the data necessary to write news stories. . . . Reporters routinely collect information in databases, analyze public records with spreadsheets and statistical programs, [and] study political and demographic change with geographic information system mapping" (*Wikipedia*). The birth of computer-assisted reporting is attributed to journalist Philip Meyer, as described in Chapter 12.

Corporate credibility. A term used in this book (Chapter 6) to describe the voluntary release of data on corporate operations—including financial operations, environmental/social/governance measures, and more—to improve a company's brand, attract investment and partnerships, respond to public and stakeholder concerns, and generally build trust in the company. Proposed by the author as an alternative to "corporate accountability" or "corporate transparency."

Corporate social responsibility (CSR). A broad term that has been defined as "the integration of business operations and values, whereby the interests of all stakeholders including investors, customers, employees, the community, and the environment are reflected in the company's policies and actions" (www.csrwire.com). Corporate social responsibility, or CSR, can include anything from a company's efforts to reduce pollution to its charitable donations and youth employment programs. The concept has been criticized by some business leaders, who believe it distracts from a company's core goals, and by activists, who believe companies may use CSR to improve their image without addressing core operational or policy issues. Recently, many companies have referred instead to **ESG measures**—environmental, social, and governance—which can be more specific and can be released as **Open Data**.

Crowdsourcing. Coined by Jeff Howe and Mark Robinson in *Wired* magazine in 2006. Howe's definition, from a blog post written shortly after the article appeared: "Simply defined, crowdsourcing represents the act of a company or institution taking a function once performed by employees and outsourcing it to an undefined (and generally large) network of people in the form of an open call. This can take the form of peer-production (when the job is performed collaboratively), but is also often undertaken by sole individuals. The crucial prerequisite is the use of the open call format and the large network of potential laborers." More recently, "crowdsourcing" has been used as a general term to describe online collaboration around data and information, with more than 40 definitions by one count. See Chapters 9 and 10 for a discussion of collaborative approaches. (Blog post by Jeff Howe at http://crowdsourcing.typepad.com/cs/2006/06/crowdsourcing_a.html.)

Data. From the federal government's central data hub at Data.gov: "A value or set of values representing a specific concept or concepts. Data become '**information**' when analyzed and possibly combined with other data in order to extract meaning, and to provide context. The meaning of data can vary depending on its context" (www.data.gov/glossary). Data is distinguished from the more general "information" because it can be stored, represented, and analyzed by computers in quantitative ways. Text in documents is often referred to as "unstructured" data to contrast it to the organized data found in computer databases.

Data discovery. The ability to find useful data through a natural, intuitive search process, similar to the experience of using Google or another search engine. This includes the ability to "discover" data that the user may not have known was relevant to a topic of interest. This is also sometimes called "data exploration." See discussion of Enigma.io in Chapter 4.

Data enclave. "[A] tool that allows the sharing, among a closed community of researchers, of datasets that are too sensitive to share broadly" (www.norc.org/Research/Capabilities/Pages/data-enclave. aspx). A data enclave is maintained, for example, by the research organization NORC at the University of Chicago.

Data exhaust. "[T]he digital trail that people leave in their wake [is called] 'data exhaust.' It refers to data that is shed as a by-product of people's actions and movements in the world. For the Internet, it describes users' online interactions: where they click, how long they look at a page, where the mouse-cursor hovers, what they type, and more" (Mayer-Schönberger and Cukier, *Big Data*, 113). Other examples include different kinds of data from cell-phone records, such as numbers called or the location of the caller.

Data-hugging disorder. A tongue-in-cheek term used by **Open Data** advocates to describe the tendency of government agencies to hold on to the data they manage and resist releasing it.

Data scraping. Programming a computer to access certain kinds of websites and systematically copy the desired information into a database. (For example, searching credit card-related sites to compile a database of terms and fees.) A technique that can turn unorganized, dispersed, publicly available data into structured, usable **Open Data**, but at some effort and expense.

Database. "A database is an organized collection of data. The data is typically organized to model relevant aspects of reality (for example, the availability of rooms in hotels), in a way that supports processes requiring this information (for example, finding a hotel with vacancies)" (*Wikipedia*). A database organizes the information in one or more **datasets** so that it can be used for analysis and problem solving.

Datapalooza. Originated by U.S. Chief Technology Officer Todd Park when he was at the Department of Health and Human Services, a datapalooza brings together government experts, entrepreneurs, businesses, and others to celebrate and find new uses for government Open Data. The Health Datapalooza was the first such event and is the largest, but datapaloozas have also been held for energy, education, and other sectors.

Dataset. From the Data.gov glossary: "A dataset is an organized collection of data. The most basic representation of a dataset is data elements presented in tabular form. Each column represents a particular variable. Each row corresponds to a given value of that column's variable. A dataset may also present information in a variety of nontabular formats, such as an extended mark-up language (**XML**) file, a **geospatial data** file, or an image file, etc." (www.data.gov/glossary).

Demand-driven data disclosure. The author's term for a process of consultation that would involve subject matter experts, application developers, industry, consumer groups, and others meeting with government agencies that manage data in order to help them identify and release datasets that will be most useful to the public.

ESG reporting. Public reporting on environmental, social, and governance factors in a company's operations. The term is sometimes used interchangeably with **corporate social responsibility** but seems to be increasingly used to describe a more measurable, quantitative approach than CSR. May be reported as **Open Data** voluntarily, under government reporting requirements, in response to requests from advocacy organizations, or in some other way.

eXtensible Business Reporting Language. See **XBRL**.

eXtensible Markup Language. See **XML**.

Five-star linked Open Data. A set of categories developed by Sir Tim Berners-Lee, inventor of the World Wide Web, to denote different levels of **Open Data** from least to most useful. They range from simply making data available on the web in any form with an **open license** that allows its reuse (one star) to providing it as machine-readable **Linked Data** (five stars). Underscores the concept that data can be released with different degrees of "openness," but that all Open Data requires public availability online and an open license allowing reuse. (5stardata.info).

Geospatial data. Data relating to the physical location of a person, organization, facility, natural formation, or other entity. Geospatial data may relate to permanent location or be used to track an object or person's movements over time. Examples range from data about a smartphone's location tracked through GPS to the Environmental Protection Agency's data about the facilities it oversees in the interest of pollution control. Geospatial data can also be used to represent areas on a map, such as the outline of a county's borders, or the location on a map of a geographic feature like a lake or mountain.

Hackathon. "[An] event in which computer programmers and others involved in software development, including graphic designers, interface designers, and project managers, collaborate intensively on software projects. . . . Hackathons typically last between a day and a week in length. Some hackathons are intended simply for educational or social purposes, although in many cases the goal is to create usable software. Hackathons tend to have a specific focus, which can include the programming language used, the operating system, an application, an API, the subject, and the demographic group of the programmers" (*Wikipedia*).

Information. From the federal government's Project Open Data: "Information [according to a government definition] means any communication or representation of knowledge such as facts, data, or opinions in any medium or form, including textual, numerical, graphic, cartographic, narrative, or audiovisual forms" (project-open-data. github.io). As this definition implies, all **data** is a form of information, but not all information is in a form that can be readily analyzed as data.

Interoperability. The ability to analyze different **datasets** from different sources together without being hindered by differences in the way the data is structured or presented.

Legal Entity Identifier (LEI). From the U.S. Department of the Treasury: "The LEI is a reference code to uniquely identify a legally distinct entity that engages in a financial transaction. Currently, there are many ways to identify entities, but there is no unified global identification system for legal entities across markets and jurisdictions. The LEI is designed to be a linchpin for financial data—the first global and unique entity identifier enabling risk managers and regulators to identify parties to financial transactions instantly and precisely" (http://www.treasury.gov/initiatives/ofr/data/Documents/LEI_FAQs_February2013_FINAL.pdf).

Light-touch regulation. A term used by many in the Obama administration to describe ways that agencies can improve the manner in which regulated industries operate without telling them exactly how to operate. For example, an agency may require businesses to release more transparent data about their prices and fees—as the Department of Transportation has done with the airline industry—in the hope that market forces will then keep prices and fees in check. **Targeted transparency** is often used in light-touch regulation.

Linked Data. Linked Data assigns a web address, similar to the address for a website, to each piece of data, making it possible to connect data through the web. Unlike a conventional **database**, the connections between different Linked Data elements can expand and grow without limit. Linked Data is particularly useful for connecting and analyzing different types of data from different **datasets**, like government data from different agencies. Linked Data is central to the concept of the Semantic Web; see the benchmark article by Tim Berners-Lee, James Hendler, and Ora Lassila, "The Semantic Web," *Scientific American*, May 17, 2001.

Machine readable. "Machine-readable data are digital information stored in a format enabling the information to be processed and analyzed by computer. These formats allow electronic data to be as usable as possible. Examples of machine-readable data include formats that may be readily imported into spreadsheet and database applications. In contrast, computer files that are simply image reproductions of print disclosures or that contain only unstructured narrative text generally do not represent machine-readable formats" (Sunstein, "Informing Consumers Through Smart Disclosure," 5).

Mashup. "A mashup, in web development, is a web page, or web application, that uses and combines data, presentation, or functionality from two or more sources to create new services. The term implies easy, fast integration, frequently using open **application programming interfaces** (**API**) and data sources to produce enriched results that were not necessarily the original reason for producing the raw source data. The main characteristics of a mashup are combination, visualization, and aggregation. It is important to make existing data more useful, for personal and professional use" (*Wikipedia*). A "data mashup" is one in which the primary information combined is data—for example, a visualization that combines environmental **Open Data** with data on hospital admissions to show the relationship between air quality and asthma.

Metadata. "Metadata describes a number of characteristics, or attributes, of data; that is, 'data that describes data.' . . . For any particular datum, the metadata may describe how the datum is represented, ranges of acceptable values, how it should be labeled, as well as its relationship to other data. Metadata also may provide other relevant information, such as the responsible steward, associated laws and regulations, and access management policy" (www.data.gov/glossary). Metadata may also include measures of the quality of data.

Moore's Law. The observation, originally by Intel cofounder Gordon Moore, that computer processor power doubles roughly every two years. Also related to Kryder's Law, first proposed by Mark Kryder, Chief Technology Officer for Seagate Technology, that the storage capacity of hard drives was also doubling every two years (Ayres, *Super Crunchers*, 151–152).

Mosaic effect. The potential to piece together data from an anonymized **dataset** with other data in a way that makes it possible to discover the identities of people whose data has been collected. "The mosaic effect occurs when the information in an individual dataset, in isolation, may not pose a risk of identifying an individual (or threatening some other important interest such as security), but when combined with other available information, could pose such risk. . . . agencies must consider other publicly available data—in any medium and from any source—to determine whether some combination of existing data and the data intended to be publicly released could allow for the identification of an individual or pose another security risk" (Burwell et al., "Open Data Policy," 4–5).

MyData and **midata**. Government-led initiatives in the United States and the United Kingdom, respectively, that are designed to give individuals the data about themselves. This data is "open" in a special sense: it is not open to the general public by any means but is made available securely, person by person, to the individuals it relates to. Examples are personal health records, records of energy usage, and educational records. In some cases (such as health records from the Veterans Administration), the government itself has the data and releases it to individuals; in other cases (such as energy usage), the government may work with the companies that hold the data.

One Report. "One Report means producing a single report that combines the financial and narrative information found in a company's annual report with the nonfinancial (such as on environmental, social, and governance issues) and narrative information found in a company's '**Corporate Social Responsibility**' or '**Sustainability**' reports. . . . It involves using the Internet to provide integrated reporting in ways that cannot be done on paper, such as through analytical tools that enable the user to do his or her own analysis of financial and nonfinancial information" (Eccles and Krzus, *One Report*, 10).

Open Access. The Open Access movement has worked to make the results of scientific research, particularly publicly funded research, available to the public rapidly and at no charge. While much of this work has focused on access to reports published in scientific journals, Open Access also covers the potential benefits of sharing research data itself.

Open Data. This book describes Open Data as "accessible public data that people, companies, and organizations can use to launch new ventures, analyze patterns and trends, make data-driven decisions, and solve complex problems." This description is written to cover all kinds of publicly available data, including such sources as Twitter and data released by the private sector. Others have focused more on government Open Data and have written more detailed definitions. One influential document resulted from a 2007 meeting of 30 Open Government advocates, including the Open Knowledge Foundation, that was funded by the Sunlight Foundation. (http://sunlightfoundation.com/policy/documents/ten-open-data-principles). The federal government has used a similar set of factors to define Open Data (Burwell et al., "Open Data Policy"). A core feature of all Open Data definitions is that the data must be made available under an **open license** that allows the data to be reused. Open Data advocates generally agree that Open Data should be made available at little or no cost, but this does not seem to have been accepted as an absolute core requirement.

Open Definition. The Open Definition, first developed by the Open Knowledge Foundation in 2006, is a framework that defines "openness" generally for both data and content. In simplest terms, it states that "a piece of data or content is open if anyone is free to use, reuse, and redistribute it—subject only, at most, to the requirement to attribute and/or share-alike." More detail on the definition is at http://opendefinition.org.

Open Government. The Open Government movement, described in Chapter 13, has focused on increasing transparency, participation, and collaboration in government at the federal, state, and local levels. In practice, Open Government includes: (1) government releasing data about its own operations (transparency); (2) government being open to input from citizens (participation); (3) government engaging citizens in finding solutions to problems, for example through **hackathons** and other challenges (collaboration); and (4) government releasing data that it collects on issues of public interest, such as health, environment, and different industries—a commitment to Open Data that serves the other three principles. This last function has been dubbed "government as a platform" by tech publisher Tim O'Reilly (Lathrop and Ruma, *Open Government*, Chapter 2).

Open innovation. In his book *Open Innovation*, Henry Chesbrough of the UC Berkeley business school defines the concept as follows: "Open innovation is the use of purposive inflows and outflows of knowledge to accelerate internal innovation and expand the markets for external use of innovation, respectively. [This paradigm] assumes that firms can and should use external ideas as well as internal ideas, and internal and external paths to market, as they look to advance their technology" (http://openinnovation.berkeley.edu/what_is_oi.html).

Open license. "Broadly speaking, an open license is one which grants permission to access, reuse, and redistribute a work with few or no restrictions. . . . For example, a piece of writing on a website made available under an open license would be free for anyone to print out and share, publish on another website or in print, make alterations or additions, incorporate, in part or in whole, into another piece of writing, use as the basis for a work in another medium—such as an audio recording or a film, and do many other things" (http://opendefinition.org/guide). Creative Commons licenses are a common example of open licenses.

Open-source software. "Computer software with its source code made available and licensed with an open-source license in which the copyright holder provides the rights to study, change, and distribute the software for free to anyone and for any purpose.

Open-source software is very often developed in a public, collaborative manner" (*Wikipedia*). Open-source software often comes with some restrictions—for example, it may be sharable only with other people who sign the same license, or some kinds of reuse may require permission.

Personal data vault. Also called a "personal data store" or "personal data locker." An application that enables individuals to store their personal data safely and securely and that enables them to give third parties access to it selectively, under their own control. For example, an individual may use data from the personal data vault to fill out government forms automatically or may make it available to marketers in return for discounts or other deals (the concept of **Vendor Relationship Management**).

Personally identifiable information (PII). "Personally identifiable information (PII), as used in information security, is information that can be used on its own or with other information to identify, contact, or locate a single person, or to identify an individual in context" (*Wikipedia*).

Petabyte. A petabyte is a thousand **terabytes.**

Privacy by Design. Privacy by Design is a framework that was developed by the Information and Privacy Commissioner of Ontario, Canada, Dr. Ann Cavoukian. "Privacy by Design advances the view that the future of privacy cannot be assured solely by compliance with legislation and regulatory frameworks; rather, privacy assurance must become an organization's default mode of operation. The objectives of Privacy by Design [are] ensuring privacy and gaining personal control over one's information and, for organizations, gaining a sustainable competitive advantage" (www.privacybydesign.ca). Privacy by Design sets out seven principles, including the concept that privacy protection should be the default for information; that it should be embedded in the data; and that privacy should be protected from the time that information is gathered until it is disposed of.

Public sector information (PSI). Data and information made available by the government for public use. Public sector information is not always **Open Data**: it may not be available for free or licensed for reuse. However, under a European Union directive, member countries are now encouraged to make PSI available for reuse and to use a common portal to make it available as Open Data.

Sentiment analysis. "Sentiment analysis or opinion mining refers to the application of natural language processing, computational linguistics, and text analytics to identify and extract subjective information in source materials. Generally speaking, sentiment analysis aims to determine the attitude of a speaker or a writer with respect to some topic" (*Wikipedia*). As described in Chapter 8, sentiment analysis can be used for purposes as diverse as finding operational problems in a hotel chain or assessing satisfaction with city government agencies. While sentiment analysis is largely a form of text analysis, cues such as facial expressions and voice tone are now being analyzed together with language as well.

Smart Disclosure. "The timely release of complex information and data in standardized, **machine-readable** formats in ways that enable consumers to make informed decisions" (Sunstein, "Informing Consumers Through Smart Disclosure," 2). Smart Disclosure is designed to help consumers compare and choose between complex products and services and to find the market offerings that best meet their individual needs. Data released through Smart Disclosure can be used by innovators and entrepreneurs to create interactive choice engines for consumers. Ultimately, by enabling more informed consumer decision making, Smart Disclosure is intended to create more transparent, efficient markets for goods and services.

Social customer service. A new concept that combines social media and customer service to improve customer relations. Social customer service, discussed in Chapter 7, is intended to handle consumer complaints and concerns more cost-effectively than a call center and to enable companies to showcase good customer service through social media.

Social listening. Analyzing Twitter, Facebook, online reviews, and other social media to determine how members of the public feel about a company or its products, a movie or TV show, an organization, or any other entity.

Sustainability. "Sustainability is the capacity to endure. . . . For humans, sustainability is the potential for long-term maintenance of well-being, which has ecological, economic, political, and cultural dimensions. Sustainability requires the reconciliation of environmental, social equity, and economic demands" (*Wikipedia*). In a business context, "a sustainable corporation is one that creates profit for its shareholders while protecting the environment and improving the lives of those with whom it interacts . . . . Sustainability in practice can be seen as the art of doing business in an interdependent world" (Savitz and Weber, *The Triple Bottom Line*, x).

Tagging. "In information systems, a tag is a . . . keyword or term assigned to a piece of information. . . . This kind of **metadata** helps describe an item and allows it to be found again by browsing or searching. Tags are generally chosen informally and personally by the item's creator or by its viewer, depending on the system" (*Wikipedia*). Tagging is a process that can either be done professionally or by the public, by releasing **Open Data** and inviting users to tag different pieces of data as they see fit.

Targeted transparency. A term used by the Transparency Policy Project at Harvard's John F. Kennedy School of Government. "Instead of aiming to generally improve public deliberation and officials' accountability, targeted transparency aims to reduce specific risks or performance problems through selective disclosure by corporations or other organizations. The ingeniousness of targeted transparency lies in its mobilization of individual choice, market forces, and participatory democracy through relatively light-handed government action" (Fung et al., *Full Disclosure*, 5). A classic example is the Toxics Release Inventory, which successfully reduced pollution by publicizing data on the amount of pollution produced by specific factories. Targeted transparency is a major tool of **light-touch regulation**.

Terabyte. An amount of data equal to a thousand gigabytes. This has been calculated to be the amount of information in 60 piles of typed paper stacked as tall as the Eiffel Tower, though the original source of this calculation is obscure. See **petabyte**.

Text analysis. A methodology dating back to the 1950s for extracting meaning from text in natural language. Text analysis forms the basis for **sentiment analysis**.

Triple Bottom Line. Attributed to "sustainability guru John Elkington," the Triple Bottom Line is the idea that "businesses need to measure their success not only by the traditional bottom line of financial performance (most often expressed in terms of profits, return on investment [ROI], or shareholder value) but also by their impact on the broader economy, the environment, and on the society in which they operate" (Savitz and Weber, *The Triple Bottom Line*, xii).

Vendor Relationship Management (VRM). A concept developed by Doc Searls, author of *The Intention Economy*, as a system in which consumers will be able to manage the ways in which marketers contact them through control of their own personal data. Described as the inverse of Customer Relationship Management (CRM), the process by which marketers analyze and use customer data.

XBRL (eXtensible Business Reporting Language). A computer language increasingly used to communicate business and financial data electronically. "Extensible Business Reporting Language (XBRL), referred to by the SEC as 'interactive data,' is a freely available standard designed to express business information in a standardized electronic format through the use of electronic 'tags.' Every piece of business information—such as revenues or short-term liabilities, innovation or strategy, tons of carbon emissions, or lost time [due to] accidents—can have an electronic tag (called **metadata)** that enables access to this information over the Internet" (Eccles and Krzus, *One Report*, 68).

XML (eXtensible Markup Language). From Data.gov: "XML was developed for several purposes, one of which is to make the metadata of documents more directly available. XML, when properly used, tags information in a document so that computers can automatically extract it to help provide users with capabilities such as searching, browsing, and information discovery. Along these lines, an important emerging property of XML involves providing mechanisms for tracking versions of a document. When used, it allows the history of a document to be made available to others—an important capability for tracking legislation, policy guidance, and decision memos" (http://www.data.gov/developers/blog/primer-machine-readability-online-documents-and-data).

Chapter Notes

Author's note: This book mentions a large number of online companies and quotes descriptions found on their websites. In most cases, where websites can easily be found from the company name, I have not given the web address here. Web URLs are noted when they do not directly match the company name or when they refer to a specific part of a website. Please see the Selected Bibliography for full citations of some of the works noted here.

Introduction

1 President Obama's remarks on Open Data: http://www.whitehouse. gov/the-press-office/2013/05/09/remarks-president-applied-materials-inc-austin-tx.
2 McKinsey, "Open Data," 6.

Chapter One

8 Gavin Starks quote: From "Opening Government" conference at Open Data Institute, London, November 10, 2012.

8 Tim Berners-Lee bio: http://www.theodi.org/people/timbl.

9 Description of Open Data: For definitions of government Open Data, see Burwell et al, "Open Data Policy," and Sunlight Foundation, "Ten Principles for Opening Up Government Information," http://sunlightfoundation.com/policy/documents/ten-open-data-principles.

9 History of Internet: http://en.wikipedia.org/wiki/Internet and http://en.wikipedia.org/wiki/DARPA.

10 President Obama quote: http://www.whitehouse.gov/the-press-office/2013/05/09/remarks-president-applied-materials-inc-austin-tx.

12 For an overview of Big Data: See Mayer-Schönberger and Cukier, *Big Data*.

12 "devotes only two-and-a-half pages to Open Data": Mayer-Schönberger and Cukier, *Big Data*, 116–118.

14 "no one is sure exactly what they'll be worth": For a critique of the value of Big Data, see James Glanz, "Is Big Data an Economic Big Dud?" *The New York Times*, August 18, 2013 (http://www.nytimes.com/2013/08/18/sunday-review/is-big-data-an-economic-big-dud.html?pagewanted=all).

14 For more about the Open Data 500, see the website of the GovLab (http://thegovlab.org); Wyatt Kash, "GovLab Seeks Open Data Success Stories," *Information Week Government*, September 19, 2013. (http://www.informationweek.com/government/information-management/govlab-to-showcase-top-businesses-using/240161518); and Colby Hochmuth, "Open Data 500 Gives Voice to Companies Using Government Data," *Fedscoop*, September 23, 2013 (http://fedscoop.com/open-data-500-govlab-joel-gurin/).

15 Deloitte's "archetypes": Deloitte, "Open Growth", 3.

15 Quote from Deloitte: Deloitte, "Open Growth", 8.

17 "About This Book" section: Sources for material described in chapter descriptions are found in the notes for the relevant chapters.

Chapter Two

24 Weather data: The figure of $31.5 billion as the economic benefit of weather forecasts in the United States comes from the National Oceanic and Atmospheric Administration and the National Weather Service, "Value of a Weather Ready Nation," October 13, 2011, 13 (http://www.ppi.noaa.gov/wp-content/uploads/PPI-Weather-Econ-Stats-10-13-11.pdf). That report points out that "These benefits far exceed the $5.1 billion spent annually by both private and public weather bureaus on generating forecasts." See also Clay Johnson, "How Did Weather Data Get Opened," *The Information Diet*, August 9. 2010 (http://www.informationdiet.com/blog/read/how-did-weather-data-get-opened); and National Oceanic and Atmospheric Administration, "Societal Impacts of NOAA, (http://www.ppi.noaa.gov/economics/societal-impacts). An additional estimate of $1.5 to $2 billion for private-sector meteorology comes from David B. Spiegler, "The Private Sector in Meteorology—An Update," June 2007, American Meteorological Society, 18 (http://www.ametsoc.org/boardpges/cwce).

24 GPS data: U.S. Chief Technology Officer Todd Park has quoted a figure of $90 billion for GPS data here and elsewhere: Philip Yam, "How to Kick-Start Innovation with Free Data," *Scientific American*, March 23, 2013 (http://www.scientificamerican.com/article.cfm?id=how-to-kick-start-innovaton). Because this number came from an industry study, an estimate of "tens of billions" is more conservative (personal communication from Nick Sinai, June 2013).

24 Kundra quote: Vivek Kundra, "Digital Fuel of the 21st Century: Innovation Through Open Data and the Network Effect," Joan Shorenstein Center on the Press, Politics, and Public Policy,

Harvard College: Discussion Paper Series, January 2012, 16 (http://www.hks.harvard.edu/presspol/publications/papers/discussion_papers/d70_kundra.pdf).

24 Panjiva: Alex Howard, "Panjiva Uses Government Data to Build a Global Search Engine for Commerce," *O'Reilly Strata*, December 6, 2012 (http://strata.oreilly.com/2012/12/panjiva-government-data-platform.html).

25 Google's uses of GPS and mapping data: Author's phone interview with Vint Cerf, October 10, 2013; email to author from Meredith Whittaker, October 10, 2013; Lance Whitney, "Google to Profit From Self-Driving Cars by Decade's End – Analyst," CNET, July 9, 2013 (http://news.cnet.com/8301-1023_3-57592837-93/google-to-profit-from-self-driving-cars-by-decades-end-analyst/); and Sean Kane, "Video: Google Finally Explains the Tech Behind Their Autonomous Cars," *Popular Science*, October 19, 2011 (http://www.popsci.com/technology/article/2011-10/googles-explains-tech-behind-their-autonomous-cars).

25 Foursquare: Erin Griffith, "Foursquare Explore Is Amazing. but Only for a Very Small Group of People," *PandoDaily*, June 28, 2013 (http://pandodaily.com/2013/06/28/foursquare-explore-is-amazing-but-only-for-a-very-small-group-of-people).

25 Uber: Megan McArdle, "Why You Can't Get a Taxi," *The Atlantic*, April 2, 2012 (http://www.theatlantic.com/magazine/archive/2012/05/why-you-cant-get-a-taxi/308942).

26 President Reagan and GPS: "Global Positioning System," *Wikipedia* (http://en.wikipedia.org/wiki/Global_Positioning_System).

26 Cell-phone design: "The Evolution of Cell-Phone Design Between 1983–2009," *Web Designer Depot* (http://www.webdesignerdepot.com/2009/05/the-evolution-of-cell-phone-design-between 1983-2009).

26 Weather Underground: Erica Ogg, "Weather Underground Upgrades Tablet Weather App with a Lot More Sources of

Data," *GigaOm*, July 11, 2013 (http://gigaom.com/2013/07/11/weather-underground-upgrades-tablet-weather-app-with-a-lot-more-sources-of-data).

27 "one of the largest buys of a new-era analytics company": Ashlee Vance, "Monsanto's Billion-Dollar Bet Brings Big Data to the Farm," *BloombergBusinessweek Technology*, October 2, 2013 (http://www.businessweek.com/articles/2013-10-02/monsanto-buys-climate-corporation-for-930-million-bringing-big-data-to-the-farm).

28 David Friedberg quotes: Interview with the author at The Climate Corporation, San Francisco, April 12, 2013.

31 Health data: McKinsey, "The 'Big Data' Revolution in Health Care," 8.

32 "The industry is here": Comment by Alex Howard to the author.

32 "about 80 percent . . . getting health information online": Pew trend data on total online activities (survey data for September 2010).

32 "an all-out crazy party of data": Martin Tisné, "An 'All-Out Crazy Party' . . . Of Data," *Harvard Business Review* blog, March 19, 2013 (http://hbr.org/special-collections/insight/scaling-social-impact/an-all-out-crazy-party-of-data).

33 Todd Park quotes: Keynote on second day of Health Datapalooza, June 4, 2013. See also Simon Owens, "Can Todd Park Revolutionize the Health Care Industry?" *The Atlantic*, June 2, 2011 (http://www.theatlantic.com/technology/archive/2011/06/can-todd-park-revolutionize-the-health-care-industry/239708).

34 Interview re: Aidin: Eric Whitney, "Datapalooza: A Concept, a Conference, and a Movement," *NPR.org*, June 7, 2013 (http://m.npr.org/news/Business/189565146).

35 Shadbolt quote: Interview with the author, New York, April 19, 2013.

35 Starks quote, "What we're trying to do here": Interview with the author, London, April 2, 2013.

36 Starks quote, "One perspective": E-mail to the author, June 11, 2013.

37 Mastodon C, Locatable, Open Corporates, and Honest Buildings: Interview by the author at the Open Data Institute, London, April 2, 2013.

38 *Forbes* on Honest Buildings: Yoni Cohen, "Meet Honest Buildings, A Yelp And LinkedIn For Greener Buildings," *Forbes*, March 7, 2012 (http://www.forbes.com/sites/yonicohen/2012/03/07/meet-honest-buildings-a-yelp-and-linkedin-for-greener-buildings).

39 Average price of apps: Erica Ogg, "The Average Price of an iPhone App is 19 cents—and It'll Probably Keep Shrinking," *GigaOm*, July 18, 2013 (http://gigaom.com/2013/07/18/the-average-iphone-app-price-is-now-0-19-and-itll-probably-keep-shrinking).

41 Brightscope and Department of Labor: Vivek Kundra, *ibid*, 13–15.

Chapter Three

43 For a general online resource on Smart Disclosure: See http://www.data.gov/consumer/community/consumer. The term *Smart Disclosure* was coined by Sophie Raseman at a planning meeting for the White House Task Force on Smart Disclosure, which had previously been using the term *smart data*.

46 Definition of Smart Disclosure: Sunstein, "Memorandum: Informing Consumers Through Smart Disclosure," 2.

46 For reporting and blogging around the March 2012 Smart Disclosure summit: See Charles S. Clark, "White House Summit Cranks Up Push to Better Inform the Public," *Government Executive*, April 2, 2012 (http://www.govexec.com/management/2012/04/white-house-summit-cranks-push-better-inform-public/41654); Cass Sunstein, "Informing Consumers Through Smart Disclosure," *The White House* blog, March 30, 2012 (http://www.whitehouse.gov/blog/2012/03/30/informing-consumers-through-smart-disclosure); Alex Howard, "What Is Smart Disclosure?" *O'Reilly Radar*, April 1, 2012 (http://radar.oreilly.com/2012/04/what-is-smart-disclosure.html).

46 Task Force on Smart Disclosure report: National Science and Technology Council, "Smart Disclosure and Consumer Decision Making."

46 RECAP: Thaler and Sunstein, *Nudge*, 95–96.

46 "a total of $13 billion a year": Bar-Gill cited in Cass Sunstein, "Show Me the Money," *New Republic*, October 5, 2012 (http://www.newrepublic.com/article/books-and-arts/magazine/108153/show-me-the-money).

46 "in a piece for *Harvard Business Review*": Richard H. Thaler and Will Tucker, "Smarter Information, Smarter Consumers," *Harvard Business Review*, January-February 2013.

47 "in his recent book": Sunstein, *Simpler*, 98–100.

48 "more than 80 million Americans have access": Nick Sinai, phone interview with the author, May 17, 2013.

48 "Green Button . . . more than 16 million homes": Nick Sinai, phone interview with the author, May 17, 2013.

50 Choice engine business models: National Science and Technology Council, "Smart Disclosure and Consumer Decision Making," 29.

51 UnitedHealth Group: "UnitedHealthcare's myHealthcare Cost Estimator™ Now Available in Virtually All Markets Nationwide," Press Release, May 15, 2013 (http://www.unitedhealthgroup.com/Newsroom/Articles/Feed/UnitedHealthcare/2013/0515MyHealthcareEstimatorAvailable.aspx).

52 "according to Colorado Public News": Eric Whitney, "Attention Health Care Shoppers: Colorado's New Price List for Providers," *Colorado Public Radio/Kaiser Health News*, May 16, 2012 (http://www.kaiserhealthnews.org/stories/2012/may/16/colorado-health-care-price-list-database.aspx).

52 U.S. Department of the Treasury Resource Center: Finance Data Directory (http://www.treasury.gov/resource-center/financial-education/Pages/fdd.aspx); Sarah Gearen, "Innovators Using Federal Data to Help Consumers Make Informed Decisions," *U.S. Department of the Treasury* blog, April 16, 2013 (http://www.treasury.

gov/connect/blog/Pages/Innovators-Using-Federal-Data-to-Help-Consumers-Make-Informed-Decisions.aspx).

53 Zillow using data from state and local vs. federal sources: Personal communication from Mike Nelson, August 8. 2013.

53 "A post on the White House blog": Todd Park and Steven Van-Roekel, "The American Dream, Aided by Open Government Data," *The White House* blog, August 7, 2013 (http://www.whitehouse.gov/blog/2013/08/07/american-dream-aided-open-government-data).

53 Quote from Zillow: David Sasaki, "Advice for Open Data Startups" (personal blog), July 17, 2013 (http://davidsasaki.name/2013/07/advice-for-open-data-startups/?utm_source=feedly).

54 "In his January 2013": President Barack Obama, State of the Union Address, February 12, 2013 (http://www.whitehouse.gov/state-of-the-union-2013).

54 "the president announced a plan to push even harder": Frank James, "Polite Reception For Obama College Plan Belies Hurdles," *NPR: It's All Politics*, August 22, 2013 (http://www.npr.org/blogs/itsallpolitics/2013/08/22/214556995/polite-reception-for-obama-college-cost-plan-belies-hurdles); Tamar Lewin, "Obama's Plan Aims to Lower Cost of College," *The New York Times*, August 22, 2013 (http://www.nytimes.com/2013/08/22/education/obamas-plan-aims-to-lower-cost-of-college.html?pagewanted=all).

55 GreatSchools.org finances: E-mail from Alan Simpson, August 5, 2013; GreatSchools.org Annual Report.

56 Ogi Kavazovic quotes: Interview with the author, March 28, 2013.

56 Statistics on Opower's effectiveness: http://opower.com; Matt David, Environmental Defense Fund, "Behavior and Energy Savings: Evidence from a Series of Experimental Interventions," 2011 (http://opower.com/uploads/library/file/5/edf_behavior_and_energysavings.pdf).

56 National Broadband Map: Available at www.broadbandmap.gov.

57 "Measuring Broadband America": The original 2011 report, follow-up annual reports, and a discussion of methodology are available at http://www.fcc.gov/measuringbroadbandamerica/.

57 "Measurement Lab, or M-Lab": Details on M-Lab are available at www.measurementlab.net.

58 "Open Data is available for anyone to review and use": See https://code.google.com/p/m-lab/wiki/HowToAccessMLabData.

58 Vint Cerf quotes: Phone interview with author, October 2, 2013.

58 "the Iranian government slowed down the network": Collin Anderson, "Dimming the Internet: Detecting Throttling as a Method of Censorship in Iran," *Cornell University Library*, draft submitted June 18, 2013 (http://arxiv.org/abs/1306.4361/).

59 "a global map of network neutrality": See netneutralitymap.org/.

59 Schwark Satyavolu: Phone interview with the author, June 13, 2013.

60 British choice engines: Mark Sweney, "How Meerkat Aleksandr Orlov Helped Increase the Market for TV Ads," *The Guardian*, January 15, 2010 (http://www.guardian.co.uk/media/2010/jan/16/aleksander-orlov-price-comparison-ads).

61 *Which?* magazine": "Is the Price Right?," *Which?*, August 2013, 32–35.

61 Description of ideas42: E-mail from Will Tucker, August 8, 2013.

62 Ogi Kavazovic quotes: Interview with the author, Arlington, VA, March 28, 2013.

62 Nigel Shadbolt quotes: Interview with the author, New York, April 19, 2013.

64 Paul English quote: Geoff Colvin, "Kayak Takes on the Big Dogs," *Fortune*, September 27, 2012 (http://management.fortune.cnn.com/2012/09/27/kayak-paul-english/; http://www.bloomberg.com/news/2012-11-08/priceline-buys-kayak-for-1-8-billion-expanding-in-travel.html).

65 Giant Food: Obituary, "Mother of Consumerism Esther Peterson: Nutritional Labeling, Open Dating, Unit Pricing Among Her

Contributions," *Baltimore Sun*, December 24, 1997 (http://articles.baltimoresun.com/1997-12-24/news/1997358044_1_esther-peterson-nutritional-labeling-unit-pricing).

65 Quotes from Isaacson: e-mail to the author, August 2, 2013.

66 Quotes from Breslin-Barnhart: e-mail to the author, August 5, 2013.

Chapter Four

68 Hudson Hollister quotes: Interview with the author, Washington, DC, March 27, 2013.

68 Data Demo Day: http://www.datacoalition.com/index .php?option=com_content&view=article&id=39.

68 Examples of companies in different categories: Hudson Hollister interview with the author, Washington, DC, July 30, 2013.

69 "Take Palantir Technologies": "Palantir Technologies," *Wikipedia* (http://en.wikipedia.org/wiki/Palantir_Technologies).

70 Quotes from Eaves: David Eaves, "The Value of Open Data: Don't Measure Growth, Measure Destruction," *Eaves.ca*, April 25, 2013 (http://eaves.ca/2013/04/25/the-value-of-open-data-dont-measure-growth-measure-destruction).

71 $181 million website: Clay Johnson, "What Is the Future of Open Government?" *Department of Better Technology* blog, April 15, 2013 (http://www.dobt.co/What-Is-The-Future-Of-Open-Government).

71 "Johnson and others wrote persuasively": Clay Johnson, "The Healthcare .gov Fiasco," *Department of Better Technology blog*, October 7, 2013 (http://blog.dobt.co/post/63381111778/the-healthcare-gov-fiasco); Alex Howard, "How the First Internet President Produced the Government's Biggest, Highest-Stakes Internet Failure," *BuzzFeed Politics*, October 13, 2013 (http://www.buzzfeed.com/alexhoward/how-the-first-internet-president-produced-american-governmen).

71 RFP-EZ cost reduction: Karen G. Mills and Todd Park, "RFP-EZ Delivers Savings for Taxpayers, New Opportunities for Small

Business," *OSTP* blog, May 15, 2013 (http://www.whitehouse
.gov/blog/2013/05/15/rfp-ez-delivers-savings-taxpayers-new-
opportunities-small-business).

72 "also called . . . Semantic Web": The concept of Linked Data was
introduced in an article by Tim Berners-Lee, James Hendler, and
Ora Lassilla, "The Semantic Web," *Scientific American*, May 2001.

72 Quotes from OpenGov Inc.: Interview with the author, Palo Alto,
CA, April 11, 2013. For more on OpenGov, see Yuliya Chernova,
"With Palo Alto on Board, OpenGov Aims for Transparency in
Dozens More City Governments," *The Wall Street Journal: Venture
Capital Dispatch*, July 11, 2013 (http://blogs.wsj.com/venturecapi-
tal/2013/07/11/with-palo-alto-on-board-opengov-aims-for-trans-
parency-in-dozens-more-city-governments/).

74 Merritt quotes: E-mail to the author, August 5, 2013.

74 Datamarket and import.io: Mayer-Schönberger and Cukier,
Big Data, 121.

75 Bronfman quotes: Interview with the author, New York, May 23,
2013. See also Chris Velazco, "And the Winner of TechCrunch
Disrupt NY 2013 Is . . . Enigma!" TechCrunch, May 1, 2013 (http://
techcrunch.com/2013/05/01/and-the-winner-of-techcrunch-
disrupt-ny-2013-is-enigma).

79 "Peace Corps of Geeks": Smolan and Erwitt, *Human Face of Big
Data*, 165.

79 150,000 data scientists: McKinsey Global Institute, "Big Data: The
Next Frontier for Innovation, Competition, and Productivity," 104.

Chapter Five

81 Carl Malamud and SEC: Tauberer, *Principles and Practices of Open
Government Data*, 11–12.

82 "The move to XBRL": For background on the federal government's use of XBRL, see xbrl.sec.gov.

82 Blaszkowsky quote: E-mail to the author, June 12, 2013.

83 "a report from the Columbia Business School": Trevor S. Harris and Suzanne Morsfield, "An Evaluation of the Current State and Future of XBRL and Interactive Data for Investors and Analysts," Columbia Business School, Center for Excellence in Accounting and Security Analysis, White Paper Number Three, December 2012, i and ii (http://www4.gsb.columbia.edu/filemgr?&file_id=7313146).

83 Call Reports: U.S. Department of the Treasury, Office of Financial Research, "2012 Annual Report," 114–115 (http://www .treasury.gov/initiatives/wsr/ofr/Documents/OFR_Annual_ Report_071912_Final.pdf).

83 "Robocop": David Blaszkowsky e-mail to the author, June 12, 2013.

83 Members of SEC Advisory Committee: http://www.sec.gov/News/ PressRelease/Detail/PressRelease/1365171488168#.UgO4- 5KTjQg.

84 Quotes from the report of the Investor Advisory Committee to the SEC: "Recommendations of the Investor Advisory Committee Regarding the SEC and the Need for Cost Effective Retrieval of Information by Investors (Adopted July 25, 2013)," 1 (http://www .sec.gov/spotlight/investor-advisory-committee-2012/data-tagging- resolution-72513.pdf).

84 "On one end of the spectrum is SigFig": Michael Carney, "Sig- Fig rakes in $15M to Continue Its Assault on the Financial Advisory Status Quo," *PandoDaily*, July 2, 2013 (http://pandodaily .com/2013/07/02/sigfig-rakes-in-15m-to-continue-its-assault-on- the-financial-advisory-status-quo).

85 Quotes from Ballow: E-mail to the author, August 2, 2013.

86 "a New York conference on sentiment analysis": From Sentiment Analysis Symposium, New York, May 8, 2013.

86 KredStreet: Jon Evans, "Big Data Could Cripple Facebook," *Tech- Crunch*, March 30, 2013 (http://techcrunch.com/2013/03/30/ big-data-could-cripple-face-book)

88 Taggart quote: Interview with the author, London, April 2, 2013.

88 "implement a Legal Entity Identifier (LEI) system": For background on the Legal Entity Identifier initiative, see U.S. Department of the Treasury, Office of Financial Research, "2012 Annual Report," Chapter 5 (Promoting Data Standards) (http://www.treasury.gov/initiatives/wsr/ofr/Documents/OFR_Annual_Report_071912_Final.pdf).

88 On Deck Capital: J.J. Colao, "Need a Business Loan? Impress the Algorithm, Not the Loan Officer," *Forbes*, April 15, 2013 (http://www.forbes.com/sites/jjcolao/2013/03/27/need-a-business-loan-impress-the-algorithm-not-the-loan-officer/).

89 Kimmelman and Fitzpatrick quotes: Interview with the author, London, April 3, 2013. See also Amy Wilson, "Duedil Hunts for Buried Treasure in Small Businesses," *The Telegraph*, October 9, 2012 (http://www.telegraph.co.uk/finance/businessclub/9596506/Duedil-hunts-for-buried-treasure-in-small-businesses.html).

90 "Nonprofits Are Corporations, Too": Aspen Institute report, Beth Simone Noveck and Daniel L. Goroff, "Information for Impact: Liberating Nonprofit Sector Data," The Aspen Institute, 2013 (http://www.aspeninstitute.org/sites/default/files/content/docs/events/psi_Information-for-Impact.pdf). Also see Beth Simone Noveck, "IRS: Turn Over a New Leaf, Open Up Data," *Forbes*, May 21, 2013 (http://www.forbes.com/sites/bethsimonenoveck/2013/05/21/irs-turn-over-a-new-leaf-open-up-data).

91 President Obama's budget proposal: Cinthia Schuman, "Obama's FY14 Budget Includes a Score for 'Big Data,'" *The Aspen Idea* (blog), April 15, 2013 (http://www.aspeninstitute.org/about/blog/score-big-data).

Chapter Six

93 Carbon Disclosure Project funds: Carbon Disclosure Project website (as of June 2013) (https://www.cdproject.net/en-US/Pages/About-Us.aspx).

94 Dodd-Frank: "Dodd-Frank Wall Street Reform and Consumer Protection Act," *Wikipedia* (http://en.wikipedia.org/wiki/Dodd%E2%80%93Frank_Wall_Street_Reform_and_Consumer_Protection_Act).

95 Extractive Industries Transparency Initiative: U.S. Department of the Interior website (http://www.doi.gov/EITI/index.cfm).

95 "to no one's real satisfaction": Clive Crook, "The Good Company," *The Economist*, January 20, 2005 (http://www.economist.com/node/3555212); Deborah Doane, "The Myth of CSR," *Stanford Social Innovation Review*, Fall 2005 (http://www.ssireview.org/articles/entry/the_myth_of_csr).

95 Trading for Good: Interview with Philip N. Green and Kay Allen, London, April 2, 2013.

95 CSR and ESG: Eccles and Krzus, *One Report*, 123 ff.

96 *Green to Gold* quotes: Esty and Winston, *Green to Gold*, 8, 282.

96 *Triple Bottom Line* quotes: Savitz and Weber, *The Triple Bottom Line*, x–xii.

97 Prestbo quote: Cited in Esty and Winston, *Green to Gold*, 31.

97 "Unilever . . . may exemplify . . . sustainabililty": Mark Gunther, "Unilever's CEO Has a Green Thumb," *Fortune*, June 10, 2013 (http://money.cnn.com/2013/05/23/leadership/unilever-paul-polman.pr.fortune/index.html?pw_log=in).).

98 Top 100 sustainable companies: Amanda White, "How Many Top 100 Sustainable Companies Do You Invest In?" *top1000funds.com*, February 1, 2012 (http://www.top1000funds.com/news/2012/02/01/how-many-top100-sustainable-companies-do-you-invest-in).

98 "An extensive study by Deutsche Bank": "Company Performance Linked to CSR, Deutsche Bank Finds," *Environmental Leader*, June 15, 2012 (http://www.environmentalleader.com/2012/06/15/company-performance-linked-to-csr-deutsche-bank-finds).

98 "An even more comprehensive analysis": Eccles and Krzus, *One Report*, 124.

98 Kaplan quote: Eccles and Krzus, *One Report*, 93.

99 Soyka book quotes: Soyka, *Creating a Sustainable Organization*, 251–253.

99 Soyka quotes: E-mail to the author, August 1, 2013.

100 Ravenel quotes: E-mail to the author, August 5, 2013.

100 Use of Bloomberg ESG data: Bloomberg, "2012 Sustainability Report," 15 (http://www.bloomberg.com/bsustainable/wp-content/themes/wp_sustain13_theme/report/BloombergSustReport2012.pdf.)

100 Wallace quotes: Phone interview with the author, August 5, 2013.

100 Global Reporting Initiative: https://www.globalreporting.org.

101 White quote: Allen White, "Swamped by Sustainability Indicators That Fail to Drive Transformation," *The Guardian* Sustainable Business blog, August 7, 2013 (http://www.theguardian.com/sustainable-business/blog/sustainability-indicators-corporate-transformation).

101 Reporting by S&P 500 and Fortune 500 companies: G&A Institute, "Number of Companies in S&P 500® and Fortune 500® Reporting on Sustainability More Than Doubles from Previous Year, According to New Analysis by Governance & Accountability Institute," News Release, December 17, 2011 (http://www.ga-institute.com/nc/issue-master-system/news-details/article/number-of-companies-in-sp-500R-and-fortune-500-R-reporting-on-sustainability-more-than-doubles-1.html).

101 KPMG study: Cited in Mike Wallace, "GRI Update: Global Trends in Sustainability Reporting," Keynote to International Society of Sustainability Professionals, May 2013 (http://www.slideshare.net/ MAWallace).

102 Definition of One Report and quote on use of Internet: Eccles and Krzus, *One Report*, 9, 10.

102 Krzus on use of One Report: Personal communication, March 7, 2012.

103 Soyka quote: E-mail to the author, August 1, 2013.

103 Wallace quote: Phone interview with the author, August 5, 2013.

103 Goleman quote: Goleman, *Ecological Intelligence*, 9–10.

104 O'Rourke quotes: Interview with the author in San Francisco, April 11, 2013. Also see Claire Cain Miller, "On Web and iPhone, a Tool to Aid Careful Shopping," *The New York Times*, June 14, 2009 (http://www.nytimes.com/2009/06/15/technology/internet/15guide.html).

108 H&M and Gap petition: Steven Greenhouse, "Major Retailers Join Bangladesh Safety Plan," *The New York Times*, May 13, 2013 (http://www.nytimes.com/2013/05/14/business/global/hm-agrees-to-bangladesh-safety-plan.html).

Chapter Seven

112 Yhprum's Law: Paul Resnick, Richard Zeckhauser, John Swanson, and Kate Lockwood, "The Value of Reputation on eBay: A Controlled Experiment," Working Paper (University of Michigan), March 12, 2004, 29.

112 "their accuracy has come into question": Tom Slee, "Some Obvious Things About Internet Reputation Systems," *Whimsley*, September 29, 2013 (http://tomslee.net/2013/09/some-obvious-things-about-internet-reputation-systems.html); Gary Bolton, Ben Greiner, and Axel Ockenfels, "Engineering Trust: Reciprocity in the Production of Reputation Information," March 25, 2012 (http://ben.orsee.org/papers/engineering_trust.pdf).

112 Garfield/Levy quote: Garfield and Levy, *Can't Buy Me Like*, 7, 9.

113 Kerfye Pierre and bill shock: John D. Sutter, "U.S. Aims to Regulate Mobile 'Bill Shock,'" *CNN.com*, October 13, 2010 (http://www.cnn.com/2010/TECH/mobile/10/13/fcc.bill.shock/index.html).

114 Bill shock agreement: Edward Wyatt, "Wireless Users Will Get Alerts on Excess Use," *The New York Times*, October 17, 2011 (http://www.nytimes.com/2011/10/17/technology/fcc-and-wireless-carriers-agree-to-alerts-to-fight-bill-shock.html?emc=eta1).

115 "In 2012, the Consumer Financial Protection Bureau (CFPB)":
CFPB complaint database can be accessed at http://www
.consumerfinance.gov/complaint. More details are available
at http://www.consumerfinance.gov/complaintdatabase and
http://www.consumerfinance.gov/reports/a-snapshot-of-com-
plaints-received-3.

115 Ayres paper: Ian Ayres, Jeff Lingwall, and Sonia Steinway, "Skeletons in the Database: An Early Analysis of the CFPB's Consumer Complaints, *Yale Law and Economics Research Paper No. 475*,
July 17, 2013 (http://papers.ssrn.com/sol3/papers.cfm?abstract_
id=2295157).

115 "A recent article in *American Banker*": Rachel Witkowski, "Customers Are Now Banks' Greatest Regulatory Threat," *American
Banker*, September 11, 2013 (http://www.americanbanker.com/
issues/178_176/customers-are-now-banks-greatest-regulatory-
threat-1061975-1.html). See also Amy Fontinelle, "Why Banks
Are Scrambling to Hear Your Complaints," Forbes, October 25,
2013 (http://www.forbes.com/sites/investopedia/2013/10/25/
why-banks-are-scrambling-to-hear-your-complaints/).

116 Social media predicting CFPB complaints: Brandon Purcell and
Nick Baldocci, "Leveraging CFPB Complaint Database Analysis to Improve Customer Experience," Beyond the Arc monthly
webinar series, January 31, 2013 (http://beyondthearc.com/
downloads/BTA-Webinar-CFPBAnalysis-1-31-13.pdf).

116 Powell and Fouty quotes: Interview with the author, New York,
April 17, 2013.

118 Ripoff Report: "Ripoff Report," *Wikipedia*, (http://en.wikipedia
.org/wiki/Ripoff_Report).

119 Yelp and revenue: Michael Luca, "Reviews, Reputation, and Revenue: The Case of Yelp.com," Working Paper 12-016, Harvard
Business School, September 16, 2011 (http://www.hbs.edu/fac-
ulty/Publication%20Files/12-016.pdf).

119 UC Berkeley study: Michael L. Anderson and Jeremy R. Magruder, "Learning from the Crowd: Regression Discontinuity Estimates of the Effects of an Online Review Database," *The Economic Journal* 122, no. 563 (2012): 957–989.

119 Glassdoor quotes: From background material for the author's June 2010 meeting with Glassdoor principals.

120 Study of bad online reviews: David Streitfeld, "Why Web Reviewers Make Up Bad Things," *The New York Times*, July 15, 2013 (http://bits.blogs.nytimes.com/2013/07/15/why-web-reviewers-make-up-bad-things).

120 Amazon self-promoting authors: David Streitfeld, "His Biggest Fan Was Himself," *The New York Times*, September 4, 2012 (http://bits.blogs.nytimes.com/2012/09/04/his-biggest-fan-was-himself).

120 Michael Jackson campaign: David Streitfeld, "For Michael Jackson Battle, Trying to Even the Score," *The New York Times*, January 25, 2013 (http://www.nytimes.com/2013/01/21/business/a-casualty-on-the-battlefield-of-amazons-partisan-book-reviews.html?pagewanted=all).

120 Kindle case: David Streitfeld, "For $2 a Star, an Online Retailer Gets 5-Star Product Reviews," *The New York Times*, January 26, 2012 (http://www.nytimes.com/2012/01/27/technology/for-2-a-star-a-retailer-gets-5-star-reviews.html).

120 Yelp sting: David Streitfeld, "Buy Reviews on Yelp, Get Black Mark," *The New York Times*, October 18, 2012 (http://www.nytimes.com/2012/10/18/technology/yelp-tries-to-halt-deceptive-reviews.html?_r=0).

121 Estimate of 5 percent fake reviews: Author interview with Kristin Muhlner, Washington, DC, March 29, 2013.

121 Gartner estimate of fake reviews: "Gartner Says By 2014, 10–15 Percent of Social Media Reviews to Be Fake, Paid for by Companies," Press Release, September 17, 2012 (http://www.gartner.com/newsroom/id/2161315).

121 Bing Liu estimate of fake reviews: Trinity Hartman, "Bing Liu: The Science of Detecting Fake Reviews," *Content Ping*, May 18, 2012 (http://www.contentping.com/social-media-2/bing-liu-the-science-of-detecting-fake-reviews).

121 Kristin Muhlner quote: Interview with the author, Washington, DC, March 29, 2013.

122 One billion tweets every three days: Smolan and Erwitt, *The Human Face of Big Data*, 150.

123 APIs for using data from Twitter (examples): https://dev.twitter.com/docs and https://dev.twitter.com/docs/faq#rest-api-v11.

123 Gnip as Grand Central: "Gnip," *Wikipedia* (http://en.wikipedia.org/wiki/Gnip).

123 Datasift pricing: http://datasift.com/platform/pricing.

123 Taplin quote: The Governance Lab Experiment (conference), New York, April 19, 2013.

123 Margetts quote: Interview with author, London, April 5, 2013.

124 Fertik quotes: Interview with the author, Redwood City, CA, April 11, 2013.

125 Fertik quote: E-mail to the author, August 7, 2013.

127 Fertik quote: E-mail to the author, August 7, 2013.

127 Powell quote: Interview with the author, New York, April 17, 2013.

Chapter Eight

129 For general background on sentiment analysis and marketing: See Kevin Randall, "Market Research 3.0 Is Here: Attitudes Meet Algorithms in Sentiment Analysis," *FastCompany.com*, September 18, 2009 (http://www.fastcompany.com/1363805/market-research-30-here-attitudes-meet-algorithms-sentiment-analysis); Seth Grimes, "Market Research + Sentiment Analysis = New Insight," *Breakthrough Analysis*, October 24, 2012 (http://breakthroughanalysis.com/2012/10/24/market-research-sentiment-analysis-new-insight).

130 Grimes quotes: Interview with the author, Takoma Park, MD, March 28, 2013.

131 Summly: Victor Luckerson, "Why Is That 17-Year-Old's $30 Million News App Even Legal?" *Time*, March 27, 2013 (http://business.time.com/2013/03/27/why-is-that-17-year-olds-25-million-news-app-even-legal).

131 "She noted that Quertle": Quertle is at http://www.quertle.com, Compendia Bioscience is at http://www.compendiabio.com, and H3 Biomedicine is at http://www.h3biomedicine.com/home. Their collaboration to mine data from The Cancer Genome Atlas from National Cancer Institute is at http://www.h3biomedicine.com/press-release-details/54. Thanks to Maureen McArthur Hart for alerting me to these applications.

132 "Grimes runs a twice-a-year conference on sentiment analysis": From Sentiment Analysis Symposium, New York, May 8, 2013.

133 Wittes Schlack quote: From Sentiment Analysis Symposium, New York, May 8, 2013.

133 Use of sentiment analysis by Unilever: Seth Grimes, "Sentiment Analysis: A Focus on Applications," *BeyeNetwork*, February 19, 2008 (http://www.b-eye-network.com/view/6897).

133 Bluefin: Smolan and Erwitt, *Human Face of Big Data*, 170.

134 Use of sentiment analysis by European telecom firms: Joe Mullich, "Opposition Research: Sentiment Analysis as a Competitive Marketing Tool," *DataInformed*, December 10, 2012 (http://data-informed.com/opposition-research-sentiment-analysis-as-a-competitive-marketing-tool).

134 Muhlner quotes: Interview with the author in Washington, DC, March 29, 2013.

136 "the mayor told the *Washington Post*": Julie Zauzmer, "Mayor Gray Celebrate's D.C.'s Good Grades," *The Washington Post*, July 9. 2013 (http://www.washingtonpost.com/local/mayor-gray-celebrates-dcs-good-grades/2013/07/09/b830fd8c-e8d3-11e2-aa9f-c03a72e2d342_story.html).

136 "an earlier *Washington Post* piece critiqued": Mike DeBonis, "Just How Useful Is Grade D.C.?", *The Washington Post (blog)*, April 3, 2013 (http://www.washingtonpost.com/blogs/mike-debonis/wp/2013/04/03/just-how-useful-is-grade-d-c/).

137 "*The Wall Street Journal* praised": Sarah Portlock, "In D.C., Social-Media Surveillance Pays Off," *The Wall Street Journal*, November 28, 2012 (http://online.wsj.com/article/SB1000142 412788732471250457813353003391 6570.html).

137 Problem of sarcasm: Katherine Rosman, "The Strange Science of Translating Sarcasm Online," *The Wall Street Journal*, October 30, 201, (http://online.wsj.com/article/SB100014240529702033355 04578088763796519732.html).

137 "claim impossible accuracy numbers": Seth Grimes, "Never Trust Sentiment Accuracy Claims," *Social Media Explorer*, July 17, 2012 (http://www.socialmediaexplorer.com/social-media-monitoring/never-trust-sentiment-accuracy-claims/).

138 Antiterrorist use of sentiment analysis: Karl Rethemeyer, personal communication, May 14, 2012.

138 Advice for smaller companies: Angela Hausman, PhD, "Social Media Analytics: Sentiment Analysis," *Hausman Marketing Letter*, June 28, 2013 (http://www.hausmanmarketingletter.com/social-media-analytics-sentiment-analysis).

139 Grimes quote: Email to the author, August 2, 2013.

Chapter Nine

141 Crowdsourcing: For ongoing news and information about this approach, see the "industry website," www.crowdsourcing.org.

141 "40 different definitions": Brabham, *Crowdsourcing*, 2.

142 InnoCentive description as "the pioneer . . .": Press release, "Inno-Centive Announces Enhanced Collaboration Tools for Problem Solvers," April 2, 2012 (http://www.innocentive.com/innocentive-announces-enhanced-collaboration-tools-problem-solvers).

143 Spradlin quote: Phone interview with the author, May 22, 2013.

143 Kaggle challenges (as of June 2013): http://www.kaggle.com/competitions; also see Derrick Harris, "Kaggle Now Has 100K Data Scientists, but What's a Data Scientist?" *GigaOm*, July 11, 2013 (http://gigaom.com/2013/07/11/kaggle-now-has-100k-data-scientists-but-whats-a-data-scientist).

144 TopCoder competition: Press release, "TopCoder's Open Community Challenge Process Yields 970 Fold Increase in Speed for Big Data Genomics Sequencing Algorithm," February 7, 2013 (http://www.topcoder.com/pressroom/topcoders-open-community-challenge-process-yields-970-fold-increase-in-speed-for-big-data-genomics-sequencing-algorithm).

144 University of Washington AIDS research: Sarika Bensal, "One Point for Crowdsourcing: Gamers Solve Protein Structure of AIDS-like Protein," *Forbes* September 28, 2011 (http://www.forbes.com/sites/sarikabansal/2011/09/28/crowdsourcing-gamers-solve-protein).

144 "Noveck has long been an Open Government pioneer": Noveck, *Wiki Government*, throughout.

146 "In his influential book *Future Perfect*": Johnson, *Future Perfect*, 94.

146 Noveck quotes: Interview with the author, New York, May 31, 2013.

147 StackOverflow business model: "What Is Stack Overflow's Business Model?" (http://meta.stackoverflow.com/questions/79435/what-is-stack-overflows-business-model).

147 Matt Kaufman quote: E-mail to the author, August 2, 2013.

147 Research on Wikipedia: Stacey Kuznetsov, "Motivations of Contributors to Wikipedia," *ACM SIGCAS Computers and Society Newsletter* 36, no. 2 (2006) (http://staceyk.org/personal/WikipediaMotivations.pdf). See also Joachim Schroer and Guido Hertel, "Voluntary Engagement in an Open Web-Based Encyclopedia: Wikipedians, and Why They Do It," *Media Psychology* 12, no. 1 (2009): 96–120 (http://citeseerx.ist.psu.edu/viewdoc/download?doi=10.1.1.86.2761&rep=rep1&type=pdf).

147 Info Army: Ingrid Lunden, "InfoArmy Retreats After Crowd-sourced Research Business Goes Through The Floor. All Reports Now Free," *TechCrunch*, February 1, 2013 (http://techcrunch .com/2013/02/01/infoarmy-retreats-after-crowdsourced-research-business-goes-through-the-floor-all-reports-now-free/?utm_source=feedburner&utm_medium=feed&utm_campaign=Feed% 3A+Techcrunch+%28TechCrunch%29).

148 NASA: http://data.nasa.gov.

148 National Archives: http://www.archives.gov/citizen-archivist.

148 USAID: Author interview with Stephanie Grosser, December 14, 2012. Also, Shadrock Roberts, Stephanie Grosser, and D. Ben Swartley, "Crowdsourcing to Geocode Development Credit Authority Data: A Case Study," *USAID*, June 2012 (http://transition.usaid.gov/our_work/economic_growth_and_trade/development_credit/pdfs/2012/USAIDCrowdsourcingCaseStudy.pdf).

148 National Archives and 1940 census data: E-mail from Miriam Nisbet to the author, June 12, 2013.

149 Simpson quotes: Interview with the author, Oxford, April 5, 2013.

150 Cell Slider: Liat Clark, "Citizen Science Project Crowdsources Identification of Cancer Cells," *Wired* (UK), October 24, 2012 (http://www.wired.co.uk/news/archive/2012-10/24/cancer-research-crowdsourcing).

151 "Wikipedia represents about 100 million hours": Shirky, *Cognitive Surplus*, 14.

151 SkyTruth analysis of BP oil spill: Neely Tucker, "SkyTruth, the Environment and the Satellite Revolution," *The Washington Post*, July 31, 2013 (http://skytruth.org/washington-post-magazine-skytruth-the-environment-and-the-satellite-revolution/).

151 SkyTruth and FrackFinder: Unsigned blog post, "FrackFinder: Mapping and Tracking Fracking Sites With Your Help," *SkyTruth* blog, July 31, 2013 (http://blog.skytruth.org/2013/07/frackfinder-mapping-and-tracking.html).

151 Mechanical Turk: https://www.mturk.com/mturk/welcome. Accuracy of Mechanical Turk: Jakob Rogstadius et al., "An Assessment of Intrinsic and Extrinsic Motivation on Task Performance in Crowdsourcing Markets." Presented at the Fifth International AAAI Conference on Weblogs and Social Media, Association for the Advancement of Artificial Intelligence, 2011. Retrieved from https://www.aaai.org/ocs/index.php/ICWSM/ICWSM11/paper/view/2778.

152 "Clay Shirky summarized the power of collective intelligence": Shirky, *Here Comes Everybody*, 104.

153 Spradlin quotes: Phone interview with the author, August 5, 2013.

Chapter Ten

155 Jay Bradner: "Jay Bradner: Open-Source Cancer Research," *TEDx*, May 2011 (http://www.ted.com/talks/jay_bradner_open_source_cancer_research.html).

157 Tensha: Press release, "Tensha Therapeutics Completes $15 Million Series A Financing to Advance Selective Bromodomain Inhibitors for Cancer and Other Disorders," September 12, 2011 (http://www.tenshatherapeutics.com/pdf/tensha_press_release_9_12_11.pdf).

157 SARS: Surowiecki, *Wisdom of Crowds*, 158ff.

157 "I believe the reinvention of discovery": Nielsen, *Reinventing Discovery*, 10.

158 Bermuda Agreement: Nielsen, *Reinventing Discovery*, 7.

159 Pollock quotes: Interview with the author, London, April 4, 2013.

159 MIT study: Heidi L. Williams, "Intellectual Property Rights and Innovation: Evidence from the Human Genome," *Journal of Political Economy* 121, no. 1 (2013): 1–27.

159 Research Data Alliance quote: http://rd-alliance.org/about.html.

159 Brain research initiative: Jonathan Gray, "Will Obama's New $100M Brain Mapping Project Be Open Access?" *Open Knowledge Foundation* blog, April 4, 2013 (http://blog.okfn.org/2013/04/04/

will-obamas-new-100m-brain-mapping-project-be-open-access).

160 Fox Foundation quote: Press release, "The Michael J. Fox Foundation Launches New Arm of Parkinson's Progression Markers Initiative Studying At-Risk Populations in Parkinson's Disease," April 23, 2013 (https://www.michaeljfox.org/foundation/publication-detail.html?id=472&category=7).

160 Michael J. Fox and PPMI—"full, open access": PPMI Publications Policy, May 28, 2010, 1 (http://www.ppmi-info.org/wp-content/uploads/2010/07/PPMI-Publication-Policy.pdf).

160 Material on Kathy Giusti: Linda Tischler, "Using Data to Treat Cancer and Drive Innovation," *Fast Company*, April 15, 2013 (http://www.fastcompany.com/3007768/creative-conversations/using-data-treat-cancer-and-drive-innovation. Also "Kathy Giusti," *Wikipedia*, (http://en.wikipedia.org/wiki/Kathy_Giusti).

161 For more on PatientsLikeMe: See "Jamie Heywood: Healthcare Revolutionary," *TED* (http://www.ted.com/speakers/jamie_heywood.html).

161 GSK support for AllTrials: Press release, "GSK Announces Support for AllTrials Campaign for Clinical Data Transparency," February 5, 2013 (http://www.gsk.com/media/press-releases/2013/ GSK-announces-support-forAll-Trials-campaign-for-clinical-data-transparency.html).

161 GSK PR problem: Pratap Chatterjee, "Medical Trial Data Activists Score Win Over Glaxo," *CorpWatch* blog, February 7, 2013 (http://www.corpwatch.org/article.php?id=15816).

162 Pharmaceutical industry opposition to AllTrials: Ian Sample, "Big Pharma Mobilizing Patients in Battle Over Drugs Trials Data," *The Guardian*, July 21, 2013 (http://www.guardian.co.uk/business/2013/jul/21/big-pharma-secret-drugs-trials); Katie Thomas, "Breaking the Seal on Drug Research," *The New York Times*, June 29, 2013 (http://www.nytimes.com/2013/06/30/business/breaking-the-seal-on-drug-research.html?pagewanted=all).

163 Aaron Swartz: "Aaron Swartz," *Wikipedia* (http://en.wikipedia. org/wiki/Aaron_Swartz).

163 RECAP at Princeton: http://www.recapthelaw.org. This "RECAP" has no relationship to the "RECAP" approach recommended by Thaler and Sunstein, described in Chapter 3 of this book.

164 Case brought against Swartz: Tim Cushing, "U.S. Government Ups Felony Count in JSTOR/Aaron Swartz Case from Four to Thirteen," *TechDirt*, September 18, 2012 (http://www.techdirt. com/articles/20120917/17393320412/us-government-ups-fel-ony-count-jstoraaron-swartz-case-four-to-thirteen.shtml).

164 JSTOR an unlikely target: http://about.jstor.org/10Things.

164 Elsevier profits: "The Price of Information," *The Economist*, February 4, 2012 (http://www.economist.com/node/21545974).

164 Academic Spring: "Academic Spring," *Wikipedia* (http:// en.wikipedia.org/wiki/Academic_Spring).

165 Access2Research: "Access2Research," *Wikipedia* (http:// en.wikipedia.org/wiki/Access2Research).

165 Petition campaign: On We the People website at https://petitions .whitehouse.gov/petition/require-free-access-over-internet-sci-entific-journal-articles-arising-taxpayer-funded-research/wDX-82FLQ.

165 Petition response: On We the People website at https://petitions .whitehouse.gov/response/increasing-public-access-results-scien-tific-research.

165 Holdren memo: Holdren, Memorandum for the Heads of Executive Departments and Agencies.

166 Champions of Change: http://www.whitehouse.gov/champions/ open-science; http://www.whitehouse.gov/sites/default/files/ microsites/ostp/openscience_release_6-18-13.pdf.

166 FASTR: Meredith Schwartz, "FASTR Aims to Speed Open Access to Government-Funded Research," *Library Journal*, February 21, 2013 (http://lj.libraryjournal.com/2013/02/oa/fastr-aims-to-speed-open-access-to-government-funded-research).

167 Eisen quote: Video at http://en.wikipedia.org/wiki/File:PhD_ Comics_Open_Access_Week_2012.ogv.

167 "half of all scientific papers published in 2011": "Open Access Reaches a Turning Point," *Science-Metrix News*, August 2013 (http://www.science-metrix.com/eng/news_13_08.htm).

167 "papers . . . were cited more often": Heather A. Piwowar and Todd J. Vision, "Data Reuse and the Open Data Citation Advantage," *PeerJ*, October 1, 2013 (https://peerj.com/articles/175/).

168 Jack Andraka: Lia Steakley, "Teen Cancer Researcher Jack Andraka Discusses Open Access in Science, Stagnation in Medicine," *SCOPE* (Stanford Medicine), June 3, 2013 (http://scopeblog.stanford .edu/2013/06/03/teen-cancer-researcher-jack-andraka-discusses-open-access-in-science-stagnation-in-medicine); "Winning the Top Award at Intel ISEF 2012 Kicks off Amazing Year for Jack Andraka," Society for Science & the Public, April 30, 2013 (http://societyforscience.typepad.com/ssp/2013/04/winning-the-top-award-at-intel-isef-2012-kicks-off-amazing-year-for-jack-andraka.html).

168 *New England Journal* article: Martin Frank, PhD, "Open but Not Free—Publishing in the 21st Century," *New England Journal of Medicine*, February 28, 2013, 787–789.

169 Pollock quotes: Interview with the author, London, April 4, 2013.

170 Goroff quotes: Email to author, June 16, 2013.

171 "In their influential book *Wikinomics*": Tapscott and Williams, *Wikinomics*, 163–166.

172 Bradner quotes: Phone interview with the author, August 9, 2013.

173 Eli Lilly and Open Innovation: See https://openinnovation.lilly .com/dd/.

173 GlaxoSmithKline and Open Innovation: Press release, "Funding Boost for GSK's Open Innovation Research into Diseases Affect-ing the Developing World," May 3, 2013 (http://www.gsk.com/ media/press-releases/2013/funding-boost-for-gsks-open-innova-tion-research-into-diseases-af.html).

173 "As the authors of *Wikinomics* point out": Tapscott and Williams, *Wikinomics*, 172–173.

Chapter Eleven

177 McNealy quote: http://technologizer.com/2009/11/09/great-tech-quotes.

178 Data brokers: See Lois Beckett, "Everything We Know About What Data Brokers Know About You," *ProPublica*, March 7, 2013 (http://www.propublica.org/article/everything-we-know-about-what-data-brokers-know-about-you).

178 "Parents of schoolchildren have raised alarms": Corinne Lestch and Ben Chapman, "New York Parents Furious at Program, inBloom, That Compiles Private Student Information for Companies That Contract with It to Create Teaching Tools," *New York Daily News*, March 13, 2013 (http://www.nydailynews.com/new-york/student-data-compiling-system-outrages-article-1.1287990). See also Stephanie Simon (Reuters), "School Database Loses Backers as Parents Balk Over Privacy," in *Chicago Tribune*, May 29, 2013 (http://articles.chicagotribune.com/2013-05-29/news/sns-rt-us-usa-education-databasebre94s0yu-20130529_1_student-data-database-school-districts).

178 "Gun owners are worried": J. David Goodman, "Newspaper Takes Down Map of Gun Permit Holders," *The New York Times*, January 18, 2013 (http://www.nytimes.com/2013/01/19/nyregion/newspaper-takes-down-map-of-gun-permit-holders.html?emc=eta1). See also Kevin Miller, "Senate Amendment Bans Release of Gun Owner Information," *Morning Sentinel* (Maine), April 18, 2013 (http://www.onlinesentinel.com/news/senate-amendment-bans-release-of-gun-owner-information_2013-04-18.html?pagenum=full).

180 "The Fair Credit Reporting Act": "Fair Credit Reporting Act," *Wikipedia* (http://en.wikipedia.org/wiki/Fair_Credit_Reporting_Act).

180 "Significantly, as *The New York Times* put it": Natasha Singer, "An American Quilt of Privacy Laws, Incomplete," *The New York Times*, March 30, 2013 (http://www.nytimes.com/2013/03/31/technology/in-privacy-laws-an-incomplete-american-quilt.html?pagewanted=all).

180 "a right to access and correct personal data": The White House, "Consumer Data Privacy," 48.

181 Dempsey quotes: Interview with the author, San Francisco, April 12, 2013.

182 Sinai quote: Interview with author, May 17, 2013

183 For more on Pentland's ideas: See interview with Pentland, "Reinventing Society in the Wake of Big Data," *Edge*, August 30, 2012, and Alex "Sandy" Pentland, "The Data-Driven Society," *Scientific American*, October 2013, 78-83.(http://www.edge.org/conversation/reinventing-society-in-the-wake-of-big-data).

183 TrueCar: World Economic Forum, "Unlocking the Value of Personal Data," 30. Also see "TrueCar," *Wikipedia*.

184 New Deal on Data: Alex Pentland, "Reality Mining of Mobile Communications: Toward a New Deal on Data," in *The Global Information Technology Report 2008–2009: Mobility in a Networked World*, eds. Soumitra Dutta and Irene Mia (World Economic Forum, 2009), 79 (http://hd.media.mit.edu/wef_globalit.pdf).

185 "The World Economic Forum has produced": World Economic Forum, "Unlocking the Value of Personal Data."

185 "it would take 30 days": Mike Masnick, "To Read All of the Privacy Policies You Encounter, You'd Need to Take a Month Off from Work Each Year," *TechDirt*, April 23, 2012 (http://www.techdirt.com/articles/20120420/10560418585/to-read-all-privacy-policiesyou-encounter-youd-need-to-take-month-off-work-each-year.shtml).

185 "Organizations need to engage . . .": World Economic Forum, "Unlocking the Value of Personal Data," 4.

186 Definition of personal data vaults: World Economic Forum, "Unlocking the Value of Personal Data," 29.

186 "Putting individuals in charge of their data": Searls, *The Intention Economy*, throughout.

187 Personal.com and Privacy by Design: Josh Galper, e-mails to the author, August 4 and 5, 2013.

187 Personal.com in *The Economist*: "Personal Data: Know Thyself," *The Economist*, December 15, 2012 (http://www.economist.com/news/business/21568438-data-lockers-promise-help-people-profit-their-personal-information-know-thyself/print).

187 Fee charged by Personal.com: Bill Flook, "Yes, Personal.com Is Charging. But It's Got Something Bigger in Mind," *Washington Business Journal*, June 5, 2013 (http://www.bizjournals.com/washington/blog/techflash/2013/06/personalcom-is-now-charging-but-its.html?ana=RSS&s=article_search&utm_source=dlvr.it&utm_medium=twitter).

188 Personal.com, DMV, and Department of Education: Josh Galper, e-mail to the author, June 14, 2013.

188 "20 million . . . federal student aid": http://www.ed.gov/about/offices/list/fsa/index.html. See also Kate Freeman, "Apply for Scholarships in a Flash with 'Personal for Education' App," *Mashable*, January 8, 2013 (http://mashable.com/2013/01/08/personal-for-education).

188 "30 million hours each year": Press release, "Personal Launches 'Personal for Education' at White House Event," October 9, 2012 (https://www.personal.com/personal-launches-personal-for-education).

188 World Economic Forum on form-filling: World Economic Forum, "Unlocking the Value of Personal Data," 29.

189 Fertik quotes: Interview with the author, Redwood City, CA, April 11, 2013.

191 "had yet to turn a profit": Natasha Singer, "A Vault for Taking Charge of Your Online Life," *The New York Times*, December 8,

2012 (http://www.nytimes.com/2012/12/09/business/company-envisions-vaults-for-personal-data.html?pagewanted=all).

191 Peter Fader quote: Tom Simonite, "If Facebook Can Profit from Your Data, Why Can't You?" *MIT Technology Review*, July 30, 2013 (http://www.technologyreview.com/news/517356/if-face-book-can-profit-from-your-data-why-cant-you).

191 Katrina Lerman blog post: Katrina Lerman, "Go Sell Yourself: Adventures on the Open Data Market," *Verbatim*, July 31, 2013 (http://blog.communispace.com/learn/go-sell-yourself-adventures-on-the-open-data-market/#_msocom_1).

192 Searls blog post: "For Personal Data, Use Value Beats Sale Value," *Doc Searls Weblog*, February 13, 2012 (http://blogs.law.harvard.edu/doc/2012/02/13/for-personal-data-use-value-beats-sale-value).

194 Josh Galper quotes: e-mail to the author, August 5, 2013.

Chapter Twelve

199 Meyer research with University of Michigan: Susan Rosegrant, "Revealing the Roots of a Riot," *Institute for Social Research* (undated) (http://home.isr.umich.edu/sampler/revealing-the-roots-of-a-riot).

199 Meyer on *Precision Journalism*: http://www.unc.edu/~pmeyer/book.

200 Lewis quotes: Interview with the author, Washington, DC, March 28, 2013.

202 Court decision: Maurice Tamman, "Federal Judge Lifts Ban on Public Access to Medicare Data," *Reuters*, May 31, 2013 (http://www.reuters.com/article/2013/05/31/us-medicare-lawsuit-idUSBRE94U1AE20130531). Court decision available at http://hr.cch.com/hld/FloridaMedicalAssociationvDeptof-HealthEducationandWelfare.pdf.

202 ProPublica on dialysis and Grassley quote: Author interview with Paul Steiger of ProPublica, New York, January 25, 2013; Robin Fields, "Feds to Follow ProPublica, Release Dialysis Clinic Data,"

ProPublica, March 29, 2011 (http://www.propublica.org/article/
feds-to-follow-propublica-release-dialysis-clinic-data). For other
ProPublica projects, see Prescriber Checkup at http://projects
.propublica.org/checkup, Dollars for Doctors at http://projects
.propublica.org/docdollars, and Nursing Home Inspect at http://
projects.propublica.org/nursing-homes.

203 Atlanta schools: "Cheating Our Children," ongoing online
archive of coverage in *Atlanta Journal-Constitution* (http://www.ajc
.com/s/news/school-test-scores); Michael Winerip, "Ex-Schools
Chief in Atlanta Is Indicted in Testing Scandal," *The New York
Times*, March 29, 2013 (http://www.nytimes.com/2013/03/30/
us/former-school-chief-in-atlanta-indicted-in-cheating-scandal
.html?pagewanted=all&_r=0).

203 *Guardian* crowdsourcing: "Datablog + MPs' Expenses," ongoing
online archive of coverage in *The Guardian* (http://www.guardian
.co.uk/news/datablog+politics/mps-expenses).

204 Geithner quotes: Lloyd Grove, "Too Big to Fail? Geithner Says
No," *The Daily Beast*, May 17, 2011 (http://www.thedailybeast
.com/articles/2011/05/18/too-big-to-fail-timothy-geithner-says-
no-at-hbo-movie-screening.html).

205 Quote on Lehman Brothers: Basel Committee on Banking Supervi-
sion, "Report and Recommendations of the Cross-border Bank Resolution Group," Bank for International Settlements, March 2010.

205 Dodd-Frank: "Dodd-Frank Wall Street Reform and Consumer
Protection Act," *Wikipedia*.

206 Taggart quote: David Meyer, "Want to Follow the Money? Open
Corporates Uses Open Data to Expose Corporate Structures,"
GigaOm, July 12, 2013 (http://gigaom.com/2013/07/12/want-to-
follow-the-money-opencorporates-uses-open-data-to-expose-
corporate-structures).

206 Cameron quote: Prime Minister David Cameron's Speech to the
World Economic Forum in Davos, January 24, 2013. Available on the

official site of the British Prime Minister's Office, www.number10 .gov.uk.

207 Miller quotes: Interview with the author, New York, April 17, 2013.

207 Ad Hawk: http://adhawk.sunlightfoundation.com.

208 POGO: Author interview with Scott Amey, January 16, 2013; see http://www.pogo.org.

208 Good Jobs First: Author interview with Phil Mattera, December 13, 2012; see www.goodjobsfirst.org.

208 "Their data was one of the main sources": *New York Times* series, "The United States of Subsidies," interactive application at http://www .nytimes.com/interactive/2012/12/01/us/government-incentives .html. Originally published as three-part series, December 1–3, 2012.

208 BizVizz: Tom Roston, "BizVizz: A Mobile App Inspired by a Documentary Film," *POV* (PBS website), February 4, 2013 (http:// www.pbs.org/pov/blog/docsoup/2013/02/bizvizz-a-mobile-app-inspired-by-a-documentary-film/#.URGmnej8V5b).

211 "what I'd call a new era": The term *corporate credibility* was suggested by Mitchell Belgin in a conversation with the author.

Chapter Thirteen

213 "on a trip to a technology center in Austin": Philip Rucker, "In Austin, Obama Plans to Announce Steps to Boost Economy," *The Washington Post: Post Politics*, May 9, 2013 (http://www.washingtonpost .com/blogs/post-politics/wp/2013/05/09/in-austin-obama-plans-to-announce-steps-to-boost-economy).

213 President Obama's remarks on Open Data Policy: http://www. whitehouse.gov/the-press-office/2013/05/09/remarks-president-applied-materials-inc-austin-tx.

214 "the policy got some extensive play on Slate": Alexander B. Howard, "The Best Thing Obama's Done This Month," *Slate: Future Tense*, May 15, 2013 (http://www.slate.com/articles/technology/

future_tense/2013/05/open_data_executive_order_is_the_best_
thing_obama_s_done_this_month.single.html).

214 Quotes from advocates on Open Data Policy: Nick Sinai and
Haley Van Dyck, "Recap: A Big Day for Open Data," *OSTP* blog,
May 10, 2013 (http://www.whitehouse.gov/blog/2013/05/10/
recap-big-day-open-data).

214 Quote from Nick Sinai: Telephone interview with the author,
May 17, 2013.

215 "10,000 different information systems used in the federal government": Jared Duval, *Next Generation Democracy*, 174, describing
Vivek Kundra, "Opening Doors: Finding Keys to Open Government," panel discussion, Center for American Progress, Washington, DC, March 20, 2009.

216 "On January 21, 2009": Barack Obama, Memorandum, "Transparency and Open Government."

217 Participatory budgeting: Daniel Altschuler, "Participatory Budgeting in the United States: What Is its Role?" *Nonprofit Quarterly*
blog, April 18, 2013 (http://www.nonprofitquarterly.org/policy-
social-context/22157-participatory-budgeting-in-the-united-
states-what-is-its-role.html).

218 David Cameron quote: Letter to the British Cabinet, July 7,
2011, reprinted in "The Government's New Transparency Initiatives: What Data Will They Release and How Big a Deal Is
It?" *The Guardian Datablog*, July 7, 2011 (http://www.guardian
.co.uk/news/datablog/2011/jul/07/government-transpar-
ency-data-releases#cameron).

218 For the U.S. commitment to the international Open Government
Partnership: See "Open Government Partnership: National
Action Plan." Also see the Partnership's website at http://www
.opengovpartnership.org.

218 Paul Maltby quotes: Interview with the author, London, April
4, 2013.

218 "between about $3 billion and $9 billion": Deloitte, "Market Assessment of Public Sector Information." Also see Stephan Shakespeare, "Shakespeare Review: An Independent Review of Public Sector Information," May 2013 (https://www.gov.uk/government/uploads/system/uploads/attachment_data/file/198752/13-744-shakespeare-review-of-public-sector-information.pdf); Anna Leach, "Public Data Will Boost Business, Report Says," *The Wall Street Journal*, May 15, 2013 (http://blogs.wsj.com/tech-europe/2013/05/15/public-data-will-boost-business-report-says); and Stephan Shakespeare, "Shakespeare Review," *YouGov*, (http://yougov.co.uk/news/2013/05/15/shakespeare-review).

218 "about 30 to 140 billion euros": Vickery, "Review of Recent Studies on PSI."

219 EU vote: Tom Brewster, "EU Heralds Open Data Boom After Parliament Votes for New Rules," *TechWeekEurope*, June 13, 2013 (http://www.techweekeurope.co.uk/news/eu-heralds-open-data-boom-after-parliament-vote-118978). The estimate of 40 billion euros in value from releasing new Open Data comes from Vickery, "Review of Recent Studies on PSI."

219 G8: U.K. Cabinet Office, "Policy Paper: G8 Open Data Charter and Technical Annex."

220 Sunlight on error in USASpending.gov: Sunlightfoundation.com/clearspending.

220 "ARRA. . . has shown that better data is possible": Andrea Peterson, "Here's How the Recovery Act Became a Test Case for Open Data," *The Washington Post: The Switch*, September 16, 2013 (http://www.washingtonpost.com/blogs/the-switch/wp/2013/09/16/heres-how-the-recovery-act-became-a-test-case-for-open-data/).

220 "prevent tens of millions of dollars in waste and fraud": Savings of $60 million cited by Hudson Hollister in interview with the author, Washington, DC, March 27, 2013.

221 Hudson Hollister quotes: Interview with the author, Washington, DC, March 27, 2013.

222 Nisbet quotes: Interview with the author, Washington, DC, March 28, 2013.

222 Use of FOIA by journalists and businesses: "Frequent Filers: Businesses Make FOIA Their Business," *Society of Professional Journalists*, July 3, 2006 (http://www.spj.org/rrr.asp?ref=31&t=foia).

222 "*The Wall Street Journal* reviewed": Brody Mullins and Christopher Weaver, "Open-Government Laws Fuel Hedge-Fund Profits," *The Wall Street Journal*, September 23, 2013 (http://online .wsj.com/news/articles/SB100014241278873242023045790530 33444112314).

223 For a discussion of FOIA reform: See "One Step Forward, One Step Missed: House Committee Approves Limited FOIA Improvements," *Center for Effective Government*, March 21, 2013 (http://www.foreffectivegov.org/one-step-forward-one-step-missed-house-committee-approves-limited-foia-improvements).

224 "Cass Sunstein followed this philosophy": Sunstein, *Simpler*.

224 "targeted transparency": Fung, Graham, and Weil, *Full Disclosure*, 6.

225 Sean Moulton quotes: Interview with the author, Washington, DC, March 27, 2013.

225 Quote on impact of TRI: Hamilton, *Regulation Through Revelation*, 8; also see Fung, Graham, and Weil, *Full Disclosure*, 188.

227 CARFAX data sources: http://www.carfax.com/about/data_ sources.cfx.

227 *Consumer Reports* on hospital data: "How Safe Is Your Hospital?" *Consumer Reports*, August 2012 (http://www.consumerreports .org/cro/magazine/2012/08/how-safe-is-your-hospital/index. htm); "Safety Still Lags in U.S. Hospitals," *Consumer Reports*, May 2013 (http://www.consumerreports.org/cro/magazine/2013/05/ safety-still-lags-in-u-s-hospitals/index.htm).

227 Kevin Merritt quotes: E-mail to the author, August 5, 2013.

228 "Newsom describes in his book": Newsom, *Citizenville*, throughout.

228 "an office of New Yorkology": Alan Feuer, "The Mayor's Geek Squad," *The New York Times*, March 24, 2013.

229 Theresa Pardo quote: E-mail to the author, June 14, 2013. See also Center for Technology in Government at http://www.ctg .albany.edu.

230 Huduma assessment: Rakesh Rajani speaking at Open Up! conference, London, November 13, 2012.

230 Success of RosPil: Paul M. Healy, Karthik Ramanna, and Matthew Shaffer, "Case Study: Rospil.info," Harvard Business School, February 14, 2012 (http://hbr.org/product/rospil-info/ an/112033-PDF-ENG).

230 SARPAM: Jose Alonso, personal communication, November 2012; see also www.sarpam.net.

231 Poderopedia: Jessica McKenzie, "Chilean Anti-Corruption Resource: A Crowdsourced Database of Social and Political Connections," *TechPresident*, May 17, 2013 (http://techpresident.com/ news/wegov/23893/chilean-anti-corruption-resource-crowd-sourced-database-social-and-political-connections).

233 Problems with EPA data: Personal communications to author from Steve Young, David Smith, and Michael Alford.

Chapter Fourteen

235 Zurich: Zurich Insurance Company, "A Structured Insight into the Complexity of Global Risks: The Zurich Risk Room," 2010 (http://www.zurich.com/internet/main/sitecollectiondocuments/ insight/zurich-risk-room-brochure.pdf).

236 Relationship Science: Andrew Ross Sorkin, "A Database of Names and How They Connect," *The New York Times*, February 11, 2013 (http://dealbook.nytimes.com/2013/02/11/a-database-of-names-and-how-they-connect).

236 Food Genius: Derrick Harris, "How to Build a Business Around Data in 7 Easy Steps, Explained with Food," *GigaOm*, July 4,

2013 (http://gigaom.com/tag/food-genius). Also see Kevin Fitchard, "How Food Genius Built the Ultimate Test Kitchen Out of Menu Data," *GigaOm*, December 21, 2012 (http://gigaom .com/2012/12/21/how-food-genius-built-the-ultimate-test-kitchen-out-of-menu-data).

Index

INDEX

About the Author

JOEL GURIN BRINGS A UNIQUE BACKGROUND TO HIS WORK ON Open Data. He began his career as an award-winning science journalist, became a leader and innovator in magazine and online publishing, led a White House task force on consumer-focused data and information, and now helps lead a foundation-funded program on Open Data and Open Government.

Gurin began work as a science writer and editor immediately after graduating from Harvard University with a degree in biochemical sciences. He has won the top science-writing awards from the American Association for the Advancement of Science and the National Association of Science Writers. He is the coauthor with William Bennett of *The Dieter's Dilemma*, which introduced the setpoint theory of weight control, and edited the book *Mind/Body Medicine* with Daniel Goleman, author of *Emotional Intelligence*. Gurin was the editor and cofounder of *American Health* magazine, the first health publication to win the National Magazine Award for General Excellence.

Gurin had a long and successful career at Consumers Union, the nonprofit publisher of *Consumer Reports*, where he began as science editor, soon became editorial director, and then served as executive vice president for almost a decade. As EVP of Consumers Union, Gurin launched and grew *Consumer Reports*' website, ConsumerReports.org. Under his leadership, it became the world's largest information-based paid-subscription site: it now has more than three million active paid subscribers.

In December 2009, Gurin joined the Obama administration as Chief of the Consumer and Governmental Affairs Bureau of the Federal Communications Commission. He conceptualized and served as Chair of the White House Task Force on Smart Disclosure, which studied how government Open Data can help consumers choose their best options in services like healthcare, financial services, education, and energy. He is now senior advisor to the Governance Lab at New York University, which studies how to use Open Data and citizen engagement to improve the ways we govern and thus improve people's lives. He lives in Scarsdale, New York, with his wife, Carol; they have three grown children.

31192020792790